Lucy McR

365 DAYS WILD

A RANDOM ACT OF WILDNESS FOR EVERY DAY OF THE YEAR

WILLIAM COLLINS

For my mum, Alison, and my daughter, Georgiana.
I wish you had met.

William Collins
An imprint of HarperCollins*Publishers*
1 London Bridge Street
London SE1 9GF

WilliamCollinsBooks.com

First published in Great Britain by William Collins in 2019

2020 2022 2021 2019
2 4 6 8 10 9 7 5 3 1

Printed in China by RRD Asia Print Solutions

MIX
Paper from
responsible sources
FSC™ C007454

DISCLAIMER
The activities and content of this book are the author's and do not necessarily reflect Wildlife Trust policy. The author and publisher expressly disclaim any responsibility for any effects arising in any way from the advice, information, recipes, activities or products referred to or described in this book.

CONTENTS

Introduction

My wild life

Growing up in rural Leicestershire, I was lucky to experience a wild childhood, scouring every tree, every park, every field and every hedgerow for adventure, running (relatively) wild and free.

As I got older, things changed; that innate love of nature faded (although it never disappeared) as I discovered boys, make-up and the shackles of modern school curriculum. When I was thirteen, my mum got very ill with cancer. She died three years later. As I've grown older, I've realised that I didn't start to grieve properly for years: not until I was at university. I now believe that this grieving process was triggered, and ultimately overcome, by rediscovering my love of nature: a love that I'd forgotten until then.

In my twenties I began to reconnect with nature. I met my now husband, Rob Lambert, who is a hardcore birder and twitcher, inevitably falling down that rabbit hole myself. By the age of 28 I'd seen over 400 different species of bird in Britain (Rob has seen well over 500!). The more I immersed myself, the more I learned about the challenges facing our modern environment. I knew I wanted to make a difference. This sense of purpose, more time spent outdoors, a love of the natural world and an increasing knowledge of it, helped to bring the peace of mind that I had lacked since losing my mum.

Now, a handful of years later, my whole life revolves around nature. I have fallen in love with new landscapes – the Highlands and Islands of Scotland, the Isles of Scilly, the Somerset Levels, North Norfolk. And my wild life has become even more exciting with a new little traveller to share adventures with. I wrote this book while I was pregnant, and in September 2018, Rob and I welcomed Georgiana Tean Lambert into our lives. Georgie already has a wild life of her own, visiting Kent to see a beluga whale in the Thames at one week old; exploring the Isles of Scilly by land, air and sea at a month; and watching for birds and wildlife every day. She has enriched our wild experiences and lives.

I work for a wildlife charity called The Wildlife Trusts, engaging hundreds of thousands of people with wildlife and helping them to fall in love with it, too. As part of my job, I helped to set up the annual campaign 30 Days Wild to encourage people to do something wild every day for 30 days. This book takes that campaign a step further – why not live all 365 days of the year with nature in mind?

I hope that this book will give you plenty of ideas for your own wild adventures. Wildlife and wild places are much closer than you think, so have a fabulous time finding your own wild life.

The Wildlife Trusts

No matter where you are in the UK, there is a Wildlife Trust standing up for wildlife and bringing people closer to nature near you. Their work is returning wildlife to our towns and countryside and touching the lives of millions of people, young and old, from all walks of life. Each of the Wildlife Trusts believes that everyone can make a positive difference to their local environment – whether schools, councils, farmers, businesses or individuals – and that by working together we can achieve nature's recovery on land and at sea.
Visit their website at **wildlifetrusts.org**.

Wildlife Watch

Wildlife Watch is the junior branch of The Wildlife Trusts and the UK's leading environmental action club for kids. Taking part in Wildlife Watch is an exciting way to explore your surroundings and get closer to the wildlife you share it with. And the best thing about being a member is that by joining Wildlife Watch you'll be helping your local Wildlife Trust to care for the wildlife where you live!
Visit **wildlifewatch.org.uk**.

The 30 Days Wild Campaign

Setting up the Wildlife Trusts' 30 Days Wild Campaign inspired me to write this book. The campaign encourages people to get outdoors every day in June by providing them with inspiring ideas: 'Random Acts of Wildness'. Once June is over, we ask them to stay wild and The Wildlife Trusts are there to help. Put simply, The Wildlife Trusts believe that all our lives are better when they're a bit wild.

You don't have to do something every single day, but by becoming more aware of your natural surroundings, enjoying the wonders nature can bring and occasionally even giving it a helping hand, most people will find that they feel better. It becomes unconscious, too: people always ask me, 'when do you find time to go birdwatching?' The simple answer is that I am always birdwatching and enjoying wildlife: whether I'm on a train, at work, at home or spending time with friends. And it's wonderful.

What is a Random Act of Wildness?

A Random Act of Wildness is any little thing that you can do as part of an average day, that allows you to experience, learn about or even help nature near you. It can take a few seconds – like taking a moment to smell a wildflower on the way to work; or a few hours – like creating a

whole area for wildlife in your garden. Some Random Acts of Wildness don't have to take any time at all, but instead are all about making little changes to your daily routine that will ultimately be better for wildlife, like buying a re-usable coffee cup or using products that are good for the environment. To help you, I have pulled together my top 365 Random Acts of Wildness, but that doesn't mean you shouldn't get creative and make up your own. The best Random Acts of Wildness immerse you (if only for a few seconds) in nature, setting your senses alight. Smelling freshly fallen rain, tasting the sweet explosion of a fresh blackberry as you pop it in your mouth, wriggling your toes in the icy waters of a stream, waking up to birdsong. It's not just about seeing, but experiencing the wild in every way possible.

Wild, happy and free

When it comes to letting the wild into your life, a little will go a long way. That's why Random Acts of Wildness are perfect: they're quick and simple to do, and when put together they add up to a big change – for you and for wildlife.

We all instinctively know it: spending time outdoors is good for us. After all, we are part of nature, so it makes sense that getting your daily wildlife fix will do you the world of good. There's lots of science out there now that underpins this, too: spending time in nature makes us happier and healthier. Just like eating a balanced diet and exercising helps our minds and bodies, wildlife and wild places help us to get active, encourage us to be more social, improve our confidence and creativity, and help us cope with stressful life events. Nature can help us recover from illnesses, cope with grief and loss, and even help people to manage mental health problems, like anxiety, stress and depression. In many ways, it's the ultimate medicine – and it's free.

There's no excuse for not getting the whole family involved, too. Nature is great for all ages and can have the biggest impact on the young and the elderly, so take the kids, grandma and grandpa and anyone else you can find on this wild adventure with you.

Everyday wild

Random Acts of Wildness aren't about trekking to distant wild lands, climbing mountains or getting lost in dense jungles – they are about the wild near you. If you want to experience nature every day, it has to be local. It's also been proven that doing something wild every day can have a significant impact on your health and happiness: this isn't about an annual nature fix by going on an exotic holiday, it's about discovering how amazing the nature on your doorstep already is.

Wild places are all around us. Each one is home to very different kinds of wildlife, but all of them can be fun to explore. I want to help you make the ordinary extraordinary. As an introduction, I've pulled together some of my favourite wild places and I hope that as you begin your wild adventure, you'll get to experience some (or all) of these landscapes. They can all be found right here in the UK: proof that you don't have to look far to find your own wild life.

Wild places

Gardens

Finding the wild every day has to start close to home, and every garden has the potential to become a wild place, no matter how small. If you don't have a garden, you could work your magic on a balcony or transform communal spaces with your neighbours. Domestic gardens in the UK are thought to take up over 430,000 hectares. Imagine the difference we could all make for wildlife if every garden was wildlife-friendly: we could create the UK's biggest nature reserve!

There are a few key things that you can do to make sure your garden is a wild garden. Some of these are full-blown Random Acts of Wildness, so they're covered in detail later on, but think simply about what wildlife needs to feel safe, secure and at home: food, water and shelter. A garden bursting with bugs will also attract birds and other animals. By making sure that your insects have some cover (grass, log piles or compost heaps, for example) and plenty of food (nectar- and pollen-rich plants), you'll be encouraging other wildlife in, too. Avoid using slug pellets and pesticides. If you have room, even the smallest of ponds will bring huge diversity, and you can support wildlife by providing feeders and nest boxes.

In the spring and summer, look out for a whole range of beautiful butterflies fluttering among the flowers, like painted ladies, peacocks or small tortoiseshells. A healthy population of moths and beetles will attract bats to your garden, too. Birds like house sparrows, starlings, blackbirds, robins, wrens and dunnocks are quintessential garden species that can be seen all year round, and you might also attract a variety of tits and finches. If you've got a pond, common frogs and common toads might make themselves at home, and a small hole in your fence will make your garden accessible for hedgehogs.

Parks and churchyards

I've always loved the way that parks can bring people together. Whether a children's play area or a vast, green common, these places can be great for getting your daily wild fix. The same can be said of churchyards. Quiet places of tranquil reflection, the peaceful atmosphere in a churchyard can help you hone in on birdsong. In the winter, scan the tops of berry-laden trees (like rowan or holly) for thrushes, which will feast on these tiny fruits: song and mistle thrushes love these areas, and redwings and fieldfares may stop over, too. An open grassy park will be great for green woodpeckers. Hedgehogs love to rummage around in fallen leaf litter, while baby rabbits might be seen taking their first unsteady steps. Even foxes and badgers use these areas to explore. A park or churchyard can be a magical place at sunrise, so wrap up warm and experience the dawn chorus, or welcome in spring by noting when you first see snowdrops or daffodils shooting up.

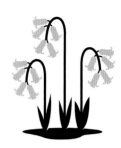

Towns and city centres

With so many people living or working in cities now, it's important to be able to find the wild in the urban jungle. Surrounded by concrete, glass and high rises, it can be hard to imagine how any wild animal could find a home here, but trust me when I say that cities can be unexpected places in which to have a really wild experience. Birds will use the tall buildings as makeshift cliff faces, building their nests and raising their young high up to avoid predators. Gulls, ducks and pigeons all use this tactic, and now peregrine falcons have adapted their lifestyle, too. In many of our major cities, peregrines can be seen swooping and diving among the buildings. Foxes, deer and hedgehogs make the most of our cities, and being so used to people you can often get much closer to them. With so many towns built on rivers, otters can occasionally pop up, and cormorants and herons may choose to fish along the banks. Flowers will grow in pavement cracks and overgrown, abandoned sites (known as 'brownfield' sites) can become quickly colonised by a range of birds, bugs and mammals.

Woodlands and forests

I was lucky enough to grow up near to a woodland, where I was allowed to play and explore with my friends. At the time, it seemed like the biggest forest in the world, full of hiding places, trees to climb and hidden treasures. 'My' woodland is in fact little more than a spinney, but with its criss-crossing paths and hidden wonders it isn't any less magical. In the spring, it's carpeted with bluebells; the trees are covered in budburst and birds bellow out their chorus. In the summer, it's alive with butterflies, and as the autumn sets in, fungi erupt from every tree or rotten branch, and mushrooms sprout from the leaf litter. It's a typical broad-leafed woodland, with dappled light, lush undergrowth, a strong earthy smell and a healthy population of crows, rooks and jackdaws. Smaller birds, like finches, are regulars, along with great spotted woodpeckers, treecreepers and nuthatches. In the spring, wild garlic fills the air with a pungent smell. If you take time to explore a woodland near you, you might also spy tawny owls, jays, muntjac and other deer, as well as badger setts and fox dens.

Little copses and spinneys like this can be found all over the place, but there are of course much bigger forests to explore. Trees are either deciduous (lose their leaves in the winter) or evergreen, which hang on to their leaves or needles all year round. Depending on the kind of woodland you're in, you'll see different wildlife wherever you go. The Forest of Dean in the southwest is home to wild boar; while forests in the north of England and Scotland might contain red squirrels, pine martens or specialist birds, like the capercaillie of the Caledonian pine forest in Inverness-shire. Forests in the south of England can be home to beautiful butterflies like purple emperors or white admirals, and wildflowers like red campion and orchids. No matter how big or small, woodlands are perfect for a wild adventure.

The coast

Britain is a coastal country. From stretching sand dunes to pebbly beaches, foreboding tidal mudflats to rocky cliffs, as an island nation we love to be close to the sea. Living in the Midlands, I try to get to the coast as often as possible for my dose of vitamin 'sea'. Whether it's a gentle stroll on the sand (with a quick litter-pick thrown in), scanning out to sea for whales, dolphins or porpoises that might be seen (Britain has an amazing variety of marine species), or heading out on a boat to watch seabirds or seals, our shores offer endless possibilities for experiencing wildlife. Discover starfish, crabs and shellfish living in rockpools, wonder at wading birds like sanderling and turnstone as they scurry along the shore, and enjoy the overwhelming noise (and smell!) of a seabird colony teeming with puffins, guillemots, razorbills, gannets and gulls.

Fields, farmland and meadows

Fields and farmland are pretty much what you'll think of when you imagine the countryside: over two-thirds of the land in the UK is farmed in one way or another. The best farmland to enjoy wildlife on is managed in a traditional way: thick hedges, smaller fields and a mix of crops or grasses. This is farmland at its best: where you'll find barn owls, kestrels and yellowhammers; huge flocks of finches, partridges and buntings. They're making the most of the seeds and grasses on offer, as are the many small mammals that might live here – voles, mice and shrews. The bigger fields that only have one crop growing in them, like rapeseed, aren't as rich in wildlife, but you can still scan down the hedges for a wildlife surprise. Look for boxing brown hares in March, or skylarks singing loudly overhead. Meadows are a much rarer habitat, brimming with wildflowers, lush grasses and, in the summer, hundreds of butterflies, moths and other insects. Most meadows are protected now and carefully managed using traditional methods; flowers like poppies, oxeye daisies, bee orchids and cornflowers are particularly stunning.

Hedgerows and country lanes

Okay, so hedgerows and country lanes aren't really wild places in themselves, but you can often find wildlife around the edges of them. I've included them because they're ideal foraging spots in the spring, summer and autumn. They're wonderful places to find edible gems like elderflowers, wild rosehips, blackberries, damsons, sloes and crab apples, and this feast will bring in great wildlife, too: birds, mammals and insects. Just make sure you have correctly identified any fruits, nuts, fungi or berries before you tuck in, as you could accidentally eat something poisonous.

Rivers, streams and ditches

Who doesn't love *Wind in the Willows*? The picturesque scene of a gently meandering river, lined with lush green vegetation, overhanging willow trees and reeds sprouting along the banks. Smaller brooks babble alongside fields, canals cut straight paths through our towns and countryside, and smaller ditches might lurk beneath a hedgerow or in a woodland. All can be bursting with wildlife: a healthy river might be home to water voles, kingfishers or maybe even otters. Stately grey herons or little egrets will stand motionless in the water, and of course there may be fish, too. Rivers and streams make wonderful locations to experience wildlife; search among the reedbeds

in the summer for more elusive wildlife like sedge warblers or Cetti's warblers – even if you don't see them, you'll hear them! Always be wary near these waters though; some rivers and streams are perfect for a wild swim, while others may hold fast currents beneath their serene surfaces. Make sure you know the waterway well if you're planning to do more than walk beside it.

Lakes, ponds and wetlands

Lakes and ponds are hugely diverse wild places, which offer delights all year round to any wild explorer. They vary season by season, so if there's one near you, make sure you check back throughout the year to see how it changes. Wetlands come in all shapes and sizes; from reservoirs to old quarries; Scottish lochs to woodland ponds; marshland, bogs and fens. These places are all about the ducks, geese and swans in the winter, as well as otters and water voles. In the summer, you might get visitors like the osprey, a huge bird of prey that only eats fish. You'll also be in for a treat with elegant dragonflies and damselflies in the summer, too. Great crested grebes perform an elaborate courtship dance in early spring, while moorhens and coots will be around all year. Wading birds like oystercatchers and redshanks might skitter around the edges looking for food in the mud. A vast wetland with plenty of reedbed might even have birds like marsh harriers or bitterns.

Mountains, moorlands and uplands

For most people living in the UK, mountains and moorlands are the settings for wild and romantic novels (*Wuthering Heights*, anyone?), or maybe holiday destinations. Most of us don't live nestled among snowy peaks or on the tops of windswept hills. I've included them here though, because these landscapes are so different from any other and because they make up a third of our land. A walk atop the hills might bring you into contact with red grouse, wading birds that breed on the high tops (like dotterels or golden plovers) or birds of prey like peregrines, merlins or hen harriers (which are now very rare in England). You might also be lucky enough to see a mountain hare or red deer. The flowers and plants make the uplands really special; heather will look at its most beautiful in late summer, and you can also look out for wildflowers, bracken and bilberry. Sphagnum mosses make up much of the vegetation in blanket bogs (and let's face it, 'sphagnum' is a great word, too).

A note on nature reserves

I haven't included nature reserves as one of my favourite habitats because each one is unique: it's hard to generalise and compare. The experiences you can have on them vary so much that they're not a habitat in their own right – rather they are made up of a mosaic of ecosystems. They are of course great places to explore and discover wildlife. The Wildlife Trusts have the biggest network of nature reserves in the UK, and 93 per cent of people living in England live within six miles of one of these special wild places. They're always carefully managed and protected for wildlife, so can be perfect if you'd like to take up volunteering in your local area. A lot of them will have 'hides' – special buildings, usually made from wood (glorified sheds) – that you can sit in to watch the wildlife up close. Hides are an acquired taste: most of them can be a bit draughty and you have to sit very quietly so as not to disturb the nearby wildlife. I wouldn't recommend hides as places to inspire children; stick to the immersive experiences where they can get hands-on and run around a bit. For the seasoned wildlife-watcher, though, they can be tranquil and enjoyable. Many nature reserves have special 'designations' – meaning that they're protected for a reason – and many can't allow dogs in. When on a nature reserve, always stick to the paths; don't pick any plants or disturb the wildlife.

Really wild life

The UK is a hugely diverse country, full of so many different animals that it would be impossible to list them all. I have pulled out the main groups of animals you might encounter on your adventures, with a few ideas on the best ways to enjoy them. Where you could have a really wild experience, it'll be listed as a full-blown Random Act of Wildness, and I'll give some handy hints and tips on the best ways to get up close and personal to our star species.

Fur

There are loads of different species of mammals living on land in the UK; we know most of them from children's books – Mr Badger, Ratty and Mole from *Wind in the Willows*, or Beatrix Potter's Mrs Tiggy-winkle – but in reality they're quite difficult to see. Squirrels, rabbits and foxes might be spotted easily in towns, villages and cities, but having a wild encounter with a hedgehog, badger, water vole or otter is much trickier. There are also seventeen species of bats living in the UK, not to mention different kinds of mice, voles and shrews;

a family of mammals called the 'mustelids' (which includes stoats and weasels); mountain and brown hares; two species of squirrel (the native red, which is now only found in the northern parts of England, Northern Ireland and Scotland; and the non-native grey, now found across much of England and Wales); and no fewer than six species of deer. Add to these, animals like beavers and wildcats, and you'll see that there's an awful lot of fur out there. Most mammals are highly secretive or nocturnal, and some are incredibly rare, but I've included several Random Acts of Wildness that will help you get a little bit closer to our furriest of neighbours. None of our mammals are dangerous or predatory to humans, but some will give you a nasty nip if you venture too close. Never try to stroke or pet wild mammals; if you find an injured mammal, phone a local wildlife rescue centre.

Feathers

There's a reason why birdwatching is so popular in the UK, and that's because of the sheer variety of species it's possible to see in a day, month, year – or even a lifetime. Around 220 species breed here, but we also get lots of birds arriving in the autumn to spend the winter, jetting off to warmer climates as the weather gets colder, or just passing through on their migration. Field guides can help you identify individual species, as can birding websites. Every wild place and every part of the UK will have different kinds of birds living in it, so look out for different species wherever you go. Gardens are the best place to start practising your identification. When you see a new bird, make a note of where it is (on a bird feeder, in a field, on a lake), what it looks like (colours, size, structure), any features that make it stand out (a long, pointy bill, for example) and what it's doing. When you get home, you'll be able to look it up online or in a book. With so many birds to choose from, it's best to get the hang of the common birds first before trying your hand at anything rarer.

Flippers

Marine mammals are often forgotten about when we think about British wildlife, but around the UK are many different species of whales, dolphins, porpoises and seals. Seals are the easiest to enjoy, as they come up on to beaches to breed, play in the shallows and rest. There are only two species that live here: the grey seal and the common (or harbour) seal. If in doubt about which you're looking at, remember that greys look more like dogs, with long snouts, while common seals look more like cats, with shorter noses. To see whales, dolphins and porpoises (also known as 'cetaceans'), your best chance is to go out on a boat. There are lots of hotspots for cetaceans around the UK that will enable you to see different species, but the most commonly sighted are harbour porpoises (which are very shy), common dolphins (which love to bow ride on the front of boats), bottlenose dolphins (big, acrobatic and dark grey) and minke whales.

Fins

Unless you're an avid fisherman, the fish you have the best chance of seeing is the Atlantic salmon, as they leap from the water on the way to their breeding grounds upstream. Weirs and waterfalls are not going to stand in the way of this amorous beauty, as they fight their way up-river. Other species that you might see as they disappear down the gullet of a heron include trout (rainbow and brown), bream, carp, perch and pike. If you see a kingfisher beating up a tiny silver fish, you're probably looking at a minnow.

Scales

With just six species of reptiles in the UK, snakes and lizards are an easy group to get your head around. There are three snakes – the adder, smooth snake and grass snake; the sand lizard; the common lizard; and the slow worm, which despite looking like a snake is actually a legless lizard! Only adders are venomous (though not deadly), but they're so shy that your chances of seeing one are slim. Any encounters with these gorgeous creatures are special. They will bask on warm, sunny days, soaking up the rays, but are very easily disturbed; they will sense your footsteps as you approach, and will probably beat a hasty retreat before you get close. You might encounter grass snakes in your garden; they like to lay eggs in compost heaps. These gentle creatures are a sign of a healthy and thriving garden and are best left undisturbed.

Slime

This is a bit of an unfair title for amphibians, but let's face it, most of them are quite slimy. Amphibians in the UK are a pretty simple bunch: two frogs, two toads and three newts. In your average garden pond, you might find the common frog, common toad or smooth or palmate newt. Frogs and toads are easy to separate: the former are smooth, shiny and hop; the latter are warty, appear dry and crawl. Newts are like tiny dragons that live in your pond, and these species are hard to separate. The rarer and protected great crested newt is larger, warty, dark along the back and with a bright orange belly, splotched with black. There are also populations of marsh frogs and natterjack toads living in very specific areas where they are protected.

Legs

Okay, I lied. Not everything in this group has legs. Invertebrates make up the biggest of the wildlife groups I've listed here: there are 45,000 species in the UK! These can be split into 25 major insect groups, including grasshoppers, beetles, bees, butterflies, moths and dragonflies; 'arthropods' like spiders and woodlice (these guys have the skeleton on the outside); and then everything else, like snails, slugs and worms. It's easy to be a bit grossed out by bugs, but remember: life on earth as we know it depends on them. A third of what we eat is dependent on insects, including fruit, honey and chocolate. Up close and personal, bugs can be the most beautiful creatures in the UK, as well as the most helpful, and they're literally everywhere: we just need to help you find them!

Petals

Wildflowers are often markers of the seasons: for example, snowdrops signal the coming of spring and oxeye daisies follow the summer sun across the sky. Bluebells and foxgloves will blossom in a woodland, while other species, like orchids, prefer carefully cultivated meadows. Even the seashore has wildflowers: thrift and sea holly. A wildflower meadow in full blossom will be alive with bees, butterflies and other pollinators, drinking in the sweet nectar, and is best viewed throughout the spring and in early summer. A riot of colour, wildflowers have a delicate and understated beauty; if you can make room for them in the garden, do! Don't pick them though; instead, buy from a garden centre or cultivate your own in your garden.

Bark

There are more than 50 species of native trees and shrubs in the UK: three native conifers – yew, Scots pine and juniper; shrubs like holly and guelder rose; and also broadleaf deciduous trees, including many well-known favourites such as ash, silver birch, elm, maple and, of course, oak. Lots of trees are identified largely by their flowers, fruits or nuts, or by the shape of their leaves. Deciduous trees will drop their leaves in the winter, and this can make for one of the most spectacular times of year: watching a woodland change colour in the autumn is magical, and who doesn't love searching around for acorns

or conkers as they fall from the trees? Some trees are also fabulous for their edible bounty, with treats like elderflower, which blossoms in late spring; blackthorn (or 'sloe'), which makes a favourite tipple, sloe gin; and crab apple. As always when foraging, enlist the help of an expert until you know what you're doing: lots of berries in the UK are poisonous to humans.

Spores

Don't be alarmed, but there are over 15,000 different species of fungi in the UK. Gulp (or not, as the case may be)! If nothing else, get to know some basic fungi as the names are totally enigmatic, onomatopoeic and downright fun. Some of them look really weird as well. Fly agaric is your typical toadstool: red with white spots, with fairies living underneath it. Beefsteak fungus looks like (you'll never guess) a sirloin sticking out of the side of an oak tree. Stinkhorn is funny on all sorts of levels. Jelly ear fungus, often found on elder, looks like a human ear, and puffballs are hugely satisfying in being perfectly spherical. I'm not often going to tell you not to do things in this book, but I am making an exception in this instance: do not eat a single slither of wild fungus unless you know that it is edible. The safest way to learn is with an expert forager, and I'd absolutely urge you to do this if you're after some food for free.

Wild kit – what do I need?

Most of the Random Acts of Wildness in the book are designed to be done with minimal equipment. There are just a few key items that will make your wild adventures even more exciting and comfortable...

Warm and waterproof clothing

Who are we kidding? Our beloved British weather is totally unpredictable, and if you're not prepared it can put a dampener on the wildest of adventures. This is especially true if you're getting the kids involved in your newfound love for the wild: children need to feel warm and safe to have fun and really get stuck in, so making sure they're comfortable will make everything a lot easier.

Wellies

If you can get your hands on a good pair, do. There's nothing worse than having cold, wet toes as you trudge through the wild, and a lovely pair of wellies coupled with cosy, thick socks will do the trick.

A thermos flask

Even in the summer, it can get a bit chilly outside, and loads of Random Acts of Wildness will be hugely enhanced with a warming mug of hot chocolate, a strong coffee or a nice cup of tea. Whatever your favourite tipple, investing in a good thermos flask for those chilly days, early mornings and late evenings will be money well spent.

Binoculars

If you're really getting into your wild adventures, it might be time to invest in a pair of binoculars, which will help you explore wildlife and wild places in more detail, and cause the minimal amount of disturbance to sensitive wildlife. They're not just great for birds, but will come in handy for scanning the sea for marine life and watching mammals, too. You can pick up a good pair for around £100, and as with anything, the more you spend, the better the quality. Lots of nature reserves and visitor centres have demonstrations where you can test different pairs to see which ones are best for you.

A field guide or two

As a book addict, my house is simply teeming with field guides for every different kind of animal you can think of: birds, butterflies, whales, dolphins, moths, bats, mammals, wildflowers, fungi and more. You don't need all of these: when you're starting out, there are loads of free websites that can help with identification. You can also download field guides as apps on to your smartphone. But if you're like me, and love the feel of a book in your hands, buying one or two of your choice might be a good investment. Pick your favourite Random Acts of Wildness and work out which ones you need from there. If you're getting into foraging, I would recommend buying a book that you can take with you, so you're always aware of what you're picking.

A smartphone or camera

This may seem counter-intuitive. After all, we're trying to get you outside into the wild and away from all that technology. But a smartphone or camera can be very useful to document your adventures, help you with identification and, of course, take photographs. Just don't get addicted to it and don't let it replace your wild adventures.

How to use this book

The Random Acts of Wildness have been ordered roughly by season, although most can be done at any time of year: just do whatever takes your fancy on the day. Though most activities are great for kids, some – like the DIY gin recipes – are not, so parents, please supervise. As well as lots of really Random Acts of Wildness in the book, you'll notice that there are some common themes that appear throughout.

Wild words
There are lots of 'wild words' for you to learn and try to use in everyday conversation. Words are magical things. They're full of mischievous ideas, paint beautiful pictures, and tell us stories of the world around us. Lots of people grow up without knowing what these words are and what they really mean: are apples and blackberries fruits or phones? Are chatrooms more important than clovers, catkins and conkers? Of course not. We can all make room for a little more nature in our brains by learning some wild words, sharing them with other people and putting them into practice by having amazing wild experiences. The words scattered throughout the book are my favourites. See if you can use them. What are your favourites? You can even make up your own words – that's how language is born!

Think before you buy
Again, there are lots of these tips included. They don't require much effort at all – just a little bit of conscious thought when you're out doing your regular weekly shop. Every time we clean our houses, do the dishes, take a shower, get crafty, eat takeaway food, and so on, we're having an impact on planet Earth. Help is at hand, though – I've pulled together some easy switches to make in your everyday life that will allow you to do your bit for Mother Nature.

Identify a wild species
In every chapter there are examples of wild plants and animals described (with photos) that should help you feel more confident in identifying some of the most common species you might see every day. From bees to trees, grasses to fungi, there are interesting hints and tips to guide you in figuring out what species you're looking at. Don't worry – you don't have to remember all of these by heart (I certainly can't!); just keep referring to the book if you're not sure. If you find that you really love learning about a certain group of plants or animals, think about investing in field guides for those species.

Unexpected Random Acts of Wildness

Unexpected animal enounters can happen anywhere and at any time. Some of them can be completely accidental, while others are even more magical than you expected. They can happen to anyone, too. I've included some of my own unexpected Random Acts of Wildness to show you how, once you begin to immerse yourself in a wild life, you can encounter unbelievable species. The eight included in this book are some of my most enchanting wildlife experiences – from bow riding dolphins to breaching humpback whales and encounters with badgers and natterjack toads. There are a lot more I could have picked from, too. Once you start your own wild life, you'll find that you have your own moments. I've also included a few hints and tips to show you the best way to have a similar experience.

Staying happy and safe in the wild

I don't want to impose lots of rules on your time in the wild: this is about what you can do, and not what you can't. That said, being sensible and looking after nature while you're out enjoying it will ensure it thrives for future generations. All the activities in this book are meant to be carried out responsibly, and it is your responsibility to ensure that all Random Acts of Wildness keep yourself and the natural world safe. Whether you're climbing a tree, dipping your feet in the water or tasting a wild blackberry, take care.

The Countryside Code

There's a simple code to follow when you're out enjoying wild places, for the benefit of both people and wildlife. You can find a copy of the full code online at gov.uk/government/publications/the-countryside-code, but here are the key points:

Respect other people. Many people, just like you, love spending time in wild places – they live there, work there or go there for pleasure. So when you're exploring, stick to footpaths and leave gates the way you find them (whether they're open or closed). Climb over stiles and through gaps, never over walls or fences. Treat farm animals and vehicles with caution and respect, giving them a wide berth. If you see a problem, let the local landowner know.

Protect the natural environment. Take as many photos as you like – but never pick wildflowers or dig up trees to take home. Make sure that all litter gets collected. Don't light fires or drop cigarette butts. Dogs must always be kept under control and cleaned up after, and make sure to respect local rules: if an area doesn't allow dogs, it's for

a reason. There might be ground-nesting birds or a rare habitat that needs protecting, or livestock in the area. It's your responsibility to find out what these rules are, and the internet is a great place to start.

All wild plants are protected under the Wildlife and Countryside Act (1981) and it is illegal to dig up or remove a plant without permission. Some species are specially protected (these can be found on Schedule 8 of the Wildlife and Countryside Act (1981)).

Prepare to enjoy the outdoors. Stay safe by doing a little prep if you're going into wild areas: look up your location online or in an up-to-date guidebook. Remember, you may not have phone signal, so always let someone know where you're going. The weather can change quickly in the uplands, so be prepared with warm clothes, waterproofs and something to eat or drink. Follow local signs and guidance.

Wild swimming

Wild swimming can be great fun, but it must be enjoyed responsibly and safely. This book gives no guidance as to locations or specific situations, so before taking a dip, make sure that you have researched your activity thoroughly, looking at local conditions, legal access and your own physical suitability for the swim. Give fishermen a wide berth and respect local landowners' wishes. Before getting in the water, check for changing or rip tides, strong currents, weed or debris in the water, cold or deep water, or anything else that could cause harm. There are loads of online forums and websites that can provide information about the best swimming locations – these are the best place to start. Even better – join a local wild swimming group, who can offer support, activities, events and social opportunities, too!

Wild foraging

Many wildlife sites don't allow commercial foraging, so keep your foraging for domestic use only. Some sites don't allow foraging at all, so always check for local guidance and legal protection – it's illegal to pick some species. Some plants and fungi are poisonous to humans, so be 100 per cent sure of identification and edibility before you eat any. Courses are a great place to start or go out with an expert to pick up top tips. Books and the internet are good resources, too, but if there are any doubts on identification, it's best not to eat it. Only forage where there is a lot of food to be had and only take what you need. Leave plenty for local wildlife populations, which may depend on it.

Be respectful, be responsible, and have wonderful adventures!

Start a wild diary

Welcome to the start of your wild adventure – 365 Days Wild! I promise, you are going to have a really wild time and you're going to love every second. There are 365 Random Acts of Wildness here for you to try out. Every single one will encourage you to fall in love with, learn about or even help wildlife and wild places near you. So, what are you waiting for?

As you start doing more and more Random Acts of Wildness, you might forget what you've done already, so start a wild diary. You could either buy or make one and decorate it with drawings or sketches, or even fallen leaves and pressed petals. The most important thing about your diary is that it will help you reflect on all the different Random Acts of Wildness that you've already done, and plan what you might do next.

Write down everything you do and, if you're feeling arty, you could draw little pictures or even stick in things that you find – feathers, leaves and so on. You could include notes about wildlife you've seen, like birds or insects; who you were with at the time; and where you went.

But that's only the beginning – as well as what you've done, make a note of how those Random Acts of Wildness have made you feel. Did you feel excited, calm, relaxed, nervous, grumpy, inspired, tired, joyful? Be completely honest with yourself and make a note of anything you think or feel as you're doing your Random Act of Wildness that day.

This will also give you a little reminder to do something wild every day, as you'll want to write it down. If you miss a day – that's fine. We all lead hectic lifestyles and finding that wild time can be tricky. Hopefully your diary will help you make time, no matter where you are or what you're doing.

Finally, as you're filling up the pages, don't forget to look back on what you've been doing, and remember all the Random Acts of Wildness you've done. How does it make you feel when you re-live those memories? Hopefully you'll begin to see how amazing a wild life really is.

Find your local patch

Wildlife and wild places are all around us. You just have to know where to look and what you're looking for. Wildlife can find a home in the most unusual of places, so start with those you know well: your garden, your neighbourhood and any regular journeys you make, such as to work or school. Is there a park or churchyard within a mile or two? Maybe there's even a local nature reserve. This is your 'patch' – a little bit of the world that you can get to know better than anyone else. Take the first step towards exploring your local wildlife and within a short space of time you'll become a local patch expert.

To start with, you won't need anything other than your senses. As you get more confident, you may need a website, app or book to help you identify wildlife, and perhaps a pair of binoculars, but these aren't essential. Identify an area near you that looks promising: lush, green and with some wildlife.

Exploration is about using all your senses, so start by looking and listening for wildlife. Can you hear birds singing? Can you see different flowers? Do the leaves have different shapes? Begin by noticing one or two little things every day in your patch and make a note of them in your diary (or on a blog or calendar).

Try and get back to your patch every few days (or if you're feeling ambitious, every day!) and build on what you've already noticed: what else is there? Is anything new? Is the weather changing what's happening? Try different times of day as well, keeping notes all the time. If you're struggling to identify wildlife while you're there, take photos or notes or make sketches.

Keeping lists of the wildlife you've seen and how it's changed over the seasons will bring a huge sense of achievement. And reflecting on your memories will bring a sense of connection with your very own wild patch.

Search for mini wildness

Habitats don't have to be huge to be diverse – it's all about your sense of perspective. Nature can find a way to flourish even in tiny spaces. See if you can spot wildflowers, dandelions or grasses sprouting out of the sides of walls, between cracks in the pavement, or even in the gutters above. You'll see a jumble of weeds growing up near the roof of a house or an office building. That's all part of the magic. Lichens and mosses love to grow in fresh, clean air on any available surface, on benches, trees, the sides of buildings, so open your eyes to these undiscovered wild places and see what you can spot. Remember, weeds are just plants that are growing in the 'wrong' place. We should be celebrating weeds, not uprooting them! Next time you see a dandelion or some daisies, before you seek vengeance, take a moment to appreciate just how pretty they are.

Timelapse a tree

Is there a tree you go past every day on the way to work, or one near your house, in a street or local park? This Random Act of Wildness will only take a few seconds and a camera phone, but you'll need to go back to your tree at least twelve times over the course of a year – your 365 Days Wild. Focusing on a local tree will make this as easy for you as possible, especially if it's a tree you pass every day. All you need to do is take a photograph. Try and get the whole tree in, from the roots to the very end of the twigs. Save the photo (you'll need it again), then repeat as often as you can, making sure that you return to the exact same spot each time to take the photograph. You could do this once a month, once a fortnight, once a week, or even daily if you like a challenge! You're creating a timelapse of your tree, and as you look back through your photos you'll begin to see the subtle changes that we take for granted – when the first buds appear, when the tree is full and lush, when the leaves begin to change colour and fall, and when the branches are bare and naked. If you can keep it up all year round, you'll get a diary for your tree. You could print your photos off and create a collage, or if you're a techy whizz then you could create a single display or even a video of them on your computer – perfect for sharing with friends!

Lift up a log

Look for a log that's been lying on the ground a good long time. This could be anywhere – in a woodland, in your garden, in the park. Carefully, using gloves if you like, lift one end and see what might be lurking in the cracks. To us, this may not look like much, but a fallen log, decaying inside, with lots of bits rotting away, creating a yummy, woody mulch, is the perfect mini ecosystem for all sorts of invertebrates, or maybe even amphibians like frogs or newts. The trick is to be gentle, and don't pick anything that looks too heavy. Just peek underneath – what can you see? Look for brightly coloured beetles, like ladybirds, or earwigs scurrying for cover. Centipedes and millipedes will love this damp, dark hideaway, and slugs and snails might tuck themselves into the cracks. Even if you don't know the species, see how many different creatures you can spot. When you're finished, make sure to lay the log back down exactly where you found it. That's somebody else's home, after all!

Inhale a wild scent

Make the most of your most underappreciated sense today: smell. The natural world is bursting with gorgeous (and some not so gorgeous!) aromas, and they only take a few seconds to enjoy if you've got a jam-packed day. Try and find different wild smells, even if you're in the city and think that you're confined to fast-food joints, car emissions and whatever other unpleasantness might be lurking about.

Trees have a smell, bushes and flowers have a smell, freshly fallen rain on a hot pavement has a smell. It's about taking a bit of time in your day to find something wild and see what it smells like. In the spring and summer, target wildflowers growing in unusual places or wild in mini meadows. In the winter, it might be more challenging, but see what you can find. My personal favourites are gorse flowers, pine needles and the dank smell of a woodland after it has rained.

Keep a window list

Pick a window with a view either from your house or your workplace. Make sure that it's got a bit of variety, so overlooking a garden or your street, a park or green space, or a few trees. Keep a pen and a notebook on the windowsill. Every time you see a new animal from the window, make a note of it. You can only include wildlife that you see from that window, so other rooms in the house or workplace don't count. Look carefully at all the different places where wildlife could be hiding – in the tops of trees, flying overhead, buried in bushes, perched in the distance. Don't forget to check for insects crawling along the window ledge, too! Once you've been looking for a few days, you'll find that you know this familiar scene much better than you did before. You'll also become a bit obsessed. If you want to challenge yourself further, get a friend involved and ask them to do the same from a window of their choice; you can compete for the best window list!

THINK! THINK! THINK!

THINK! THINK! THINK!

THINK! THINK! THINK!

THINK! THINK! THINK!

8

COMPOST

9

10

11

BUMBARREL

(n): Old name for the long-tailed tit, so called for the shape of their nest, which is almost spherical, with a little hole at the front.

Think before you buy

Peat-free compost has been around for years, and it's a must-have for the conscientious gardener. Traditional composts contain a substance called peat, which is mined from peaty bogs around the world. It's taken years to form and is a hugely valuable resource when left out in nature – it locks up carbon, helping to fight climate change, and is a great habitat for plants, mosses and beasties. The processes involved in extracting it are devastating huge areas of the countryside. So next time you're shopping for compost, insist on peat-free. Even better, make your own (find out how on page 218).

Relax under a rainbow

This Random Act of Wildness requires the right type of weather, but when it happens you should savour the beauty. When there is rain in the air and the sun breaks through the clouds, rainbows can form in the atmosphere, arching over the earth. This natural spectrum of light is caused by sunlight refracting and reflecting through the moisture and raindrops. We've all seen them, so rather than ruing the rain, take a minute to stop and relax under this natural light show. Does it get stronger or begin to fade? Is it a full arch or broken by clouds? Sit back and admire it – what's your favourite colour shining in the sky?

Change your perspective

This Random Act of Wildness is simple, but surprisingly good for you! Rather than looking down at your phone, change your perspective and look up. Give your neck a rest, stretch your muscles and search for birds in unusual places, insects above you, or even just clouds racing by overhead. You might see gulls, like kittiwakes, nesting on top of buildings, or wagtails hunting on rooftops, pumping their tails as they go. Peregrine falcons love cityscapes, using the buildings like cliffs and crags. All of that looking down can't be good for you, so eyes to the skies today and enjoy the sun, rain or wind on your face!

Learn a wild word

Bouncing along from tree to tree, look out for little black, white and pink bumbarrels moving through in flocks. They are, of course, long-tailed tits. Long-tailed tits stick together. In early spring, they'll begin to build intricate, teardrop-shaped nests of moss, feathers and spider webs. You may see young, non-breeding birds helping their older relatives, getting the nest ready and ship-shape for the eggs and chicks. They huddle together at night, packed tightly on a branch. Other great nicknames for these gorgeous little fellas include prinpiddle and mumruffin.

Pick up a piece of plastic

Plastic can be one of the worst things for nature and our environment. Most plastics don't break down naturally on their own, and even the biodegradable ones can take years and years. Sadly, we're almost completely reliant on plastic products and packaging – me as much as anyone – and when discarded outside it can cause serious problems for our wildlife. It can be accidentally eaten by birds and mammals, who might mistake it for food. If it makes its way into rivers, it'll soon be in the sea, where it can be eaten by fish, whales and dolphins. In short, there's no place for plastic lying around on the ground.

Challenge yourself today to pick up a piece of plastic litter that's been left on the ground. If you can, take it home and recycle it, but at the very least pop it in a bin. You might find drinks bottles, old sweet wrappers, food packets and random bits that don't make any sense at all. If you can, use a pair of gloves and wash your hands afterwards. This little Random Act of Wildness might save a little life – that's definitely one worth doing for today!

Jump over puddles (or in them!)

Any good at long-jump? No, me neither. The great thing about trying to jump over puddles is that it's just as much fun when you end up in them. On a lush rainy day, don your wellies and unleash your inner wild child. If you've got little ones in your life, this is a great way to motivate them to spend some time outdoors, even in the wet weather.

Find a spot with lots of puddles – try to avoid the really muddy ones. Big brown puddles full of squelchy mud may look appetising, but be aware that it's easy to slip and lose a welly. Have you ever got your shoe stuck in the suction of thick, oozing mud? It's all fun and games until your foot pops out and you fall over! Once you've got your course, challenge everyone to jump over every puddle – start with the smallest ones and work your way up to the biggest. It's up to you if you allow a run up or if you all go from a standing start. You can give points for the biggest jumps or the most stylish. Remember: if you've got to drive or have a long walk home, take some spare socks and a towel – there's nothing worse than cold, wet feet.

Walk on the wild side

Walking is a good form of exercise – one that we mustn't underestimate. When you're tired and you've had a long day, it can be hard to motivate yourself to get up and out of the house to stretch your legs. I certainly struggle at times. Walking in the local area gives me a motivation and I feel much better for it. I use the step counter on my phone to set myself targets, and take the opportunity to explore some wild places that I have never been to before, even if they are only minutes away: the canal, local footpaths across fields, and longer walks along the river. I spot wildflowers, which I never notice when I'm driving or running, and because I am motivated by the step counter (and not my time, speed or distance) I'm at liberty to stop and examine them and take photos. Sometimes I borrow a dog from a neighbour (which they appreciate, too!).

This is an easy one to do and a great way to get a nature fix, whether it's just for a few minutes at lunchtime or a longer weekend stroll. If you've got a packed schedule already, see where you can squeeze in a few minutes to take a nature walk, or bring a bit of nature consciously into an existing walk. On the way to school or work, try spotting birds, flowers, seeds or trees, and comparing what you experience each day. If you have a busy day, take a few minutes at lunch to explore somewhere local, and at weekends, try and prioritise a longer walk, either by yourself or with family.

Follow a snail trail

As they slowly slide along in their quest to get from a to b, snails leave a shiny trail behind them. This trail is a slime, excreted by the snail to help them keep moving, pushed along by one muscular foot. The slime reduces the friction between them and the ground, making it easier to lug their shell around (imagine carrying your home on your back all the time!). These trails, if undisturbed by rain or anything else, can make little treasure maps to follow and explore. Find a good long one and follow it – it might cover the pavement, trees, plants, leaves, furniture – anything that's in its way. The snail will just keep on sliding over everything.

At the end of the trail you might find the snail itself. If you're very gentle and very careful, lift the snail on to your hand. It will retract inside its shell at first, but if you sit patiently and quietly, it might tentatively poke its head out to inspect this new environment, waving its eyes around on long tentacles. I always think they look very inquisitive when they're doing this. You can let your snail slide all over your hand and arm, leaving a sticky, shiny slime trail on you, too! It feels very strange, but cool and quite therapeutic. Beware – the little chap might feel so at home that he'll go for a poo or a wee on you! When you're finished, gently place him back where you found him, so that he can continue on his way. Give your hands a good scrub afterwards – those trails are very sticky.

Make a yummy mud pie

All children should be taught early on the joys of making mud pies. They're not fancy or hard to make. You just have to accept that you're going to get mucky and that's the whole point. All you need is soil and water, mixed straight in the ground or in a bucket. You want a nice, gooey consistency of mud, so don't add too much water straight away. Mixing by hand is definitely the most satisfying. Once you're happy with the consistency, lift up huge great dollops and shape them into giant pancake shapes, slopping them on the floor with a satisfying splat. You can just let the mud ooze through your fingers or shape it with finesse. You can even add 'toppings' – sticks, pebbles, leaves and whatever else you find lying around. There's no real point to this Random Act of Wildness, other than the satisfaction of re-connecting with your childhood. No adult excuses, either – mud washes off skin easily, so dive right in.

Grow some tasty cress

Growing cress is a fun, easy and tasty Random Act of Wildness, especially if you don't want to spend a long time nurturing lots of house plants. It's a good practice run for the more serious stuff, and can be a great challenge for little ones in your life, too.

You will need:
- A small empty yoghurt pot – get ready to upcycle!
- Kitchen roll
- A little soil
- Cress seeds
- A watering can
- Somewhere warm and sunny, like a kitchen windowsill

1. Clean out your yoghurt pot (ideally, eat the yoghurt then rinse the pot). Line the bottom with a thick layer of kitchen roll, making sure it's nice and damp. **2.** Add a layer of soil so that it finishes a centimetre or so from the top of the pot. Sprinkle in a teaspoon of cress seeds and push them gently into the soil. Water it gently and pop it in the full sunshine. You'll need to keep it warm and moist. **3.** After a few days, you'll notice the cress appearing and you should be able to harvest it soon after – mix with salads or use as flavouring for egg sandwiches!

Take your time with celandine

Like little yellow stars shooting out of the ground rather than through the sky, the lesser celandine is a member of the buttercup family. It's one of the first wildflowers you'll see in the springtime, blossoming in woodlands, along hedgerows and near river banks. It grows very close to the ground, with shiny leaves that are shaped like the ace in a deck of cards. The flowers themselves are glossy and yellow, with between eight and twelve individual petals splaying out.

The lesser celandine can grow in gardens as well as in the wild, but is largely regarded as a weed. Yet it is perfect for those pollinators that have woken up early in the year. Before you remove it, think of all the bees and other insects that will benefit from that early source of nectar. Find some blooming near you by searching among little woodlands, along hedgerows or near rivers. It loves the damp. Snap a photo and send it to someone who might need a little bit of sunshine in their day – these flowers will brighten up even the dreariest moments as spring starts to emerge.

Share dinner with ducks

Feeding the ducks has been a favourite pastime for generations. I used to do it with my parents and grandparents and it was always bread. My theory is that my nana hated waste, so any mouldy bread would go straight to the ducks instead of the bin. Now we know that bread is bad for ducks, geese and swans (and for our rivers, too!), but that doesn't mean we should stop feeding the ducks altogether. It's a therapeutic way to spend a few minutes, either alone or with others.

Find a family of ducks nearby that maybe don't get as much attention from the public; walking a little way from other people might tempt the shyer birds out of the undergrowth. Feed them defrosted peas, corn or oats instead of bread, and don't give them too much. You don't want them to become dependent on human handouts. Rice, vegetable peelings, birdseed or mealworms are also good for them, and you can buy special duck food from most bird food suppliers, too. Scatter food in shallow water and on the grass, and enjoy the happy quacking of the ducks, geese and swans!

Don't try and feed birds by hand. Ducks tend to be gentle, but swans and geese can give you a nasty nip. Bigger birds can be intimidating to little kids (although they won't try and hurt you!). Avoid disturbing birds on nests – they need to raise their young in peace.

Read a wild book

What could be more relaxing than reading a book about nature while you're actually in nature? The genre of nature writing is generally credited to Gilbert White, in his *Natural History of Selborne*, published 230 years ago and detailing the nature all around his home village in Hampshire. Now you can find stories about wildlife and wild places for all ages and tastes. Nature writing can be descriptive, poetic, angry, sad, funny, exciting, thrilling, and it's fabulous that so many writers take their inspiration from the wild. The only way to find your favourite nature book is to start reading a few. Ask friends if they have any you can borrow, or look some authors up online to get a taste of their writing. Second-hand bookshops always have a few gems. Maybe you'll like something very narrative, or maybe you'll prefer something factually accurate, like a field guide. A lot of fiction books have nature running throughout them, too. The most exciting bit about this Random Act of Wildness is taking your book somewhere wild, so that you can immerse yourself in the words and in your surroundings.

Grow your own sunflowers

Sunflowers are big and daisy-like, and if you're not a confident grower they are a great place to start. Once fully-blossomed, the flower heads are popular with birds, like finches, as the seeds make a tasty snack for them. Tall, beautiful and striking, sunflowers can make a popular addition to your garden. April is the best time to plant, as much of the frost will have passed by then. You'll need well-drained soil that's free of weeds, and plenty of space for the flowers to grow upwards and outwards. Full sunlight is needed, as those big flowers will flourish in the sunshine, and a bit of protection from the wind and rain, too.

Rake the soil first, then plant each seed just over a centimetre into the ground and 10cm apart from its neighbours. If they all grow, you may have to spread them out even more. Water the seeds gently and keep them moist. As the seedlings come through, keep an eye out for slugs and snails and remove any that are getting too close. The sunflower should grow quickly and straight up. You'll need a cane and some string to support it as it tops dizzying heights (or it may topple over). Once the flower blooms, watch as it follows the sun across the sky, turning its head to catch all those rays!

Discover the urban jungle

Who knew that a trip to the city could be a wild experience? Whether you're a born-and-bred city-dweller or a country bumpkin, the urban jungle is a totally underappreciated habitat, full of wonderful wildlife. You just have to know where to look. The train tracks of underground stations are great places to see house mice scurrying around. Urban parks with deep lakes are perfect for ducks, geese and swans. Tall buildings have been converted into cliff faces by gulls and birds of prey, like peregrines; they use the roofs and ledges to survey the surrounding area, making the perfect launch pad for catching prey, or a safe place for raising chicks. When you're in the city, take a moment to enjoy the natural delights that the concrete jungle can offer by looking up as you walk, altering your route to go through a park or community garden, or pausing a moment by a canal or river to see what might be paddling along: coot or moorhen, or even otters, which are now found in many UK cities. Creatures we would normally associate with the countryside, like deer, foxes and owls, are all making the most of their new city environments, but night time can be the best time for a wild encounter.

23

BABY WIPES

24

25

26

NARCISSUS

(n): Bulbous Eurasian plant of a genus that includes the daffodil. Wild flowers have white or pale outer petals and a shallow orange or yellow cup in the centre.

Think before you buy

You don't have to have a baby to be addicted to baby wipes or face wipes. They're handy, easy to use and cheap enough to be convenient. They also don't go away! They're not flushable or recyclable, and a nightmare if they clog up your drains. I've recently invested in some re-usable wipes, however, and I'm completely converted. They're squares of soft flannel that come in their own sealed tub, which you fill with a little water and add lovely essential oils to. When you've finished with them, you wash them and dry them – simple. Because they're natural, they're much better for your delicate skin, too.

Scatter seedbombs

Seedbombs are like guerrilla gardening – a great way to introduce wild plants into an area that otherwise has no life in it. Simply mix peat-free compost (or garden soil) with some native wildflower seeds. Make sure you use plenty of seeds and double-check they're native to the area – you don't want to accidentally spread something that could be damaging! You can add a small amount of clay powder if you like, to help everything stick together. Add water until you have a firm, sticky mixture that you can roll with your hands into balls. Let them dry a little and then throw them into bare bits of ground in your garden.

Download a wild app

While too much screen time isn't healthy, we can use our devices for good (instead of for addictive games and internet shopping!) and connect with the natural world around us. There are some wonderful nature apps available to help you identify birds, butterflies, bees, mammals and flowers (sometimes just by uploading a picture or a sound clip of birdsong); they can help you find your nearest nature reserve or wild event; or you can use citizen science apps to record your wild sightings. A lot of apps are free or very cheap, so search for those you think will give you the best experience of wildlife around you.

Learn a wild word

Narcissus is another word for daffodil, with its drooping yellow head that delights us as it bursts into bloom in early spring. It comes in lots of different sizes and colours, usually yellow or white, with some being very tiny and highly scented, and others bigger and bolder. Most daffodils we see are escaped or hybridised varieties, but you can still enjoy wild daffodils in some woodlands or damp meadows in north or southwest England or Wales. Narcissus was a character in Greek mythology. He was so vain that he yearned after his own reflection, and as punishment was turned into a flower.

Dance with grebes

As winter turns to spring and we begin to feel the first warmth of the sun on our faces, one of the most beautiful courtship dances begins on our lakes, reservoirs and wetlands. Great crested grebes are beautiful birds – so beautiful in fact that they were hunted close to extinction for their exotic plumes. Luckily this ended in the 20th century, and great crested grebes are now widespread around the UK once more.

If you have a lake, reservoir or wetland near to you, there may be great crested grebes. Canals and gravel pits are good, too. When the mist is rising from the surface of the water, two birds, a male and female grebe, might come together and dance out in the open for you. They fluff up the plumes around their heads, bow, and then begin an intricate toing and froing with each other, sometimes shaking their heads and nodding, sometimes bowing low to the water, and standing up tall and paddling their feet frenetically. It's not dancing as we know it, but it's still cool to watch! They'll even take a beakful of weed and flick it at each other.

Try and spy the courtship dance of the great crested grebe for a Random Act of Wildness; wrap up warm and enjoy the serenity of the water, too.

Spy a hovering kestrel

If you're on a long car journey, especially if you're going to be stuck for hours on a motorway, then this is the Random Act of Wildness for you. Try and spy our most common falcon, a nippy little bird of prey called the kestrel. Kestrels are quite small, very fast, and easy to identify. They have pointed wings that curve backwards slightly and a fanned tail. The females are bigger than the males, and (as is the case all too often in the bird world) a bit plainer. If you're ever lucky enough to see a kestrel up close, the males are handsome birds, with a grey-blue face, head and tail, and chestnut red back and wings.

You're most likely to see a kestrel perched atop a telegraph pole or hovering by the side of the road. They love to hunt along grass verges, where they're looking for small mammals. You'll see them with their heads craned downwards, staring intently at the ground and using excellent eyesight to hone in on dinner. When they hover, they use very shallow, silent, fast wingbeats to keep them steady. You might see them plunge towards the ground to catch their dinner; if they're successful, they'll carry it off to a suitable location. If not, it's back to the skies to try again. See how many you can spot.

Totally urban otters

Town centres probably aren't what you picture first when you think of wildlife experiences, especially in the middle of the day in March, with the streets bustling with shoppers and concrete all around. Parts of Thetford in Norfolk are very pretty; other parts, like the spot just outside the shopping centre, not so much. That didn't matter though.

We were walking along the river on a March morning, looking for tell-tale ripples, shimmies and disturbances. It was brown with mud and not very appetising. We were in the town centre, with the river curving away from us and people everywhere, when we saw someone downstream with a camera. He was looking intently at the river. Then he turned and waved frantically, but silently, to us. He had one.

We scurried over cautiously, stopping beside the man. No one said anything, but he pointed at some ripples in the water, tantalisingly fresh. I crouched right down on the edge of the river so that I was just a couple of feet above the water's surface, and then pop! Up shot the head of an otter. There, right in front of me, looking straight at me bold as brass. I froze and tried not to make a sound, as though he hadn't half given me a fright. Even the photographer didn't raise his camera. The otter looked straight at me for a long moment, before lazily turning tail, swimming back to the centre of the river and diving down to fish again. Every minute or so he'd pop back up for air, occasionally appearing with some small, tasty morsel to crunch on and swallow.

Then he ducked down one last time and this time didn't come back up. We looked up and down the river and saw his head and whiskers appear further downstream, powerful tail swishing through the water. There was no way we could keep up, and in just a few minutes he'd disappeared completely. No doubt he knew a better spot to fish.

Do it yourself:
Otters are now popping up all over the UK in rivers, lakes and reservoirs. See if your local Wildlife Trust can recommend any good spots. You may have to go early in the morning or later in the evening and be very patient. They can be seen all year round, and you'll be able to find clues as to their presence, like otter spraint (poo) or paw prints in the mud. You'll need to be silent as they're easily spooked. If you're desperate to get a good view, then Scotland (mostly the Scottish Isles and West Coast) has reliable spots where you're almost guaranteed to see them. You may need binoculars.

Identify five gorgeous garden birds

No matter where you live, town or countryside, there's a few species of birds that make the most of our gardens. Our gardens provide shelter from the worst weather, food from our lawns and feeders, and water in birdbaths. Ornamental trees, bushes and plants can provide cover, too, and places to nest. The kind of birds you get might vary with the time of year or where you are, but there's a few favourites that you've got a good chance of seeing. We tend to take our garden birds for granted and don't think of them as being anything special, but look closer – they are some of the subtlest and most beautifully plumaged birds in the UK.

Blackbird Blackbirds are a kind of thrush. Most kids grow up being able to recognise them, as they're abundant and widely spread over the UK. The males appear jet black all over, with a beady black eye and a bright yellow-orange bill. The females are chocolate brown and mottled, slightly lighter underneath with a few darker streaks. They hop around on the ground and will be seen wrestling with a juicy worm. They also like berries, which they'll pluck from trees, and seeds, which they will pick off the ground. They rarely hang off bird feeders, preferring to forage from lawns or bird tables.

Dunnock Also known as the hedge sparrow, the dunnock is a seemingly shy and retiring little bird. They appear to skulk on the edges of bushes and in the undergrowth, looking a bit nervous as they flick their wings. Not so, in fact. They can be feisty, fiery and loud. They have a beautiful song in the spring, and when two territorial males come together then feathers can fly. They have a brown streaky back and a grey-blue face and breast, with subtle and elegant markings. They won't come to feeders, but will enjoy seeds, fruit and mealworms on the ground.

Robin I'm sure you know what a robin is, even if it's just from Christmas cards. As well as being the symbol of winter, they're also a great garden bird to have, full of personality. They have a loud tuneful voice which they use for much of the year. You might even hear them at night as they sing under streetlamps. Brown on top, pale underneath with a bright red-orange breast, the robin has been voted the UK's favourite bird. They like to forage on the ground or on bird tables, rather than hanging feeders, and are partial to mealworms. They're also sociable with humans – you might find them confident enough to come close to you or even to your hand. With other robins though, they are territorial and feisty, happy to have a scrap over anything.

Blue tit The blue tit is a beautiful bird, probably one of the most gorgeous in the UK. They're small, topping in at around 12cm, and sociable. They have a tiny bill, a lemon-yellow breast, blue wings with a white panel across the wing (called a 'wingbar'), a greenish back and a white face, with a blue cap. There's a black line around the face and going through the eye, too. They'll happily come to feeders and bird tables, eating little nuts and seeds. Don't mistake them for great tits, which are bigger, bulkier and have a jet-black cap all over.

Woodpigeon Most pigeons are seen as being a bit dull, a bit commonplace, but this does seem quite unfair. Yes, they're ungainly, and can look a bit grey and washed out, but that's not their fault, is it? Woodpigeons are grey all over, but with different shades, ranging from stormy grey on the back to a pinkish buff on the breast. They have piercing yellow eyes, an iridescent green patch on the back of the neck, and a distinctive white collar. This collar helps to distinguish them from feral pigeons, which come in all shapes and sizes. When they fly, their wings clatter loudly and they coo repetitively, with four or five notes that go up and down in pitch.

Discover the wide web

Don't you feel lucky that you don't have to build your own house? On a weekly basis? Out of materials that you've made from your own body? Well spare a moment for the much-feared spider, because this is what this diligent creature has to do over and over again if it wants to eat and sleep in relative comfort. It's fascinating to watch them at work. What's even more awesome is that human architects require years of training; spiders are born knowing how to spin their webs.

They use glands in their bodies to produce silk, which dries on contact with air and becomes incredibly strong. They'll anchor on to something sturdy and begin to craft patterns with their threads. The typical shape is a kind of star shape, with several prongs radiating out from a central point (called 'radial lines') and threads which connect these lines together (called 'orb lines'). Once the web is complete, they will lurk silently in a corner waiting for an unwitting insect to fly into the web and get caught on the sticky strands.

A great chance to admire a web is in the early morning, on a cool sunny day, as dew settles across the landscape. Droplets of water will collect on the web, making it sparkle and shine. See if you can find an elaborate web in your garden or local neighbourhood, and admire the hard work that's gone into making this beautiful structure.

Buzz with the first bee

Many bumblebee species will go into hibernation in the winter, spending the coldest months out of harm's way underground. When you see the first ones of the year, you could be looking at a queen that has freshly emerged from hibernation, looking to set up a new colony. If the winter has been relatively warm and dry, queen bees can emerge in late February and start to build their new homes. Look for big bees buzzing around patches of flowers or plants in your garden, looking for their next meal (and turn to page 111 if you want to give them a helping hand). The first bumblebee you see in the year can give you a little buzz, as it were. After so long of not seeing these beautiful insects, it is good to know that spring is on the way. Make a note of the date you see your first one. If you see a bumblebee that's active in the winter, it's probably a buff-tailed bumblebee. These industrious workers will carry on their business, making the most of scanty offerings of winter wildflowers.

Forget everything you thought you knew about seagulls

There's no such thing as a seagull! Those things you see at the seaside, or pretty much anywhere now – they're just plain old gulls. For this Random Act of Wildness, figure out what species of gull you're seeing most regularly – and try to crack the 'seagull' habit! Whatever we think of gulls, they're a formidable bunch and deserve a little respect.

Gulls have colonised huge parts of the UK now, moving far away from the sea. They're common in cities and around landfill sites, or anywhere they can scavenge a decent meal. The most commonly occurring small gull you're likely to see is a black-headed gull. In the summer, they have a dark brown cap and face (which gives them this misnomer), and in the winter, they have a little black spot just behind the eye. The biggest fellow you're likely to see is a great black-backed gull, which has a slate-dark back. Herring gulls are famous for trying to steal your chips. They're smaller than the great black-backed, but they're still large and chunky, with the piercing yellow eye, yellow bill, pale grey back and pink legs. They're noisy, unafraid and gregarious.

There are loads of other species you might see near the coast, but start with these three and see if you can tell them apart.

Plant a gutter garden

Gutter gardens are perfect for people who don't have the luxury of a big garden, but still want some beauty. They use a simple piece of guttering to create a long, thin garden that you can plant with some pollinator-friendly flowers, herbs or even fruit, like strawberries. You'll need to have end pieces for your guttering, to hold everything in, and somewhere strong to attach it to (remember, when filled with soil, plants and water, it'll weigh quite a lot): fences, walls, balcony railings, etc. A DIY store should be able to help you out with appropriate fixers. Drill some holes in the bottom to allow excess water to drain out. Fill it with a few inches of soil or peat-free compost and select the plants you'd like to grow – those that don't need a big area for roots (herbs grow really well in this environment, so you could try thyme, parsley, spearmint, chives and tarragon, for example). I've also seen succulents used. If your fence or wall can take the strain, you can layer gutter gardens one on top of the other, so that the water from the top one cascades down to those below. You'll need to keep them watered regularly, as there isn't much soil to stay damp in dry weather.

Flutter with the first butterfly

Spying the first butterfly of spring is wonderful and, depending on the weather, can happen as early as January (though March or April is more common). As the days get longer and the sun gets warmer, flowers begin to blossom, and more insects start to appear. My first butterfly of the year is usually the brimstone – a bright lemony yellow with wings shaped like leaves, with subtly pointed ends. Or it might be one of the white butterflies; a majestic red admiral; or a classy speckled wood. As soon as you get a warm day in early spring, see if you can spot anything fluttering by.

   Butterflies survive the cold winters by hibernating or migrating. Many species will find somewhere sheltered, like a log pile or shed, and remain inactive until it warms up. They can do this as an egg, a larva (caterpillar), pupa or as a fully-grown butterfly. Climate change and warmer winters have meant that butterflies are more likely to wake up in mid-winter, tricked into thinking it's spring. This can be disastrous, as there's very little food around and the weather can turn cold again quickly. Some species avoid this problem entirely – the familiar painted lady will migrate south to survive the winter!

Feed your feathered friends

Tuppence a bag? Don't worry, it's not just about pigeons. Feeding the birds is one of the most simple and effective ways that you can help wildlife in your back garden. Many birds that we're used to seeing every day are sadly in decline, and feeders are a great way to give them a helping hand. It'll also encourage a wider variety of birds into your garden, which you'll be able to enjoy from your window. Not got a garden? That doesn't have to stop you. There are now feeders designed to fit on balconies or attach straight to your window, so you can make a difference no matter how big your plot.

Here are some top tips for setting up your own feeders:

Use a variety of foods and feeders
Different birds will like different kinds of nuts, seeds and berries, as well as insects. With a feeding station, having two or three feeders with different seed mixes will bring in a variety of birds. Goldfinches are partial to niger seed. Tits, woodpeckers and starlings enjoy peanuts. Mealworms are popular with robins and thrushes. You can buy seed mixes which have lots of ingredients. You can also buy fat and suet balls, which are important in the winter as they're great sources of energy for little birds. Buy feeders appropriate for your seeds, so that the birds can get at them, and don't leave whole peanuts out in the summer – chicks and fledglings, much like babies, might choke on them. Never serve food in mesh bags, as birds can become trapped in them.

Buy from a reputable company
Much like the food we eat ourselves, everyone likes to know that they're getting a top-quality product. It's no different for bird food. Some companies have a better attitude to wildlife and the environment than others. Try to make sure that your products are from the UK and locally grown, so that they're not clocking up a huge carbon footprint, and check that those companies really care for wildlife on their farms, too.

Don't overfeed

It's really tempting to set up lots of feeders straight away and leave mounds of seed all over the garden, to draw in as many birds as possible immediately! Don't fall into this trap though. Start small and build up. It'll take the birds a while to find your feeders, and like other food, seeds and nuts will rot if they're not eaten. Lots of uneaten food can also attract unwanted guests, like rats, so make sure you clear away any leftovers and start at a steady pace.

Minimise threats from cats

Where you position your feeders is very important. You want to minimise threats from predators, especially domestic moggies: we're setting up a buffet for the birds, not a bird buffet! You have a few options to minimise the risks. If you have bushes with lots of spines and thorns, these will discourage cats from hunting there and provide cover for birds. Make sure that feeders are close enough for birds to dive for cover. Don't put feeders near to bushes and shrubs that could provide the perfect ambush for a cat, though. Give the birds enough time to react and fly away. And finally, keep them high off the ground.

Keep them clean

Hygiene can be a big problem with bird feeders and it's important that they get a regular and thorough wash. Diseases can be transmitted among birds through your feeders. Wash all feeders regularly with a gentle disinfectant, rinsing thoroughly, and allow to dry before putting more food in. If you're feeding from a bird table, wipe up droppings regularly.

Build a pop-up bird hide

A pop-up bird hide is a great way to get close to nature, although you will need a lot of patience. It'll be made much more successful if you've already got some bird feeders in the garden, as this will encourage feathered friends to get nice and close.

You will need:
- 3 wooden poles or branches
  (one long, and two half the size)
- Twine
- An old dark sheet or blanket
  (brown, blue or green is best if you have it)
- Clothes pegs
- Scissors

1. Choose where you'd like to position your bird hide, preferably so that it's facing some active garden bird feeders. **2.** Lash the top of the poles or branches together, so that the long one is at the back of your bird hide and the shorter ones are at the front. You need it to be tall enough to sit in. **3.** Cover with the blanket and secure on one side with pegs (this is your door). You'll also need to cut a small flap in the front of your hide to see out of using scissors. Make this as small as possible and only cut three sides of the square – you can then use the fourth side to peg it out of the way. **4.** It's up to you how comfy you make your hide, but you might want to consider cushions, warm clothes, an extra blanket, snacks and a drink, as well as a notebook, pen and binoculars if you have them. **5.** Make sure you go to the toilet beforehand! You don't want to be popping in and out as this will disturb the birds. Make a note of everything you spy.

Grow-your-own veggies

I've never been a dab-hand at growing my own veggies – I didn't quite have the patience or willpower to nurture those little seeds right through to life. My grandad was amazing at it and almost every vegetable we ate at his house in Wales came straight out of the garden. I especially loved picking the beans and peas, which tasted delicious fresh out of the pod. The tomatoes were sweet and plump; the carrots were crunchy; and the potatoes didn't need salt or butter to make them taste great. Growing your own is also so much better for the environment and can be cheaper, too! You might need to practise in your garden to see what works for your soil. Avoid using pesticides like slug pellets – they're bad news, not just for the slugs, but for everything that might eat the slugs, too. I started out successfully last year by growing my own herbs. Now I grow my own mint, basil (in the summer), chives, fennel, thyme and rosemary in pots in the garden, and I have grand ambitions for sage and oregano. Just read up online or ask neighbours what they're growing and see what you can conjure up out of your back garden.

Quack over the first ducklings

I challenge you not to go 'awwwwww' when you see the first ducklings of the year. The ducks that we see on rivers and canals regularly are mallard; the males have a glossy green head and the females are streaky brown. They are our most common duck. Many have also been domesticated or escaped from wild collections, so you'll find that this species tends to be quite tame and unafraid of people. You might spot ducklings as early as February or March, depending on how mild the winter has been. Mum will sit on the nest, keeping her eggs warm and dry for about four weeks, before the eggs hatch (this usually takes about 24 hours). They'll stay warm and curled up for a few hours to dry off, then it's straight out into the real world. Mother duck will lead her babies to water, and they'll learn to feed themselves straight away (unlike many other birds, where the mother has to regurgitate food). They rely on her for warmth and protection, but as they get older they will swim off more and more. They don't fledge for around 60 days! Spot the first ones of the year and watch how the family works together, and how adventurous the little ones are. Don't disturb them, though – they'll be happiest if left alone!

44 Survey like a scientist

Citizen science is the kind of science that anyone can get involved in –
you don't need training, lots of fancy equipment or special knowledge:
just your eyes, ears and a computer (or notepad). There's so much
wildlife out there, that scientists find it hard to keep a track of all
the different creatures, where they are and how they're doing. That's
where you come in. You can make a huge difference to conservation
by reporting what you've seen and where. There are lots of projects
going on all around the UK that are keen to know what you've been
seeing – you can record bees, butterflies, barn owls, garden birds,
water voles, dolphins, whales, wildflowers and lots more. Every
record you submit will be added to a vast database that will allow
conservationists to examine how a species is doing in the big wide
world, and if necessary, take action to protect it. Different science and
conservation charities run different projects, so head to the internet to
see what research projects are running at the moment.

Plant a wildflower border

Confession: I am a rubbish gardener. My flowers are quickly out-competed by dandelions and daisies and I don't have the attention span for a cultivated bed. Pruning has never been my thing. So being a wildlife gardener really takes the pressure off. As soon as you re-frame your garden as being wildlife-friendly, none of those pesky weeds matter any more: they're bursting with pollen and nectar, supporting bees and butterflies. It's why I also like wildflowers. Clear a spot in your garden so that the soil is bare and give it a good mix over – it's best to start in early spring or autumn. Then simply add a mixture of wildflower seeds. You can get these from any garden centre. Try to get species that are native and grown in the UK. Look out for cornflowers, common poppies, cowslip, common knapweed, oxeye daisies, meadow buttercup and red clover. Once the seeds are in, treat them to a sprinkling of water and, on the off-chance the ground gets too dry, keep them moist. In the late spring, you'll begin to see your flowers springing into life. You can keep the area free of unwanted weeds, but I prefer to let it colonise with other flowers and grasses, too. And the best bit? They don't require tending. Cut your mini meadow back in autumn and again in the spring, removing the freshly cut hay.

Tune in by switching off

Switching off all electronics for the day is surprisingly hardcore, depending on how far you take your commitment to go gadget-free. It will be totally worth it though, I promise. Make sure you have a plan for the day, like a wild adventure (or at least a walk), either by yourself to get some well-earned 'me' time, or with friends and family to keep you entertained. The rule: you've all got to commit. No phones, laptops, tablets, televisions, game consoles or any kind of gadget. You're allowed access to the fridge, the kettle and the cooker if you must, and maybe an alarm clock to get you up and active.

The way you frame your gadget-free day with friends and family will make or break your success. This is a brilliant challenge, and something to be proud of. It's going to be exciting, too! Making sure that everyone feels involved and enthusiastic will help your day to be a huge success.

Try to pick a day with nice weather, to start out with. A rainy or cold day can be a real challenge, especially in the middle of the afternoon when boredom might start to set in, particularly with younger kids. A warm, sunny day will naturally invite you outdoors, minimising the temptation of the internet.

When you get up in the morning, have your plan front of mind. It might help to actively turn all those electronics off and put them somewhere safe. If they're in your pocket or handbag 'just in case', you'll be so much more likely to take a peek. Get everyone involved in preparing meals, like making a hearty breakfast or preparing a picnic to take out with you. Reward yourself with little treats (like a bigger breakfast than normal, or a sneaky piece of indulgent cake in your picnic) to make the day feel extra special.

If you're going on a wild adventure, you're allowed to take your car if you must. Do consider, though, whether there's somewhere nearby that you have always wanted to explore. This might be a park, a local countryside walk or a woodland – anywhere you can stretch your legs and lose yourself in nature. Remember to print off a map, too! No turning to the satnav on your phone today to get you home. There are loads of Random Acts of Wildness that you could work into your gadget-free day. Just try to be really mindful of nature and absorb yourself in it. Make the most of this special opportunity to look after yourself, or re-connect with friends and family. If you find yourself asking questions throughout the day, like 'what's this flower?' or something similar, make a note of them and look them up in a book later (or online tomorrow). Don't be tempted to turn to your phone to ask questions now.

In the evening, the temptation will be strong to turn on the TV and give everyone some downtime, but try to be more creative. If you want everyone to stay motivated, try cooking dinner together, followed by board games or a craft session. If you're on your own, make sure you've got your favourite book handy and make the most of losing yourself in the pages (a glass of wine is optional!).

This final step is, I think, the most important. It's about reflection. As your day is ending, write down how you're feeling. You might be anxious – think of all those unchecked emails! You might be sleepy after all the exertion. You might be blissfully calm and relaxed. Either way, there's no right or wrong: this is all about you. Making notes now, just before bed, will help wind down your mind. The next day, when you wake up, re-read your notes and think about how you feel now. Did you sleep well? Are you relaxed? Are you desperate to get your tech back? Again, there's no wrong answer. Check in with anyone else that joined you and see how they found it, too. Hopefully you'll be feeling light as a feather, calm and well-rested, and most importantly I hope you enjoyed your wild day! And I hope you want to do it again!

47 Go cloud crazy

On bright, sunny days, indulge in a spot of cloud bathing. It's simple and only takes a few minutes but will make you feel wonderfully zen. Lie back on the grass and see what shapes you can see in the sky. A dinosaur? A flower? A car?

Clouds come in all shapes and sizes, occurring at different levels in the atmosphere. Those thin, wispy clouds you see high in the sky? They're cirrus clouds. They are so high up that they don't affect the weather, but just drift along peaceably. Stratus clouds are grey, dark and hang low in the sky, like thick fog. They are often associated with drizzle or snow, so aren't great for cloud gazing. Cumulus clouds are perfect for making shapes in. They are the typical white fluffy clouds that build up. They're often flat on the bottom and rounded on top, and can pile up on top of each other. They form quite low in the atmosphere, making them perfect for spotting shapes.

There's a rule of thumb that for every 20 minutes spent looking at a computer screen, you should look away for 20 seconds. Glance out of the window and challenge yourself to find a new shape or picture.

48 Spice up with wild garlic

Wild garlic has a heady aroma and pungent taste. If you walk into a damp woodland in spring, you can be hit by the strong smell of onions: it's wild garlic assaulting your senses. The flowers grow like little clusters of white stars, in little blooms on the end of a rod-straight stem. The leaves are oval-shaped, thick and dark green. This plant can be confused with the poisonous lily-of-the-valley, which has similar leaves, but your nose should give it away and the flowers look very different. Make sure of the identity before tucking in.

Unlike the garlic you buy from the shop, you eat the leaves of wild garlic, not the bulbs. It has a milder flavour too, a bit like chives. You can wash the leaves and eat them in a salad, use them in dressings (chop them up finely and let them flavour a nice olive oil), or make pesto out of them. They're highly versatile and great for fitting into whatever meal you've got on the go.

Let it grow wild

I know that the neighbours might love their perfectly manicured and pristine lawn, without so much as a daisy in sight and every blade an identical length, but that's so 20th century. Unless you're managing your garden as a football pitch or bowling lawn, let that grass grow a bit! Your Random Act of Wildness for today can be sitting back with your feet up and a cup of tea, making a conscious decision not to get the lawnmower out, and feeling really smug that you're doing more for wildlife than the snooty neighbours. Those luscious blades of grass, seed heads and wildflowers – not weeds! – are providing homes and foraging grounds for bees, beetles, butterflies and other beasties, which in turn will encourage the bats, hedgehogs, frogs and birds. If you can't quite bear to see the whole garden looking so unkempt, try leaving a wild corner, and having some patches of grass at different lengths. Feeling really brave? A patch of nettles is great for caterpillars. Go on – be a rebel!

Eat seasonally

We're all used to having whatever food we like whenever we like it. Blueberries are my weakness, even in the winter months when they're being shipped in from much warmer climates. So I've tried to adapt my cooking to suit the seasons. Rhubarb is excellent in the spring, which is when your salad veggies start to come into season, too – radishes, spring onions, watercress and so on. Make the most of juicy, sweet berries like strawberries, raspberries and blueberries in the summer months; this is the best time for peaches, apricots and other soft fruits, too. They'll taste better and they won't have had to travel far. Squashes, like butternut, pumpkin and marrow, are best in autumn and early winter, as are wild mushrooms, and in the winter make the most of wholesome and hearty vegetables like leeks, turnips, parsnips and potatoes. If you're stuck, check that your food is grown in the UK, or spend a few minutes online researching which seasonal treats you can make the most of.

Drift off (or wake up!) to wild sounds

Wherever you live, there will be a whole host of wild sounds waiting to be discovered. You just need to learn how to tune in. Try and find your favourite natural sounds nearby, then take them with you wherever you go. If you live by the sea (you lucky thing!), listen to crashing waves, squealing oystercatchers on the beach or calling curlews swooping around. If you're somewhere more built up, try listening for birdsong in the mornings or evenings, or the wind whistling through the trees, or bees buzzing between flowers.

   Once you've got your favourite sounds, make sure there's not many people around to disturb you, and record those sounds on to your phone, holding the microphone as close to the source as possible so you get a lovely, clear recording. You can then use this as a brisk alarm clock or a calming end to the day, helping you to meditate any troubles away. Close your eyes and immerse yourself in the natural soundtrack, and feel yourself step back in time to your favourite wild place. If you're going for a wild alarm clock, make sure those sounds are loud enough to cut through your snoring – we wouldn't want you to be late up now.

Feel the sting of nettle soup

Fresh nettles, when added to soup, taste a little like spinach. They're delicious and easy to find wherever you go, and foraging for them might turn around your opinion of these poor plants, so often labelled as 'weeds'. When you're foraging, wear rubber gloves to protect your hands, and gently shake off any bugs that have decided to make a home there. Only take what you need.

You will need:
- Rubber gloves
- A large saucepan
- A wooden spoon
- A blender
- 400g freshly picked nettles
- 1 tbsp olive oil, plus extra to drizzle
- 1 onion, chopped
- 1 carrot, sliced
- 1 leek, finely sliced
- 1 floury potato, finely sliced
- 1 litre stock (preferably vegetable)
- Knob of diced butter
- 50ml double cream
- Salt and freshly ground black pepper

1. Pop your gloves on, and gently wash the nettles in water, removing any dirt. Pick the leaves off the stalks. **2.** Heat the oil in your saucepan over a medium heat, and add your veggies: onion, carrot, leek and potato. Stir them to coat them with oil and add a sprinkle of salt and pepper. Let them sweat on a medium heat until they soften – about ten minutes. **3.** Pour in the stock and let the soup simmer for another fifteen minutes, until the vegetables have softened completely.
4. Stir in the nettles and allow them to wilt – no more than a minute. You may have to add them a batch at a time for space. **5.** Blend the soup, either all at once using a handheld blender or in batches. Stir in the butter and the cream, and then season to taste. Serve with a drizzle of olive oil on top.

Hear a buzzard mew

On sunny days over parks, fields and woodlands, keep your eyes to the skies and search for a majestic buzzard, circling slowly and in a stately manner. This is one of my favourite sights. Growing up, we were lucky to have a pair of buzzards in the nearby spinney, and I used to watch them circling round on warm updraughts. Buzzards are big birds of prey, with a wingspan of around 1.2m. They drift upwards on warm days, and when they're flying closer to the ground, they have powerful, slow wingbeats. They can even hover above prey, like kestrels. One of my favourite things about buzzards is their call. Before you notice them high above you, you might hear the single, powerful cry, which sounds like the mew of a cat (only much louder and more forceful). They repeat this call as they head higher into the sky, like the blast of a foghorn. You might have heard something similar in films – a lot of American and Australian films use the calls of eagles to show how wild places are, and the cry of the buzzard is similar. Listen out for it and see if you can spot the broad wings and fanned tail above.

54

THINK! THINK! THINK! THINK! THINK! THINK! THINK! THINK! THINK! THINK! THINK! THINK! THINK! THINK! THINK! THINK!

SHOWER GEL

55

56

57

CIRCINATE VERNATION

Vernation (n): The arrangement of leaves within a bud.

Circinate vernation (n): The manner in which a fern frond emerges.

Think before you buy

Shower gels usually come in plastic bottles, but not any more. You can ditch the unnecessary plastic and buy solid gels online and in high street stores that feel just as luscious and smell amazing. Aren't they just soap, then? Well they're a kind of soap, but they won't dry your skin out. They are made of mostly the same ingredients as a traditional shower gel and are concentrated, so they'll last longer than a bottle, too.

Go wild for gorse

Gorse bushes grow in abundance on heathlands, moorlands and on the coast. They're evergreen and very spiky (so wear gloves if you're foraging). Most recognisable, however, are the flowers, which are bright yellow, highly fragrant and edible. When they burst into flower, the whole area buzzes with bees. There are two species in the UK: common gorse flowers in the spring, while western gorse flowers in summer and autumn. The smell is a little coconutty in the sunshine, but the flavour is subtle and buttery. Use gorse flowers in recipes or to make tea, or sprinkle a few over salads. Dried gorse flowers taste even stronger.

Leave mud for martins

House martins turn up in the spring, after a long migration from Africa. We have a pair nest on our house every year, with little martins fledging in the summer. They nest beneath the eaves of the house, building and repairing their nest from mud. You can't attract house martins with food as they eat insects, but you can encourage them to nest nearby by making sure they have access to the right materials. Leaving a muddy puddle in your garden or yard will give them what they need. Use a watering can to top up puddles, and make sure there's soil mixed in. Start as soon as you see them arrive – around mid-April.

Learn a wild word

Circinate vernation: the two words have to be broken down to be understood. The term refers to ferns – plants that have no flowers or seeds; instead they reproduce using spores. Vernation is the formation of new leaves or fronds; in plant anatomy, it is how the leaves are arranged in a bud. In ferns, the leaves are tightly curled in a ball, so the tip is protected in the centre. Circinate vernation is the process by which the fern unfolds (rather than bursting open). They make gorgeous patterns and look beautiful close up – try and find ferns growing in a hedgerow or woodland, and look for the intricate patterns they form.

Race to find a rainbow

Nature is bright and beautiful, especially in the spring. An easy and quick way to get yourself, friends and neighbours spotting beautiful natural objects is to race them to find a rainbow. You simply need to find all seven colours of the rainbow in a given area – a local park, nature reserve or garden is perfect. Reds could be ladybirds or butterflies; yellows could be dandelions; greens could be grass and leaves; and damselflies or blue tits are perfect for your blue colours. You can be a bit creative and stretch your colour palette (including pink instead of indigo and violet) or you can be really strict. Get everyone to take photos of the colours that they find and compare what you see when your race is over. Your winner could be the team that finds the colours the fastest, or the team that has the closest colour matches – it's entirely up to you. You could even do it by yourself. Challenge yourself to find and photograph every colour of the rainbow in nature in your normal day.

Check your fishy credentials

Back when Britannia ruled the waves, many people believed that the seas were boundless in their fish stocks. It was thought that we could never run out. Sadly, this isn't the case, and many species of fish are now in decline around the UK and the world. Some, like the common skate, have been declared commercially extinct in some places. But all isn't lost, and we can all make a difference. Whether you're buying fish from a fishmonger or from a supermarket, ask questions about where the fish was caught and how – ideally, you only want to eat 'line-caught' fish and never fish from a 'bottom-trawl'. Bottom-trawling is hugely damaging to underwater environments. If you live by the sea, or are on holiday, lots of coastal communities now produce their own local seafood guides, which highlight the most sustainable fish available. If you're eating out, ask the waiting staff about where the fish is from. Take special care to ask questions about cod, haddock, salmon, canned tuna and prawns, as these commonly eaten fish are all under pressure.

Light it up with buttercups

Do you like butter? Supposedly, if you hold a buttercup up to your chin and a little yellow spot glows there, then you do! Sadly, I've tested this with a friend who doesn't like butter, and the yellow spot still appeared. It's fun to do though and a good way to get kids interacting with nature. Buttercups come into bloom in the spring and summer. They're something we all recognise – bright yellow and with five obvious, rounded petals – and something we take for granted a bit, too. Those little rays of sunshine on our lawn are great for pollinators and beautiful to look at, too. There are lots of different species of buttercups in the UK, but you're more likely to see some than others. The ones growing in your lawn? Well they are likely to be creeping buttercups. They can grow very tall, up to half a metre, and the roots can spread out a long way underground. The flowers are just a couple of centimetres across and that gorgeous buttery colour. Meadow buttercups are found, unsurprisingly, in meadows and can grow up to a metre tall. They don't have any runners, unlike the creeping buttercup. Take a moment to enjoy the bright splash of yellow that comes from the buttercup and test it out on a friend: hold the flower beneath their chin and find out if they like butter!

Meander with a river

Rivers come in all shapes and sizes, from mighty estuaries and deep channels to smaller and calmer babbling brooks. Once upon a time, not so long ago, many of our rivers weren't very nice places for wildlife. They were polluted and dirty. A lot of them are getting cleaned up now, and plants and animals can live in them once again. A wander with a river can be calming, even if it's only for a few minutes. Just the act of being so close to water will help you to unwind, but if you want to go one step further, see what you can spot and hear nearby. Wildlife collects near water, so there'll always be something good to enjoy.

The most obvious wildlife you'll encounter will be swans or ducks, moorhens or coots, but you might be in for a treat with some smaller or more unusual wildlife. Listen out for the shrill, single-note whistle of a kingfisher. If you're lucky, you might see a flash of turquoise blue as they streak past, or you might even hit the jackpot and see one perched. They love overhanging trees near the water's edge, where they can fish. In the spring and summer, sand martins might nest in a river bank. Grey wagtails have bright lemony bottoms and bounce their tails up and down while they look for insects.

Keep a close eye out for dragonflies and damselflies, too. They'll patrol up and down the edge of a river searching for suitable places to lay eggs, rest and sunbathe. Do you know how to tell the difference? Well a general rule of thumb is to look at how they're perched. If the wings are spread far apart from the body, it's probably a dragonfly. If the wings are tightly held together along the back, it's a damselfly.

Rivers can be great places to see mammals, some of which are now very rare. They can be hard to get a good look at unless you're very quiet, so instead, listen and look for some handy giveaways. If you hear a loud 'plop' by a river bank and see a furry shape very low in the water, it might just be a water vole – or 'Ratty' from *The Wind in the Willows*. These cute creatures are endangered now, so seeing one is a real treat. Otters are also a rare encounter, but their numbers do now seem to be on the increase and they can even be seen in towns and cities. If you can't get close to the animals themselves, look for their paw prints in the mud along the banks, or see if you can smell any otter spraint (or poo). It's black and sticky, sweetly-scented, and many people think it smells like jasmine!

If there's a river near to where you live or work, go back at different times of the year, and see if you can spot a new animal every time.

Blossom with cow parsley

Cow parsley is frequently taken to be a common weed. Yet as it blossoms it adds a splash of colour to our lives, growing in abundance for a few weeks, usually about May time. Try and spot the umbrellas of tiny white flowers that grow in clusters from a straight stem. It's a member of the carrot family, and if you crush the flowers between your fingers, you might recognise the aniseed-liquorice smell. You can eat the leaves in salads (known as wild chervil), but do so with caution. Hemlock looks very similar, but is poisonous, so unless you've had help from an expert forager, I wouldn't recommend this.

Forge a daisy chain

When was the last time you forged a daisy chain? The act of finding, picking and threading the daisies requires concentration and is relaxing. Don't pick more than you need and go for the little ones in your lawn (these will regrow quickly). When you pick them, leave yourself enough stem (about 3cm) to make a hole in. Make the hole using your thumbnail, and thread another daisy stem through it, so that the head rests on the first stem. Repeat this, threading a new daisy through then creating a small hole. When it's big enough, thread the first daisy together with the last to create a band. Wear it with pride!

Think before you buy

When it comes to household cleaning products, the big no-no is bleach. It's not great for you if you get it on your skin, it's awful if you accidentally inhale it, and although there's little evidence that it is directly harmful to the environment, the processes involved in the manufacture of bleach are. You can buy or make natural alternatives that are just as effective and nowhere near as harmful – try more eco-friendly cleaners, or even things like vinegar, lemon juice or bicarbonate of soda. It may seem strange, but our grannies had it right all along with their homemade household recipes!

Stretch in the garden

If you're trying to get fit or just spend a bit more time putting your body first, take your workouts or stretches into the garden, rather than sweating away in the living room. First thing in the morning on a sunny spring day, head outside and take a minute or two to gently stretch the sleep out of your muscles, by exercising your quads, hamstrings, calves, glutes, biceps and triceps. You might get some weird looks from the neighbours, but you'll feel awake and invigorated, and you'll have got your daily dose of nature too!

As with any workout programme, consult a trained professional before embarking on anything too ambitious.

62

63

THINK! THINK! THINK!

THINK! THINK! THINK!

THINK! THINK! THINK!

THINK! THINK! THINK!

64

BLEACH

65

Brew a leafy tea

Dandelions have many funny nicknames, due to their associations in folklore. My personal favourite, and apologies for those of more cultivated sensibilities, is the piss-a-bed, as supposedly dandelions have diuretic properties (put simply, they make you want to wee!). Whether this is true or not, if you like herbal teas, it's worth trying dandelion tea. As much as I love these little weeds, they're not to everyone's taste, and this is a great way to remove them from the garden without the need for weedkillers.

You will need:
- A saucepan
- A sharp knife and chopping board
- A sieve
- 1 litre water
- A couple of big handfuls of dandelion leaves and roots

1. Pop your water in the saucepan and heat gently until boiling. While you're waiting, rinse your dandelions under cold water to remove any dirt or beasties. Roughly chop the roots and leaves, making two separate piles. **2.** Add 2 tbsp dandelion roots to the water and stir together, then pop on a lid and let the tea simmer for five minutes. **3.** Remove the tea from the heat and stir in the dandelion leaves. Leave everything to soak for around 40 minutes. **4.** Strain your tea through the sieve to remove any leaves and roots, then re-heat gently to your perfect tea temperature, and serve. Just make sure there's a toilet nearby afterwards!

Follow a bumblebee

Who doesn't love seeing a bumblebee bustling on its journey from flower to flower? Their buzzing is a quintessential sound of summer. Early in the year, around March, the queen bee will search for somewhere to nest, building her intricate home and laying her first brood. These are the worker bees, and once they've developed into adults (in early summer) they'll help tend the nest and collect pollen, to feed the next brood. In the late summer, the second brood – mostly new queen bees and males – will emerge, disappearing out of the nest to reproduce. Watch as they buzz between bushes, flowers and trees, and see if you can keep up. This may sound like a simple Random Act of Wildness, but you'll soon be absorbed in their fascinating behaviour. See if you can map which flowers are their favourites, and how far they travel around the garden. Some of them will have bright yellow or orange sacs on their hind legs, carrying the pollen back home. Don't worry about being stung: keep your distance and don't disturb them.

Tiptoe through the bluebells

For a few weeks every year, from the middle of April, woodlands turn bright indigo under a carpet of bluebells, the unofficial national flower of the UK. If you tiptoe through a carpet of bluebells, you're sure to be walking somewhere that is very old, even ancient, as our oldest and most gnarly woodlands are home to the most spectacular displays. You can keep an eye out for bluebells all over the UK, apart from the Highlands of Scotland, and depending on the weather they'll bloom between April and May. They nod their little bells in the breeze, giving off a beautiful, subtly sweet smell. Folklore has it that these little bells would ring, calling fairies and goblins together in the springtime. Walking through bluebells was considered bad luck, as you might disturb the fairy spells that had been cast there. A wander through an ancient wild woodland, sticking to the paths, won't disturb the bluebells, the fairies or their spells, though. Do a little research to find your nearest ancient woodland and choose a warm sunny day with a light breeze. Inhale the sweet smell and snap a few photos if you can, and see what other wildflowers are poking their heads up, too.

Feel the world between your toes

This Random Act of Wildness is perfect for warm, sunny days when you need some refreshment and a quick dose of nature. There's different ways of doing it, so I have split it into different Random Acts – each one counts on its own as each one will feel slightly different. Take off your shoes for a few minutes and feel nature in a whole new way – through the soles of your feet. Whenever we leave the house, we throw our shoes and socks on, losing touch with wild landscapes in the process. Take a moment in your lunchbreak, or over the weekend, to re-connect with the world through your toes. It's obviously best to do this somewhere you know you're not going to stand on litter or other nasties. Just relax and really feel the textures.

69. Walk barefoot on grass
A local park or garden will do just fine. When it's warm outside, the feel of cool grass beneath your feet can be really refreshing. It can also tickle like crazy (if you're like me, anyway!), but enjoy it. If a bug wanders on to your feet, gently remove it. Concentrate on the feeling and forget about everything else for a few minutes. Hey – if it's good enough for Julia Roberts and Richard Gere in *Pretty Woman*, it's good enough for us lot!

70. Get sole-ful on sand
It's easier to kick your shoes off when you're at the beach – who wants all that sand in your shoes anyway? Make the most of the way sand changes when it's wet, so walk from the dry, powdery stuff down towards the sea, and enjoy the feeling as you hit the tideline: first of all, the sand gets cool and compact, and then as you reach the water's edge you'll sink a little way in. Feel the grains move around your toes like liquid, and enjoy the grittiness – you're getting a pedicure as well as a nature fix!

71. Make a splash in a river
Lucky enough to have a river nearby? Sitting on a river bank is relaxing in its own right, but kicking your shoes off on a hot day will take tranquillity to a whole new level. The water might be icy cold, so be prepared for a shock, but take a second to get used to it. If you sit still and quietly, all sorts of wildlife will appear around you.

72. Squelch your toes in mud

Do you remember what it's like to feel mud between your toes? I used to love the feeling as a kid, but as an adult we lose touch with those little pleasures. As your feet gently descend into the slimy goodness, you'll feel the mud suction tight around them. Wiggling your toes so that your whole foot gets a good coating is immensely satisfying. People pay good money to be wrapped in seaweed and bathed in mud now, so this is basically a free spa day, right? Be careful when walking in mud, however; make sure you don't slip and that you know how deep it is (you don't want to get stuck).

73. Tread lightly on pebbles

It can be a bit painful to walk on pebbles, so tread very gently as you explore this rocky surface beneath your feet. Choose only places with very smooth pebbles, like beaches, and be careful not to slip over. It should feel a bit like a massage though, with all of those different textures and shapes.

69–73

74 Grow borage for bees

Borage is a herb originating from the Middle East. As a non-native plant, you'll have to restrict your foraging to the garden. It has cucumber-flavoured leaves and bright blue edible flowers, which bees and butterflies love. If you plant it next to vegetables or strawberries, the flowers will attract pollinators to these plants, too. It grows easily once cultivated and can transform an unloved corner of the garden. Make sure you really want this plant to grow, however – leave it to its own devices and after a few harvests you'll have a good-sized patch, as it seeds easily. Annual, the leaves can be picked at any time and eaten fresh, but in June and July the area will blossom with beautiful indigo flowers which look like little drooping stars. The oval leaves are hairy to touch.

When you've got a nice crop of the blue borage flowers, add these to salads to bring a summery twist. If you're having a few friends over for a summer barbecue, pick some of the flowers and freeze them in ice cubes. Make up a batch of punch (alcoholic or non-alcoholic – the choice is yours) and add the cubes. As the ice melts, the flowers will float to the top, making your drinks look exotic and sophisticated. Remember to leave some for the bees, though.

BioBlitz your garden

Ever wondered what's in your garden? There's an easy way to find out! A BioBlitz is when someone intensively surveys an area over a short space of time to see how many species are living there. If this happens on the scale of a nature reserve, it can take hundreds of volunteers to cover the ground. Or you can do much smaller areas – a school playground or your garden, for example. If it's your first one, don't be too ambitious – limit your hunting to an hour and extend it in future if you're feeling adventurous. You can do a BioBlitz on your own or with friends, family or school. You don't need to be an expert, though it might help to have a pad and pen handy to record what you see; a pair of binoculars to zoom in on wildlife; and a camera to snap photos.

Scour every inch of the area – for insects, amphibians, birds, mammals, reptiles (you can include plants, too). If you can't identify something, take a photo; your friends and social media followers might be able to help. You're trying to find as many species as possible, so look in unexpected places – in log piles, under bricks, in dark corners. If you ever repeat the BioBlitz, you'll have a score to beat!

Keep an eye out for newborns

In the springtime, spotting a newborn animal can be rewarding. These young creatures are learning about the world around them, so just like babies and children, they are probably going to make a few mistakes along the way. Young rabbits might sit by the side of the road, so slow down if you're driving and catch their eyes shining in the dark.

Some baby birds look totally different to their parents; my favourite is the great crested grebe, found on rivers and lakes. The adults are graceful with long necks and elegant plumes; the youngsters look like tiny fluffy humbugs. When they're starting out, they sit on their mother's back while she ferries them across the water.

Young birds that have recently fledged from their nests can sometimes look a bit lost, perching on walls or branches and cheeping for their parents. It's important to leave these little ones alone, unless you think that they're in danger. Often the parents won't be far away, and may still be feeding their young. If you find a baby bird on the pavement or edge of a road, try and pop it somewhere undercover or high up, away from feet or predators. Don't be tempted to rescue it or take it into care – you'll probably do more harm than good.

Shimmer with mayflies

A sign of clear, unpolluted rivers, lakes and waterways, mayflies have famously short and frantic lives. They spend most of their existence as nymphs, beneath the surface of the water, and then, in just a few hours, they must emerge, display, mate and breed – that's a lot of pressure. Although they're called 'mayflies', they don't necessarily hatch out in May – they can be seen at any time of the year, but late spring is best. One species will emerge in line with the 'Mayflower', or the flowering of the hawthorn bush. Look for clouds of mayflies over a river or lake. In the evening or early morning, a great swarm of them will look beautiful in the sunlight, shimmering and swirling. If you see one perched, they have transparent wings with a lacy pattern, and three long, pointed tails. There are over 50 species in the UK, but the one you're most likely to see shimmering in great magical clouds on sunny days is the common mayfly – or green drake.

Take part in a two-minute beach clean

If you're spending the day at the beach, among the rock pools and sandcastles, take part in a two-minute beach clean. This simple forage for litter might just save a life at sea, which is hugely polluted with plastic bags, balloons, toothbrushes, bottles, cigarettes, straws and cans. These things never go away and cause havoc to sealife. They wash down rivers and float all over the world, pulled by currents, so it's important to pick up what we can and dispose of it properly.

If you have gloves, use them. There might be some sharp, nasty or even dangerous objects scattered around. If you're not sure what it is, protect yourself and don't pick it up (tell a lifeguard about anything like broken glass or needles). Gather together whatever rubbish you can and pop it safely into a bin. If you have an old bag to start with, collect everything in there. Check the tideline, where rubbish can get caught among the seaweed. When you've disposed of everything, wash your hands. To celebrate, share your beach clean on social media using #2minutebeachclean – there's an organisation that monitors beach cleans all over the world. They'll love to see you doing your bit!

Learn wild birdsong

Throughout history, birdsong has captivated us. From the sweet harmony of the nightingale to the monotonous cooing of a woodpigeon, birdsong is all around us almost constantly – even in cities. In fact, in the city, many birds like robins actually sing louder, to compete with the hubbub of the urban jungle.

To us, the melody of the blackbird may be sweet and alluring, but for the blackbird, it's life, war and romance. As he proudly tips his bill to the sky, he's calling for a mate to come and see how gorgeous he is (and what great father-potential he'll make). Simultaneously, he's proclaiming his territory against other pesky males. It's a show of pure biological masculinity – to us, it sounds lovely.

There are bird calls as well as songs. These are much shorter, less complex noises compared to the songs, which can be whole chains of notes (a bit like comparing an entire song to a couple of chords). Calls announce the presence of a predator, like an owl or cat, or can be used to contact other birds around them. They're much harder to identify as they often sound similar, especially in smaller birds like warblers.

Learning birdsong can be tricky, but the rewards are worth it. You'll get a much richer image of the world around you – whether that's your garden or a local nature reserve. Even when a bird is hidden deep in a bush or at the top of a tree, you'll know it's there. Secondly, listening to birdsong is therapeutic; there's lots of research that shows listening to birdsong can be good for your health, lowering your stress levels. Oh, and it's a great way to show off to your friends.

To make it easier for you, I've pulled out my top Random Acts of Wildness to help you get started …

79. Use a wild app

There are apps to help you learn about birdsong, from playing you calls to compare, to recording the song and telling you what it is! Personally, I think this is cheating; apps that help you test your knowledge seem to work better for me. There are loads to choose from and many of the good ones will show you photos or drawings of the birds,

79–84

tell you useful information (like where they live, if they migrate, etc.) and will have snippets of songs and calls to listen to. Don't have a smartphone? That's not a problem. You can buy CDs devoted to bird calls or use your computer to search for the information.

80. Draw what you hear

Some people can recall things much better using pictures, so rather than trying to remember sounds, have a go at drawing the noises. These could be little sketches of the noises themselves or images that remind you of the song. They can be as silly or as abstract as you like – they don't have to make sense to anyone but you. The most important thing is that when you hear a bird, it conjures an image in your head that you can associate with the bird.

81. Use word association

Have a go at writing down words that remind you of birdsong. When you hear the song again, think of the words and it'll trigger the association – this is a bit like learning the lyrics to a song to remember who sang it. The most common one that everyone knows is the great tit – 'tea-cher, tea-cher, tea-cher' or 'un-it-ed, un-it-ed' for a collared dove. You'll be able to pick out the 'lyrics' in birdsong with a bit of practice and master the basics. Some birds are even named after (or have nicknames for) their songs (the cuckoo for example). Write them down to reinforce the memory.

82. Record songs to play them back

When you're out exploring, try recording different birds using your phone or a Dictaphone. You'll be able to listen back to them and re-live that gorgeous soundscape. You'll also be able to compare your recordings to CDs or the internet, helping you to figure out exactly what you were listening to. The best time to record birdsong as a rule is in the early morning; as birds wake up and first stretch their wings, they'll be concentrating on finding food and marking their territory, especially in the spring. Some birds, like owls, are more active in the evening and at night though, so be prepared to whip your phone out and record whenever you hear something amazing.

Learn wild birdsong (continued)

83. Get out and practise!

The only way you're going to learn all of those songs is to practise outside. When you're out and about you might be able to hear lots of bird calls all at once, not to mention traffic, conversation and an orchestra of background noise. Start close to home and by learning the basics – blackbirds, wrens, robins, blue tits, starlings and so on. Once you've mastered the ones you're likely to hear every day, you can begin to widen your acoustic horizons. Explore a range of habitats – woodlands for finches, tits and woodpeckers; wetlands for ducks, swans and geese; reedbeds for bitterns and warblers; hills for grouse and curlew; beaches for wading birds. In the spring, it'll be a bit harder but more rewarding, as you'll have a lot of new sounds to tune into, too. Chiffchaffs, blackcaps and whitethroats might be confusing at first, but keep at it. Cuckoos and nightingales will only be singing in the late spring, but they have amazing songs.

84. Finding the time

One of the biggest challenges with learning birdsong can be finding the time. Fitting it into your daily routine will help, rather than having to dedicate time to it. Buy a birdsong CD or download an app, and whistle while you work. For example, instead of listening to the radio, pop some birdsong on while you're driving or on the train. The commute can be stressful at the best of times, but by listening to natural sounds you might find your stress levels decreasing and your wellbeing improving. If you're hoovering or scrubbing the bath, while away the monotony of household chores by taking this time to learn. If you're someone who likes to listen to the radio or music to unwind before bed, while your mind is relaxing, listen to bird calls to send you off to sleep. If you find yourself spending lots of time in the kitchen, pop on some bird calls while you're cooking and see what you pick up through osmosis. Or if you're exercising, rather than listening to music, try listening to a birdsong playlist. You can take this time to learn new natural sounds and you might find that by distracting yourself, you're more motivated and you can work out for longer. You won't concentrate on how hot and sweaty you're looking; instead, you'll be tuned into wildlife.

What's inside cuckoo spit?

Prepare to meet one of the cutest little bugs in the UK – the froghopper nymph. To stand a chance, though, you need to find some cuckoo spit. Start searching for it in long grass, weeds and nettles from the late spring. Despite the name, cuckoo spit has nothing to do with cuckoos – it just happens that it appears around the same time as the cuckoo starts singing. The 'spit' looks exactly that – a little blob of foamy white substance on the stems of plants and blades of grass. You can sometimes find it covering a huge area. It is secreted by the elusive little froghopper nymphs, presumably to protect them against predators. They lurk inside their home of spit, feeding and growing until they turn into adults – which can jump an astonishing 70cm into the air! As nymphs, they are tiny (around half a centimetre long) and bright green, with rather sweet-looking features. You can look inside cuckoo spit provided you are very gentle. Use a paintbrush or make-up brush to carefully move the spit, a little at a time. You should find a little green bug hidden inside. Stop when you see it so that you leave it some cover – it'll recreate the spit quickly enough, but you don't want to make it vulnerable.

86

88

87

89

CREPUSCULAR

(a): An animal active at twilight.

(a): Resembling or relating to twilight.

Scale to great heights

Climbing trees is something we should all know how to do. You might remember doing it as a child, but there's no age limit on this – you'll just need a bigger, sturdier tree! It should be healthy, with thick branches (check for decay or weakness before you start). Make sure you can see your route, and that you can easily reach the lowest branches to get up and down. Take your time, testing every branch before you put your weight on it. If you can see a fork in the branches, which looks like a lovely place to relax, why not take a book with you and enjoy some well-earned me-time, surrounded by leaves, bees and birds?

Scream with the first swifts

The return of the swift is something I look forward to every year. They scythe through the air, gliding on updraughts before diving faster than a rollercoaster. They barely ever land – only to nest and raise young – eating, sleeping and breeding in flight. They arrive in the UK in late spring, with the first big flocks often seen in May. Sickle-shaped and dark brown all over (apart from a pale chin), with a tiny fork in the tail, you can't mistake them. You'll often hear them first – they scream out as they dive, loud, brisk and drawn-out. The first time they tear through the sky each year you will feel like whooping with joy!

Fall in love with nature

Natural, green spaces can be hopelessly romantic. A meander through a lush meadow, an evening wander through a wetland, a stroll in the woods, or a stomp through a park – with the birds to serenade you and the sights and smells of nature, you'll struggle not to fall in love! It's much less formal than a dinner date, and much more sociable than a trip to the cinema. Walking through wild spaces will help you and your partner relax, find out more about each other and there's plenty to distract you in case of an awkward silence! Try it – whether it's a new relationship or just spending time with your partner. You could even pack a picnic or take a flask of hot cocoa.

Learn a wild word

As the sun sets, the shadows lengthen, and the night begins to draw in, the crepuscular animals come out to play. These are creatures of the twilight, feeding and hunting at dusk (or dawn): the turn of the day, the mysterious time between day and night. Barn owls, many species of deer, moths and beetles all become active at this time, making the most of their enhanced senses, the cover of darkness and the cooler temperatures to go about their business. It's a beautiful time of day for humans, too. Sit outside, or even with the window wide open, and enjoy the scents, sounds and shadows of the evening.

90 Admire a wild view

Find somewhere nearby where you can survey the local landscape. This could be a skyscraper in the city, a church in your village, a nearby hillside or even just a window on the top floor of your home or office. Climb as high as you can and look out over the landscape around you, taking a few minutes to piece together all of the different places that you know. How far can you see? Have you been to all those places? Are you surprised by how much green there is, or how the river bends in a way you never noticed before, or how tall those trees really are? There might be parks or gardens that you had never noticed or footpaths that lead to unknown places. Starting close and working your way outwards, make a note of all the green spaces you can see nearby, and challenge yourself to visit every single one of them.

91 Wild mint mojitos

Wild mint is a tasty addition to lots of recipes. It's fresh and green and easy to find (or grow in your back garden). Most mints have square stalks with velvety leaves that grow in pairs on opposite sides of the stalk, but of course, always make sure you know exactly what you're foraging before you taste any new plants.

You can add wild mint to tea, cakes or salads, but let's be a bit cheeky and try a wild mint mojito. This refreshing cocktail is one of my favourites, originating in Cuba. You'll need white rum (I use a double shot – 50ml), juice from one lime, a teaspoon of sugar, soda water and, of course, a handful of wild mint. Muddle the mint, sugar and lime juice together in the bottom of a glass until the minty flavour is released. Add ice, pour the rum over everything and stir together, then top up with soda water.

A mojito is the perfect way to unwind after a hard week. Pick a sunny evening, enjoy the buzz of the bees, the birds singing, and this refreshing tipple. If you want to make it with children or you don't drink alcohol, just remove the rum!

Identify five majestic woodland trees

Depending where you live, your local woodland could contain native or non-native trees, be ancient or quite young, natural or plantation. Through history we have treated our woodlands very differently, sometimes planting trees, at other times felling them. Just 12 per cent of the UK is wooded now. In parts of Scotland, you might find yourself in an ancient forest made up of Scots pine, while in the south you're more likely to see mixed broad-leafed woodland. Identifying trees can be tricky, as lots of them look similar. Look at the shapes of the leaves and the seeds they're producing (see pages 216 and 226). Think about your location, the colour of the bark and the thickness of the canopy. See what you can find in your local woodland – here are five of my favourites.

Hazel Hazel trees are commonly found in lowland woodlands and are distinctive. They can grow up to 12m high, but are often coppiced. They can live, if left unmanaged, for around 80 years, although coppicing can increase this lifespan to many hundreds of years. Unlike the traditional 'tree' shape of a straight trunk growing up tall with the canopy above, the trunk of the hazel can split very early on, with lots of individual branches twisting upwards, and with a thick canopy low down. The leaves are like rounded ovals with a point at the end, have jagged edges and lots of tiny teeth and fine hairs. The bark is grey-brown and peels off. Hazel is famous for being bendy, and in the spring a twig of fresh hazel can be manipulated and tied.

White willow Willows were made famous by Kenneth Grahame, as Ratty and Mole paddled along their river in their rowing boat. They grow near water, so their thin branches and leaves flow out over rivers, lakes and canals, drooping down to brush the surface. The branches actually sweep upwards, but they will lean over. The white willow gets its name from the silvery appearance of its leaves, which are silky and narrow and pale underneath. The cricket-bat willow, which is used to make cricket bats, is made from a cultivated type of white willow.

English oak English oaks are everybody's favourite. They grow up to 40m tall but can actually stunt their growth in order to live longer. The thick trunks can look very gnarly, spreading into sturdy branches. The canopy is spacious and lets in a lot of light, making it great for wildflowers to grow beneath, which helps insects like bees and butterflies. Acorns from oaks are unlikely to germinate, as they are a favourite with birds, deer, squirrels and rodents. An oak tree won't produce acorns for the first 40 years of its life, reaching its most fertile period at around 80 years old!

Ash Ash trees are very common in British woodlands. They are tall and proud, with smooth-ish pale brown bark, growing straight up with a domed and airy canopy. They'll often grow close together. They can live for up to 400 years naturally, or longer if coppiced. They are fabulous for wildlife, allowing lots of wildflowers and plants to grow beneath them due to the light, and supporting a range of birds and insects which use the seeds for food or the branches for nesting. The leaves can follow the sunlight throughout the day, and sometimes it looks like the whole canopy is leaning towards the sun.

Elder Elders often grow along the edges of woodlands and in hedgerows. I love them because, in the middle of spring, they shout to the world 'Look at me! Here I am', as thousands of tiny, white flowers erupt. These flowers have a gorgeous taste and are used in food and drink, including elderflower cordial. As the summer draws on, the elderflowers turn yellow and brown and the berries appear, dark red and purple, in clusters. These are a favourite of birds and mammals, so you often find elder trees growing near burrows and setts, the seeds having been deposited in droppings. Elder trees will grow to about 15m tall, with a short trunk and a few branches. The bark is grey and furrowed, and I always think it looks gnarly and twisted.

Spot Oxford ragwort

Train rides can be the perfect chance to fit in your Random Act of Wildness, by focusing on what's outside the window. Oxford ragwort is a lovely flower to spot in the spring and summer. It's a member of the daisy family, with bright yellow flowers and ragged leaves. The flower heads droop slightly, with clusters of ten to fourteen petals.

Oxford ragwort was brought to England in the 17th century as part of a collection for the Oxford Botanical Garden. As the industrial revolution hit, the new railway corridors gave it the perfect chance to spread. Look out for it, especially on scrubby patches of track.

Help a caterpillar on its way

There are over 2,600 species of butterflies and moths in the UK. Caterpillars are stage two of the butterfly lifecycle (between egg and pupa). A good place to look for caterpillars is on a sunny walk – hedgerows and verges are often covered in them on a spring or summer day. I always encounter them plodding across a pavement. They wander along, not noticing the big lumbering feet. So, do a caterpillar a favour – move it to a safe spot so that it can continue on its way. Be careful – not only are caterpillars very delicate, they can be covered in fine hairs which irritate the skin. Move them with a leaf to avoid touching them directly.

Forget me not, forget-me-nots

Forget-me-nots are one of my favourite wildflowers. In April and May, these little plants blossom into life, carpeting an area in delicate patches of bright blue. They grow quickly and easily when given the chance; the flowers are just a few millimetres across (though the plant can grow much bigger). Each flower has five petals, which overlap slightly and are bright sky blue, with a perfectly round centre of either white or yellow. They grow in woodlands, meadows and along hedges, and sometimes in gardens. If you find some, get up close and admire them. They are loved by pollinators, so let them blossom undisturbed.

Harvest a wild salad

When it's getting warmer and you feel the need for something refreshing, a salad is perfect, and nature can offer some exciting ingredients. Look out for edible leaves or wild herbs: fennel is a bit spicy, with a hint of aniseed; wild mint is refreshing. Watercress grows in ponds, and dandelions are edible, too. Keep an eye out for wild strawberries, raspberries or blackberries. You'll only need a few. Flowers can also be edible: elderflowers have a subtle flavour, rose petals are delicate, while gorse flowers are buttery. Pick only what you need, and leave the rest for nature. Read the quick guide to foraging first, and if in doubt, leave it out.

Gin three ways – part one

Gin was traditionally considered the preferred tipple of the older generation, but recently it's become the trendy drink of choice at bars and restaurants around the world. It's easy to flavour with foraged fruits and flowers; just remember the quality of the gin you use will affect the quality of the finished product. I have included three seasonal favourites for you to try, spread throughout the book (see also pages 139 and 206). They are easy to store and give away as party favours or presents, or just enjoy them yourself in cocktails or with a good-quality tonic water.

Rhubarb This one is cheating slightly, as it's unlikely you'll find an abundance of edible rhubarb growing wild in the countryside. The rhubarb we get with custard or in crumbles is a favourite in gardens, but before picking, make sure to identify it correctly: it can easily be mistaken for a plant called burdock, which, confusingly, is also nicknamed 'wild rhubarb'. It's best to harvest rhubarb directly from your own patch or from a neighbour to be safe.

   To make a batch of rhubarb gin, you'll need a bottle of your preferred gin (and an extra empty sterilised glass bottle too), a batch of washed rhubarb, chopped into 2cm-long chunks, and granulated sugar. Decant the gin into a clean bowl (don't spill any!) and add enough rhubarb to both bottles to half fill them. Pour in sugar, enough to give the stalks a generous coating. Refill the bottles with the gin and shake. Leave in a cool, dry place for four weeks or so, shaking occasionally. The gin should take on a gorgeous light pink colour, and a strong rhubarb flavour. You can decant it after the four weeks are up using a muslin cloth, or just leave the rhubarb in there.

Dig the perfect pond

A pond isn't just home to frogs and newts, but can provide life for birds, bats, insects and even snakes. Digging a pond may seem like a big step and a major job, but it's a worthy Random Act of Wildness that will make a real difference, and will help you break a sweat, too! If you go for a big one, I'll even let you count this as TWO Random Acts, as it might take all weekend.

Ponds don't have to be huge. If you're working in a tiny area, or you've got young children and you're worried about the risks, just set aside a small area and have a shallow pond. A washing up bowl dug into the ground will do – just build an area at one end with stones to create a ramp, and fill it with water.

If you want to go bigger, then you'll need to plan your pond carefully, measuring out what you need and taking your full shopping list to the garden centre beforehand. Pick an area that's nice and flat (no hills or slopes), and bright and warm. Those pond plants will need lots of warmth and sunlight to grow. Mark out the area and get digging. Make sure your pond has sloping sides so that wildlife can climb in and out easily. Anything with steep, vertical sides will cause problems for hedgehogs and other creatures that may fall in. If you have space, include a range of depths for lots of different animals – anything from a few centimetres to a metre. Once you're happy with the shape and depths of your pond, add a layer of sand, and then line with pond-liner. You can use big rocks around the edge to anchor it down. A plank of wood might be a good addition to help wildlife climb out. Fill with water (rainwater is best) and allow it to settle for at least a week, before adding some pond plants at different depths. Whatever you do, don't be tempted by ornamental fish – they'll rid the pond of wildlife! Allow your pond to develop and see what wildlife begins to use it.

Soaring with swooping swallowtails

Butterfly watching is the perfect way to spend a hot summer afternoon. Butterflies are children of the sun. They love days that stretch out from gentle sunrise to colourful sunset. They love the sweet scent of pollen in the air.

Let me introduce you to one of our most ostentatious butterflies: the swallowtail. Swallowtails are rare, only found in England in the Norfolk Broads. To see one, you must be very patient. In the meantime, the landscape of the Broads is beautiful: dappled woodlands, swaying reedbeds, waterlogged landscapes, gentle meadows. You can while away days exploring here. That's what we were doing: we'd enjoyed dragonflies skimming and darting across ponds and dykes; seen hundreds of butterflies, from the classy white admiral to the showy peacock; and heard a grasshopper warbler, a bird of the reeds, reeling away.

Then something large lifted into the air. Almost like a bird, it skimmed across the top of the vegetation, before flapping its wings frantically to hold itself steady as it supped on nectar, and then moved into full view, wings outstretched – a swallowtail.

Almost 10cm across, the black borders of the wings sloped gently backwards. Lemon yellow, deep ocean blue and with a blood red spot dead in the centre of a deeply forked tail. It was joined by a mate and the two danced together like ballerinas in elaborate costumes. They fluttered across the reeds before dropping down and disappearing entirely. For something so big and beautiful, they are the masters of disguise. Just a few seconds for this Random Act of Wildness, but sometimes that's all it takes.

Do it yourself:
The best chance you have of seeing swallowtail butterflies in the UK is in the Norfolk Broads. You'll need a warm, sunny, fragrant day in the late spring or early summer, and a special nature reserve that is carefully managed for this species. (Try Norfolk Wildlife Trust's Hickling Broad.) Check with any visitor centres to see if the butterflies have been spotted yet and how regularly before making the journey, and take a pair of binoculars with you. They might be floating out over a reedbed.

104 | Create a hedgehog highway

Hedgehogs may be small, but they can move. Those little legs may not look like much, but in a single night a hedgehog can average around 2km, with a home-range of 10–20 hectares. That's the size of a big park, a large housing estate or several farmland fields. They're foraging for food all the while, looking for juicy worms, beetles and other tasty treats. Imagine you're a hedgehog, though, living on a housing estate. You need to range over that whole estate for food, but every garden is surrounded by fences and walls. There's no point having a great garden for wildlife if wildlife can't get in, so here's a simple Random Act of Wildness to help those hedgehogs out. Team up with your neighbours to cut small holes in the bottom of your fences – they just need to be 13x13cm, and not high off the ground. A hedgehog will find those holes and make his way through. If you can do this across your entire neighbourhood, suddenly those hedgehogs don't need to rely on pavements and roads – it's much safer for them. If you can't cut a hole, try digging a small channel underneath. You can even add your hedgehog highway to the national map created by Hedgehog Street! Check out **www.hedgehogstreet.org**.

Map your wild neighbourhood

Start by getting hold of a map of your local area; you could use the internet, a local street map or even have a go at drawing your own. This can be as big or as small as you want. Two or three streets should be plenty – just the houses, roads and so on. Next, try to add the green spaces in the area, like trees, bushes, gardens, parks or any ponds that you know about, so you begin to build up a wild neighbourhood map.

When have an outline, think about where you might be likely to see wildlife, and what you might see. Birds in the trees? Insects in the bushes? Frogs in the ponds? Think about what you have noticed already and what else you could discover. Note the closest wildlife to your house, like your nearest species of tree, your nearest wildflower, your nearest dragonfly or your nearest nest of birds.

From now on, every time you see something new, mark it on the map. Soon you'll begin to see how every bush and tree and patch of grass can join to make wildlife corridors. Show your neighbours your map when you're happy with it – you might be able to identify areas where you can work together to make places more wildlife-friendly.

Build with the Lego plant

In May, the 'Lego plant' appears in abundance along the canal near my house. Until very recently, I'd forgotten how much fun this plant (called the field horsetail) could be to play with. A walk with my friend's children jogged my memory though, and I remembered being a child myself, breaking and re-building the Lego plant.

It's tall, bright green and spindly, with single thin, bright leaves growing straight out from the stem in regular circles – they almost look like branches, which spike out like points of a star every inch or so. Where these circles meet the stem, there are obvious joins (these feel rough to run your fingers over) and if you pull the stem gently near these joins, the stem should snap apart. You can do this all the way along the plant, and then have great fun trying to fix it back together again, like building a tower out of Lego. Provided you keep it upright, it should stand tall!

Field horsetail is considered a weed by many gardeners and farmers, and can be poisonous to farm animals, so if you pick it, don't scatter it around. It spreads quickly, with deep roots, so leave it where you found it. It's common in meadows, scrubland and along waterways.

Flutter with moths

What's the difference between a moth and a butterfly? People say that the two giveaways are that butterflies fly during the day and have hairless bodies, while moths fly at night and have thick, furry bodies. This doesn't always hold true, as there are plenty of moths that fly during the day, some with thin, fine bodies. The idea that moths are less beautiful is also rubbish – moths can be just as vibrant and patterned or have an understated elegance. They come in all shapes and sizes – there are over 2,500 species in the UK alone! Have a go at identifying any obvious ones that you spot, or that find their way into your bathroom at night in the spring, summer and autumn. My favourite is the small magpie moth, which turns up in our house in June. It's largely black and white, with a little yellow around the body. Garden tigers have black and white spotted upper wings, and orange and black spotted lower wings. Moths also have evocative names, like cinnabar, dark bordered beauty and chimney sweeper, so it's also worth flicking through a moth book to see what you can discover.

Build a wild hideout

Building a den is a rite of passage for children and adults; I don't know anyone who didn't enjoy doing it as a kid, or who wouldn't quite like to have a go now. They never turn out as expected, but it's first step den-in-the-woods, next step architectural genius. There are lots of ways of doing it. You can create a tipi provided you have enough long, sturdy branches and sticks and an obliging, skinny tree to place them around. Rest your biggest, strongest branches against the trunk (all the way around the edge) and then fill in the gaps with smaller branches. You can add a roof of moss or leaves for extra insulation – just make sure you leave a front door! A woodland clearing is the best place to do this, as there will be the most branches lying around. If you're in a park or garden, you may have to be a bit more creative with household items like sheets. You could use rope or branches balanced between trees (or if you're really stuck, a washing line!) and hang sheets over them to create your shelter. Just make sure you're outside, immersed in nature and having fun. If you're brave and the weather is fine, you could camp outside in your shelter – make sure it's comfy though!

Watch a butterfly emerge

Spring and early summer are great seasons for spotting one of the most beautiful natural transformations – the emergence of a moth or butterfly from its chrysalis. There are four stages to becoming a butterfly: first the eggs, which hatch into caterpillars. They do an awful lot of eating (and shed their skin a few times), before creating a chrysalis around themselves so that they can metamorphose in peace. After a while (and the time depends on the species), they hatch out as a fully-grown butterfly, often looking completely different to the caterpillar they started out as. Watching this moment is magical, as the insect breaks free, unfurls its wings and takes flight. Different caterpillars will eat different plants, like nettles or members of the cabbage family. Search around scrubby areas full of 'weeds' and see if you can find a pupa. It's best to leave them alone and go back and check on your chrysalis daily. When you begin to see movement, settle back and see if you can capture the magic moment when the butterfly or moth breaks free! They'll look a bit crumpled to start with and they'll have to dry out their wings, but soon they should be ready to take to the wing, looking fresh and ready for anything.

Try your hand at hapa zome

There's something very therapeutic about pounding things with hammers. Almost everyone enjoys it. That's why the Japanese art of hapa zome is so much fun. It simply involves dyeing bits of cotton cloth with flowers, using sheer force to knock the colour out of them. Line up some fresh flowers, leaves and buds on a piece of plain cotton, fold it over so that the flowers are completely covered, lay on some slabs or a really flat, hard and sturdy surface, and get hammering (gently)! A mallet or even a big flat rock will do – just watch your fingers! When you peel back the cotton, you should have a lovely imprint of the flowers or plants on your cotton.

Think before you buy

Very few products can claim to be completely eco-friendly. Everything we do has an impact on planet Earth. However, some are better than others, and a washing up liquid switch to a brand that uses natural, plant-based materials, rather than tonnes of foamy, fragranced chemicals, will be a start. The trick with these is to use them sparingly. You won't get the same lather as a chemical base, but you will get the same cleaning power. Don't use loads to get a lot of bubbles – just a little will do. When it heads down the drain, the impact on our rivers and seas will be much less.

Learn a wild word

As the weather warms up and the ground dries, late spring and early summer can see long periods of dry, hot weather. How refreshing is it, though, when the first fat raindrops hit the parched earth, soaking into the soil and bringing new life to browning grass. You smell the rain before you see or feel it, and this is petrichor. It's the rich, pleasant earthy smell of the first rain on warm, dry ground. It's the first and last lingering sense of a short, sharp rain shower. Even as the water evaporates from the grass and the sun comes out again, you're left with the petrichor in the air.

Decorate with nasturtiums

Nasturtiums are one of nature's little treasures: brightly coloured, found largely in gardens (or escaped from them), and totally edible with a fiery taste. You'll see them from mid-spring blossoming in housing estates, gardens and in some wild areas. My favourite foraging spot is on the Isles of Scilly, where they grow all over the place. They have orange, red and yellow floppy petals and big circular green leaves. If you're foraging, look for fresh flowers that haven't been damaged and young, soft leaves, as these have the best flavour. They are very peppery, a bit like watercress, so don't overload

110

111

THINK! THINK! THINK!
THINK! THINK! THINK!
THINK! THINK! THINK!
THINK! THINK! THINK!
¡THINK! ¡THINK! ¡THINK!

WASHING UP LIQUID

112

PETRICHOR

(n): A pleasant smell that frequently accompanies the first rain after a long period of warm, dry weather.

113

Sail downstream with an elf boat

Do you remember writing messages as a child and pushing them into bottles, to float away into the sea or down a river? Well we don't want to add any more litter to our oceans, so plastic bottles are a big no-no, but we can do something similar with natural items. A boat made from twigs or bark will do the trick nicely, and they are easy to make. You'll need a handful of sturdy twigs, some natural twine and a large leaf (like a maple leaf). Snap the twigs so that they're all about the same size (10cm or so works well). You'll need between six and eight, depending on how thick they are. You'll also need another twig the same length for the mast, but make sure this one is a bit skinnier. Lay the twigs side by side and, at one end, use the twine to tie them together – you'll need to tie your twine on to your first twig securely, then wrap the twine around each twig and tighten, so that they lie flat next to each other. Once all the twigs are wrapped together, secure with a knot around your last twig. Repeat for the other end of your raft. Push your final stick into the centre of the raft and secure with more twine if it needs it. Finally, write a message on your leaf and then turn it into a sail, by threading it on to your mast. Make sure that it floats by testing it in the sink, and then you're ready to set sail! You can either push it off to find its own way, or you can keep hold of it by attaching another longer piece of twine.

Salute the shield bug

For today's Random Act of Wildness, try and find a shield bug in your garden. They have a wide variety of great nicknames, including my personal favourite – stink bugs! They look like their name – with a shield on their back protecting them from attack. There are lots of different species and between them they eat a huge array of plants, making them easy to spot no matter where you live – look in any wild place nearby, including your garden. The hawthorn shield bug is the species you're most likely to find – bright green with a dark red hourglass shape on the shield. The native common green shield bug is marching northwards across the UK, now being found across England and Wales. They are bright green with tiny black dots and dark wings. You don't want to find out why they're nicknamed stink bugs – they release a pungent-smelling fluid when threatened, which can stain your fingers. Take a good look at them, but don't try to handle them if you want to keep your hands clean!

Identify five beautiful butterflies

Butterflies are possibly the nation's best-loved insect. They are certainly one of the most admired, with many species being bright, gaudy and intricately decorated. There are around 59 species of butterflies in the UK in the summer, although this figure does vary as butterflies alter their migration routes (because of climate change).

Many of them can be found in rare or inaccessible habitats, like mountaintops or the middle of heathlands. The ones I've picked out are my favourites, and some of the ones you're mostly likely to see in your day-to-day routine. Look for butterflies in gardens or on plants, on hedgerows and in churchyards and verges. I've tried not to pick the total show-offs; a good butterfly book or website will help you get up to speed with the species that are missing.

Brimstone These butterflies are quite big, having a wingspan of around 7cm. They're one of the first butterflies to emerge in the year, and are lime green in colour. They have a flight that reminds me of a leaf caught in the breeze, and indeed when they perch (with their wings always closed) they blend in very well with the foliage around them, looking exactly like a pale green leaf. The wings curve up to tips on the top and bottom, which do look like the tips of leaves, and the veins are obvious, too. You can see them in England, Wales and Ireland, although they are spreading north.

Comma Comma butterflies look ridiculous, with their ragged edges and mottled brown underwings, which almost exactly resemble a dead leaf. When perched, you'll see a bright orange upper wing, with paler yellow and darker brown spots. It gets its name from a single white marking on the underwing, which is shaped like a tiny white comma symbol. They have a wingspan of 5–6cm. They love nettles, so look for them around the weedy edges of woodlands or fields. Although once sharply in decline, this species is now becoming more and more common and spreading northwards.

Speckled wood Speckled woods may be one of the browner butterflies, but look closely and you'll see a rich and delicate pattern on their wings. They are dark brown, almost chocolatey, with paler patches on the wings, a pale border all the way around the outside of the wings, and little eyes in some of the spots. They're around 5cm across. As the name suggests, they favour woodlands, but will also hang out any place with trees, so gardens, parks and hedgerows. They'll perch in little patches of warm sunlight, but you'll often see them chasing each other, as they don't like to be disturbed when sunbathing.

Small white There are a few different species of white butterflies in the UK, and they can be easily confused (or even lumped together – the small white and the large white are collectively known as the 'cabbage white'). The upper wing is bright white, with one or two dark spots and very slight black tips. Underneath, when they perch with their wings held close together, they are creamy. Small whites are widespread and common in gardens and allotments, where they are known as a pest species (they like the taste of cabbages!). They are strong flyers and can vary hugely in size, from under 4cm to nearly 6cm.

Small tortoiseshell The small tortie is a beautifully patterned butterfly. Although the underwing, when perched, looks like a dead leaf, the upper wing is a fiery orange-red, with black and pale-yellow etchings along the top, black patches and spots underneath, a white spot at the wing tip and very delicate blue and black markings all around the lower edge of the wings. It is one of the most well-known of our butterflies, with males growing up to 5.5cm, and females growing over 6cm. Sadly, this beautiful creature is in decline. It's commonly found in gardens, so have a look in your own or sneak a peek at the neighbours' – any area with flowers and bushes might turn up one of these gems.

Breakfast with the birds

We all know that breakfast is the most important meal of the day. But don't just kick-start your metabolism in the morning; make the most of those few minutes by getting your nature fix at the same time, as wildlife is waking up, too. Choose a sunny morning and take your breakfast outside. Use the time to think through the day using nature as your muse. If you know it's a big day at work, crammed with meetings or stuck indoors, then this Random Act of Wildness can set you up with a positive mind. If you've got kids, this can be a great way to get them to focus before school, too. Our houses are filled with distractions – radios, televisions, toys, gadgets and general hustle and bustle. Outside, away from all this, they might eat up quicker and concentrate on the day ahead. The fresh air will wake up sleepy eyes and give an additional energy boost. Early morning is a beautiful time to tune into nature, too.

Celebrate the cinnabar

If there's a moth you need to meet this summer, it's the cinnabar. Whenever a friend asks me about a butterfly they've seen in their garden, but didn't recognise, it's almost always a cinnabar moth. And no wonder – they are beautiful. Everyone thinks that butterflies are more attractive than moths, but the cinnabar exists to prove us all wrong. They are black and bright magenta – the forewings are jet black with two pink spots and two pink stripes; the hindwings are bright pink with a dark border. They're small, but what they lack in size they make up for in beauty. You might see them in your garden, in a scrubby patch of parkland, in a meadow or woodland, or anywhere with a bit of ragwort (their favourite food – which also makes them poisonous if eaten). They fly in the daytime and at night, making them quite easy to spot. You might struggle to get close as they're skittish, but persevere. It's worth it. They have similar mothy cousins, the burnets, but these don't have any stripes – just spots. You can see the caterpillars easily, too – they have black and yellow stripes. They'll turn into pupae in the autumn and emerge in the spring.

Taste wild elderflowers

Elderflowers are the taste of summer. The flowers, tiny, white and creamy, blossom in May and June, bringing hedgerows to life and attracting bees and butterflies to the sweet nectar. Elderflower can be made into cordial, which is used to flavour lots of different drinks and desserts: it's versatile, with a subtle, yet distinctive flavour. Make sure you've identified the elderflower correctly – don't mistake it for other similar flower sprigs at this time of year. They should hang in clusters from the branches of trees, with a flat-topped appearance. The flowers are best when they have just burst open.

You will need:
- A huge saucepan with a lid
- A sieve and tea towel/muslin cloth
- A mixing bowl
- Some large sterilised glass bottles
- 30 elderflower heads
- 2 litres water
- 2kg granulated sugar
- 4 lemons, sliced
- 2–3 tsp citric acid (look in the baking sections of shops, or the chemist)

1. Rinse off the elderflowers, giving them a good shake to remove any critters or dirt. Remove as much stem as possible – it can leave a bitter taste. **2.** Heat the water in a large pan with the sugar. Once the sugar has dissolved, turn up to a boil, then remove from the heat. The water should be thick and syrupy. **3.** Add the elderflower heads, lemon and citric acid to the water and gently immerse it all in the syrup. Cover, and walk away for at least 24 hours. Some people like to leave it for longer, but I prefer the flavour after just a day – it's a matter of taste. **4.** Lay your cloth or muslin in your sieve, and place over your mixing bowl. Gently strain the liquid into the bowl, making sure it doesn't overflow. Decant into sterilised bottles (a funnel might avoid too much mess). You can drink it straight away with water, lemonade, tonic water or something stronger, or keep it in the fridge for up to six weeks. **5.** Elderflower cordial also tastes lovely with other dishes, so try using it in a salad dressing; whip a little with cream and serve with meringues and fresh strawberries; or add to a panna cotta recipe.

Find a camouflaged creature

The difficulty in this Random Act of Wildness is finding a creature that doesn't want to be found. Its appearance has evolved to remain hidden from your eyes – that's part of the challenge and part of the fun. Here's some top beasties to look out for while you're out and about exploring – remember, you'll need to look closely to be in with a chance!

The peppered moth is an amazing example of rapid evolution. In the industrial revolution, when our towns and cities were dark with smog, the peppered moth evolved to have a much darker wing pattern, to blend with the dirty surroundings. In the countryside, they remained speckled pale grey. If they land on the trunk of a tree, you'll struggle to spot one. The buff-tip moth is good at blending in, looking almost exactly like the twig of a silvery birch – only its furry head gives it away. These are both garden species, so keep an eye out. Many butterfly species will hold their wings together when perched, looking like dead leaves sticking out of the twigs. Look for species like comma, peacock and red admiral, which may be beautiful with their wings spread, and hidden as soon as their wings are closed.

Chatter with house sparrows

Perhaps the ultimate girl-next-door, the house sparrow is completely underrated and overshadowed by much flashier, showier birds in our gardens. They may be brown and they may be small, but they're fun, inquisitive, noisy, sociable and brave – which in my opinion means they deserve a Random Act of Wildness all to themselves. House sparrows will happily exploit every habitat, particularly manmade ones. They seem to love our gardens and feeding stations, wastelands, churchyards, parks and playgrounds. That said, their numbers are in decline in the UK, and you may or may not have them in your area. They occur in most towns and villages, but are less common in cities.

House sparrows love a thick hedge or bush to provide cover, and a feeding station with seed mix to gorge on. If you get a colony active in your area, try taking a break from work and just tune into the chattering of the sparrows instead. They will squabble and bicker and gossip and natter away like nothing else, and if you watch them on feeders you can see how indignant they can get with each other. They work together, though, and a quick alarm call from one of the group will send everybody scurrying for cover.

Release a muddled-up moth

This Random Act of Wildness is also a Random Act of Kindness for the day. Moths have a habit of collecting in our bathrooms, especially on warm nights when you might have accidentally left the light on. The best thing you can do is to make sure you switch off all lights when you're not using the room, but even in the few minutes you're in there a moth or two will break in. There are lots of theories about why moths are attracted to lights, but none of them has been proven. The most popular is that moths navigate using the moon, which is a fixed source of light – when you add new lights, like bathrooms or streetlights, moths become disorientated. Whatever the reason, they do respond to the bright lights and will move towards them. If you find a moth in your bathroom, gently usher it back outside again – there's no food in there for them and they can die of starvation. They want to be out in the wild where they can forage and reproduce.

Ring with the experts

It takes years of dedication to learn the skill of bird ringing. Scientists train at all hours of the day and night to catch birds using special nets, and place little rings very carefully around their legs. These rings have codes on them, which means they can be identified individually if they turn up again. We've learned some amazing things from ringing, like how far birds travel, where their migration routes take them and how they move around and interact with each other. You can only ring a bird yourself after training with the professionals, and you'll need to buy a lot of kit to do it – including a good alarm clock for all those 4am starts. It's not an easy thing to do and is a very delicate science, so don't try this yourself! What you can do, though, is find a bird ringing demonstration or event near you. In the spring and summer, these often happen on nature reserves or as part of local fetes or shows – just search the internet to see what you can find. A team of trained ringing experts will be on hand at these events to catch the birds, put the rings on and give you a chance to see these feathered friends up close. The whole programme is coordinated by the British Trust for Ornithology (BTO). Check out **www.bto.org**.

Tread carefully around toads

Toads aren't the prettiest – large, grey-brown, warty, flabby. The common toad, the one you're most likely to see, is a real brute. Unlike frogs, they are covered in rough, dry skin. This doesn't mean they're not rather cool though, so spare a few minutes for a common toad.

Common toads, like frogs, mate and lay their eggs in the early spring. Around this time, you're mostly likely to see and hear them croaking about near ponds, or find toad spawn strung out in ditches, ponds and shallow lakes. After this, the adults will disperse across dry land, looking for cool, moist places to hang out. Over the next few months, the eggs hatch into tadpoles, which feed up, grow legs and transform into toadlets. This is the most vulnerable stage of a toad's life. In the summer, toadlets will leave the safety of their home en masse. If you find the spawn in spring, it's worth checking back a few months later to see if you can watch this in action. You'll have to tread carefully – the toadlets are tiny and there will be hundreds of them. Sometimes this exodus will happen near a road, and it might be worth informing your local council to see if they can put a diversion in place.

Save a humble bee

Bees get tired; they cover an astonishing three miles a day looking for food to take back to their nests, carrying the pollen that they have collected in sacs on their legs. Even when they have a full tummy, a foraging bumblebee is never more than 40 minutes from starvation!

It's quite common, especially on colder days, to see exhausted and hungry bees on the ground. They're buzzed out and might need a helping hand. Your Random Act of Wildness for the day can be to save a life. If you find a bee on the ground, move it to somewhere safe, with plenty of shelter and flowers around to gather nectar from. Even a patch of long grass with some dandelions might do, just make sure no one can step on the poor thing. Even better, if you're near home or work, mix together a couple of tablespoons of white granulated sugar with a tablespoon of water, and place the mixture near the bee on a teaspoon or saucer. Don't use any more mixture than this, as your new friend could drown. A paintbrush soaked in sugar water is also an option, placing the tip near the bee's head. Your tired bee should smell the sweetness and take a drink. A few sips will be enough; give it a few minutes and hopefully watch it buzz away again!

Flap with bats in the dusk

There are seventeen species of bats that breed in the UK, with a few more that will turn up accidentally from the continent. They range from the tiny pipistrelle to the much larger noctule, with everything else in between. These are two of the most common species you're likely to see in your back garden. You'll need a warm, still night when there will be lots of insects buzzing around (bats will feast on moths and other flying insects). Gardens are perfect, but you can also try parks, the edges of woodlands, hedgerows, churchyards, and even just out on your street. Lakes and waterways can be good, too.

You're looking for a flickering shadow in the dusk. They can be hard to get a good view of, so, as soon as you spot one, try to think how it's flying. Is it fast and frenetic? Slow and stately? Is it diving down over water? Because you're unlikely to get a good view, the behaviour can be just as useful as the appearance. If it's flying in a sporadic fashion, very quick and darting, it could well be a common pipistrelle. This is the bat you're most likely to have an everyday experience with. Noctules fly much slower and higher in straight lines, patrolling streets. Daubenton's bats are associated with water and will take insects off the surface.

Bats find their way around using echolocation – high-pitched frequencies that bounce off objects and allow them to identify their prey. Hunting and flying at night means that their eyesight is next-to useless, so instead they've adapted to use their ears just as we use our eyes. These conversations used to be almost entirely private as they were so high-pitched, but if you've got young ears, you might just hear a bat before you see one – it sounds like a high-pitched squeaking, clicking noise. Not everyone can hear them.

We can all enjoy eavesdropping though, using bat detectors. As they echolocate, a bat detector can hear the sounds coming from the bat and translate them into lower frequencies which we can hear. A pipistrelle sounds like dripping water, while a noctule sounds like horse's hooves. Each species echolocates in a slightly different way, so this is a great way to listen in on this secret world and tell different species of bats apart. You can buy a bat detector and use a code to work out what species you're looking at; use an app connected to a detector to record the noise; or, if you just want to have a taster session, look for an event at a local nature reserve in the summertime.

Roll down a grassy green hill

There's nothing sophisticated about this Random Act of Wildness – it's just for the fun of it. It will completely immerse you in nature and stain your clothes a bit. Kick your shoes off, too – let your toes feel the cool ground. You need to find a grassy hill that's free of nettles and stones and prepare to get dizzy. On your walk up, do a quick scan for any rocks jutting out that could hurt you (or anything unpleasant you might roll in). When you get to the top, or high enough up the slope, lie on your side, stretch your hands above your head, relax and let gravity take over, whizzing you round and round down the slope.

Get crafty in the sunshine

Arts and crafts are making a comeback – the ultimate mindfulness activity. Whether you're into knitting, sewing, embroidery or crochet, there's several ways you can make your favourite crafty activity a little bit wild. You could try making a wild animal cuddly toy, like a fox or rabbit, embroidering a wild landscape, or simply taking your craft outside into the sunshine at lunchtime. You'll find that when you're surrounded by nature, you'll feel the double effects of mindfulness: wildfulness, too!

Find a wild heart

The blossoming of the dog rose tree is a beautiful sight. Dog roses are climbers, weaving their way around other shrubs, trees and bushes to gain a purchase. They grow on the edge of woodlands and hedgerows, and sometimes on derelict land, with beautifully simple flowers that blossom in the spring. The bright yellow pollen is a favourite with bees and butterflies. On windy days in summer, these petals drop off and land in hedges or on the ground. They're pinkish white and delicate, and look like little hearts scattered all around. Snap a photo of one of these hearts and send it to someone who needs to feel loved today.

Dance in a downpour

It's raining, it's pouring! Who cares? We live in a rainy country, so we might as well make the most of it. Get your umbrella out and go all 'Singin' in the Rain' for a few minutes. What a glorious feeling! Hum a ditty to yourself, sing your heart out or rock some moves and bust a groove in the rainstorm. Put on your wellies, pull up your hood and get out there. Dance in a downpour and let your troubles wash away with the rain!

Identify five wonderful wildflowers

It's very easy to overlook wildflowers. Many are small, hidden in tussocks of grass, and much of their habitat has been destroyed. And many people still frown upon them as being weeds. This is such a shame, as they're completely underappreciated, with bright colours and exquisite designs, and they're great for wildlife, too. Insects like bees adore wildflowers, so we should be doing more to bring them back and protect them. Identification can be hard, so here are some which are perfect for honing your skills. You don't need meadows to spot wildflowers; they'll pop up in the most unexpected places, in the gaps between pavements and buildings, in walls or along canals. Councils are planting wildflowers along verges and on roundabouts, too. Remember never to pick them. If you can't identify them, take a photo, make some notes or draw a quick sketch and identify them at home. Look at where they were growing, the shape of the flowers and petals, how big they were and what the leaves looked like.

Red campion Red campion blossoms just as bluebells start to go over, so our woodland floors switch from indigo to pinky-red. They love hedgerows and grassy verges, too, adding a splash of colour. They can live for years and years, blossoming in the spring and summer and dying back in the autumn. The flowers themselves are almost cartoon-like, with five heart-shaped petals clustered around a little white centre. They can grow close to white campion flowers, so they may hybridise to form pale pink blooms. The stems are long and hairy.

Common poppy Common poppies are easy to identify, due to their iconic associations with World War I. Once considered a weed, due to intensive agriculture they have declined sharply. You now see them in wildflower meadows or on roadsides. The bright red petals are filmy, round and overlap, creating a saucer shape around a yellow and black centre. They can grow tall, up to 80cm.

Oxeye daisy Oxeye daisies are hardy and robust, and grow where nothing else seems to want to. They look like much bigger versions of the little daisies you get popping up in lawns and parks. Roadside verges and wastegrounds are favourites, as well as wildflower meadows. They turn their heads across the sky to follow the course of the sun throughout the day. The flower heads appear on long stems, and although they look like one big daisy, this is actually hundreds of tiny flowers pressed together in the centre (the yellow bit), and surrounded by florets (the white 'petals').

Foxglove Foxgloves are striking, growing in great spikes from the ground all over the place. The tube-shaped flowers hang in clusters around a single stem and are usually dark pink in colour (although they can be much lighter). There's nothing else quite like them, and the flowers have often been used to depict fairy costumes, like hats. They have a series of spots running up the inside of the flower, and up to 80 of these flowers can hang together at once. Not that you would, but just as a caution, don't be tempted to eat them – they're very poisonous!

Cornflower These vibrant flowers are among the most noticeable of wildflowers, being bright electric blue in colour. Like the daisy, this isn't just one flower – a single flower head is made up of lots of different flowers, with the outer florets forming the bright blue 'petals', and dark purple flowers in the centre. Cornflowers love roadside verges, wasteland and scrub, and are often found in wildflower seed mixes, adding a splash of blue. They declined a lot when farming practices changed in the 1960s, but are making a comeback now thanks to unusual habitats, like urban meadows.

140 Spot an ugly duckling

The Ugly Duckling is a fairy-tale by Hans Christian Andersen, and has been told for generations. A little 'duckling' grows up with his brothers and sisters looking and feeling very different from all the rest, and is labelled as ugly. As he gets older he is more and more upset by this, until he realises, when he's much older, that he's no duckling at all – instead, he's a swan! I always feel very bad for this little cygnet, and indeed all cygnets: they're not ugly at all. They're gorgeous – just as cute as actual ducklings!

Cygnets are downy and a soft charcoal grey, with little black bills and eyes. They look very cuddly, but don't touch them unless you want to feel the wrath of mum, who won't take kindly to you going near her babies. They will keep that grey colour all the way through to adulthood, only becoming pure white when they reach maturity. Spy some cygnets following their parents down a canal or river or across a lake. Look out for them cruising along or curled up in a little ball near to their mother.

Be busy like an ant

Ants can live in enormous colonies – up to 15,000 in a single nest. The ones you'll see in your garden are mostly black garden ants. Their behaviour is just fascinating to watch. Following a marching ant, or even better a trail of ants, can be very mindful if you're stressed. Their world is so different to ours, but they're hardworking and strong, too.

Locate a colony of ants somewhere nearby for this Random Act of Wildness – it shouldn't be too hard in the summer. Just follow a few ants and see where they're heading. Some of them might be carrying things – like bits of leaf or twigs.

The little guys scurrying about on the ground are the worker ants. They bring food, clean the nest and tend to the queen (who is busy producing eggs). The adults appear in the summer and have wings. They're a bit bigger and have the task of setting up new colonies. It all runs like clockwork and everyone plays their part. Don't be too quick to crush an ant; instead, try and see the world from their perspective.

Encounter a wild peacock

No, there are no wild peacocks living in the UK, although you may encounter a captive one at a country estate. You might find a peacock butterfly though. These must be the showiest, loudest, most ostentatious of all the butterflies you might see in your garden. They're big, with a wingspan of up to 7cm, so easy to spot. They often perch with these wings wide open, soaking up the sun's rays. They are a riot of colour. For today's Random Act of Wildness, pick a warm sunny day in the summer, find somewhere with lots of flowers (flower-filled gardens are perfect) or a dappled, sunny woodland glade. Can you spot this intricate beauty basking in the sunshine? You might spot it flying first, with strong and purposeful wingbeats. They're unmistakable, with bright red wings and four dazzling 'eyes', which are supposed to confuse predators. These eyes are stunningly pretty, with different shades of blue fading into lilac fading into bright golden yellow, and a big splodge in the middle of each. They're fringed with white and black. They're also quite tolerant, so you may be able to get close enough to take a photo!

Enjoy demoiselles

There are two species of demoiselles in the UK – the banded and the beautiful. Related closely to dragonflies, these insects are damselflies, spotted in early summer along rivers, canals, ponds and lakes. They are enchanting, very elegant and stunningly pretty. They are the only species of damselflies to have colour in their wings, which they hold straight back along their bodies when they're perched. You might spot them on long grasses or reeds near the water's edge.

The banded demoiselle is one of my favourite insects. The males are electric blue, the females lime green, and both are iridescent. The males also have an obvious black splodge on the wing, which stands out like an eye. If they take off and fly, they seem to bounce through the air (a bit like butterflies), but I always think they look like fairies. The males will skip around trying to impress any nearby females. On a sunny day, find a spot by the water and sit very still. If you spot any little blue fairies perched in the grass or fluttering around, a favourite trick of mine is to stick my feet out over the water – your toes make the perfect spot for them to perch!

144

145

A
TOOTH-
BRUSH

146

MOONGLADE

(n): A flash
of moonlight
reflecting off an
expanse of water.

147

Cook in the sunshine

On sunny evenings, don't get trapped in the kitchen slaving away over a hot stove. Take your chopping board, vegetables and salads outside and prepare them on an outside table. If you've got peelings, you'll be able to add them straight to the compost heap! In countries where the sun shines a lot, like Australia, people rely on the 'barbie' almost as much as the oven, so try grilling meat, fish and vegetables outside over hot coals, too. Not only will they taste better than normal, they are healthier for you as you don't need oil to cook them.

Think before you buy

Nearly everyone's toothbrush is made entirely of plastic, and millions of them are binned every single year. An awful lot of these end up in our seas and that's where they will stay, literally for centuries. There are very few completely biodegradable toothbrushes on sale, as there aren't many alternatives to the plastic bristles, but there are plenty of options for bamboo or wooden handles. You can even compost some of these – just make sure you dispose of the plastic bristles in the bin beforehand.

Learn a wild word

Moonglade is a beautiful, evocative word, which describes the flash of silvery light as the moon reflects off the surface of water – of a lake, a river, a canal. There are some nights when the world just seems lit up by the moon, and the effect it makes as it dances across rippling water is magical. It's been used in poetry by Edgar Rice Burroughs, who is famous for the Tarzan series.

Tell wild stories

Storytelling is a real skill. It's a great activity to do as a family, or even as part of a school lesson. Think of all the stories you love that have nature in them – animals as characters, wild landscapes or nature topics. Then head outside and set the scene – in your favourite or most dramatic wild place. Being outside will make the experience more immersive and you can use nature to inspire your characters, the setting and the plot. Your story could be about rescue, for example a wild animal rescuing you or vice versa. You could have wild animal heroes, wild magic, wild love stories, wild tragedies – whatever inspires you! Tell your story out loud or write it down to read again.

Notice nurdles in the sand

What's a nurdle? Nurdles are tiny bits of plastic that look a bit like lentils (and are about the same size). Nearly all our plastic products are made of them. These grains of plastic are melted together by industry to create plastic goods, some of which are washed into our seas due to clumsy handling by big corporations – they can be washed overboard from boats during transport, dropped when they're being handled, or lost from factories. They are creating havoc in our oceans.

Because of their size, nurdles are often mistaken for food by fish, or ingested by marine mammals and seabirds. They collect all sorts of chemicals on them, making them toxic, and they don't biodegrade. They have started to wash up in huge numbers on beaches. Although there's no long-term solution (yet!), there are two things you can do to help. First of all, get out there and find some nurdles. You'll have to look very carefully as they are tiny. Many of them are white or clear, but they can come in any colour. Look along tidelines, paths, among the sand, in rocks or in areas where there's a lot of plastic debris. You can collect them (use gloves if you can) and store them in a jar to show people and explain why they're so harmful. Secondly, The Great Nurdle Hunt is mapping where nurdles are washing up most regularly, so become a citizen scientist and share your sightings with them!

Blow a dandelion clock

Dandelions are always labelled as weeds, but remember, weeds are just flowers growing in the wrong place. Try and shift your perceptions by appreciating what hardy little plants these are – and how great they are for wildlife. When they're in flower, the bright yellow head of a dandelion is excellent for feeding bees, butterflies and other insects. They are an amazing source of nectar for pollinators. They're also very strong-willed plants – if you've ever tried to uproot one, you'll know what I mean. If you're going to dig up your dandelions, at least don't waste them – make them into tea for yourself or feed them to chickens. Personally, I think it's best to let them grow, at least in a patch of your garden; as the weather gets warmer, the flowers will become seed heads (called 'clocks') covered in a downy, white texture that will carry the individual seeds off on the breeze. Give them a helping hand to colonise – get down on your tummy, breathe in and give a really big puff of breath over the dandelion head. Or you can play a game with children – count how many blows it takes to strip the dandelion clock of its seeds. This will supposedly tell you the time!

Examine an intricate lacewing

Lacewings are familiar garden insects that you might see in the spring and summer months. They're so delicate and small – just a couple of centimetres long at most – that they look like they might break. There are over 40 species in the UK, but the one that you'll recognise the most is the common green lacewing. This fellow is lime-coloured with green, translucent, lacy wings and brown shiny eyes. Lacewings are great insects to encourage into your garden as they munch on aphids. They'll suck all the juice out of them – yum! It's worth spending a minute or two for your Random Act of Wildness today getting up close to a lacewing. They're fragile, so don't try and touch one or move it, but check out those wings. They look like the criss-cross of a ship's rigging or a fishing net, intricate and fine. If you can get one to sit still for long enough, you could even try and sketch out the pattern.

That badger sniffed my toe

A fabulous week spent in Scotland was about to get a little better. This was my first trip to the Highlands, and I had already been blown away by several encounters with wildlife. It was gone eleven o'clock at night as I took up my perch on a low wall that encircled the lawn. I was no more than a foot above the grass, and my only company came from the midges. In the gathering dark, my keen eyes could still make out the shapes of the bushes, the house, a movement . . . I caught my breath as my black-white companion ambled into the open. A badger.

Either he was not aware of my company or he did not mind it. He pottered about in front of me, working his way across the lawn in my direction; he stopped about a metre and a half away to play tug-of-war with a juicy earthworm. The badger triumphed, and the worm snapped out of the ground. Bumbling closer – a metre: I could see the individual hairs, hear his low, foraging grumble; half a metre: his large paws and claws were clear against the grass; 30cm: I didn't dare knock away the midges. My legs were crossed, one foot hanging over the wall. The badger raised his head, cocked it to one side, and sniffed the air. A step closer – he sniffed my toe.

The moment seemed to last an age, but seconds later the sound of voices sent him scurrying for cover. His cuddly form moved with surprising agility across the grass, and his outline melted away into the dark. It took a minute to realise that my hair, arms, face and legs were crawling with midges, unpleasant certainly, but necessary for such an intimate moment.

Do it yourself:
Badgers live all over the UK, but they're surprisingly hard to see. They are shy and nocturnal, with a powerful sense of smell that sends them scurrying for cover if they sense us. To be in with the best chance, I would book yourself on to an evening guided walk or a visit to a hide. Lots of nature reserves offer these as a chance to get expert guidance and the best opportunity to enjoy these iconic creatures. They'll use peanuts and other tasty treats to bring the badgers close by, giving you the best possible experience.

Admire a noble stag

Okay, so stag beetles aren't the most common of species, but they're so awesome that they deserve their own Random Act of Wildness. This is the UK's largest beetle, growing up to 8cm long – impressive! They live in the south of England, and mostly in the east, with London being a hotspot. You can guess why they are called stag beetles – the males have fearsome-looking jaws that project from the head like the antlers on a stag. Their bodies are iridescent reddish black. Don't worry, though – those jaws won't nip you. In fact, they're surprisingly weak and harmless to humans. They need oak and rotting wood to survive, so oak piles are a good place to start looking for these magnificent creatures. Amazingly, they can live for up to six years as larvae, but for just a few weeks as adults – just enough time to reproduce and lay eggs. The best time to see them is warm summer evenings, when they'll buzz around the city looking for mates. They're so big that they look like small birds or bats flying around! See if you can spot one, and if you see one in danger (like wandering down a busy pavement) scoop it up and pop it somewhere a bit safer.

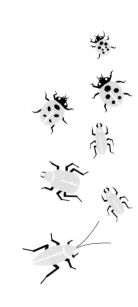

Find a hidden jewel

Beetles are the hidden jewels of the bug world. There are over 4,000 species in the UK, but this shouldn't stop you from getting up close to admire them, and trying to identify some of the easier species. The best place to start is scrubby patches of land by fields, hedgerows, rivers or parks – look for nettles and brambles and undergrowth.

Beetles are often iridescent in the sunshine. The rose chafer is a good one to spot – they can grow up to 2cm long and have a hard, shimmering green wing case, with a few creamy streaks. They love dog roses, so look for them when the flowers are in bloom. The mint leaf beetle is a real stunner – most commonly found in the south of England, it likes to hang out on mint leaves and has tiny pockmarks on its shimmering green body. It can grow to about 1cm. Smaller still, and not native to the UK, is the rosemary beetle, which hangs out on herbs in your garden. It has bright purple stripes running along its turquoise body. And proving that small really is the most beautiful, the dead-nettle leaf beetle is a firework of colour – shimmering green, blue, orange and gold. This little one is just half a centimetre long.

For this Random Act of Wildness, try and get close enough to take a photo of a beautiful beetle. See if you can identify it, too, but don't be disheartened if you can't. You've got a lot to choose from!

Skate with a pond skater

Ever wished you could walk on water? Well the pond skater can!
There's a handful of species of pond skater in the UK, ranging from
1–2cm long. You can see them from the springtime onwards (when
they come out of hibernation to lay eggs), skating around atop the
surface of ponds, shallow lakes and slow-moving streams. They
literally walk on water. This amazing feat of science is made possible
by the slight surface tension on the water, which creates a 'skin'.
Thanks to the insects' minuscule weight, which they can spread
across the surface of the water, they are able to row (or 'skate') across
this skin, using their middle set of legs to propel and steer them. Find
a pond, ditch or lake near you, and see if you can spot the pond skater
rowing across the surface. The slight weight of the insect will cause
very tiny dents in the water's surface, allowing you to see the surface
tension for yourself.

Play under the stars

Do you play a musical instrument? Sunset on a warm summer's
evening is the perfect time to take your guitar, flute or violin outside
and serenade the night, gently and quietly. A balmy evening is ideal,
with a snug blanket over your legs. Don't try and drag a drum kit or a
grand piano outside – that might be a bit ambitious! – but something
light, portable and soothing will set you (and your neighbours) up for a
lovely evening.

   If you do this Random Act of Wildness, you'll be taking part in a
piece of musical history, too. In 1924, in a garden in Surrey, Beatrice
Harrison took her cello outside and played in harmony with a
nightingale buried deep within a bush. This magical musical triumph
was broadcast across the UK on BBC radio. It was a moving piece as
the nightingale responded to the instrument, poignant, emotional
and full of joy. It was the first time people had been able to hear
wildlife broadcast live on UK radio. The show was repeated every year,
until the outbreak of World War II. Nightingales are rare now, sadly,
but you might be joined by a song thrush, blackbird or robin, singing
in the night.

156

Crystallise rose petals

Roses have a distinctive and exotic flavour that most people recognise from Turkish Delight. I love it. The petals are soft and very pretty and make elegant decorations for puddings and cakes. Try crystallising them for added texture and sweetness. The petals will begin to drop off in the summer, so harvest them when they're still fresh and pretty, but not so early that you leave the flower bud exposed.

You will need:
- Tweezers
- Baking tray
- A soft brush, like a pastry brush
  or even a clean paint/make-up brush
- Handfuls of fresh rose petals –
  around 20 or 30 for a good-sized cake
- 1 egg white, beaten
- Caster sugar, just enough to dust

1. Gently wash the rose petals in cold water and allow to dry. **2.** Holding each petal with tweezers on the baking tray, brush with the beaten egg white. You'll only need a little. **3.** Dust over a sprinkling of caster sugar, making sure the whole petal is evenly coated. I prefer to do this in batches of about ten, working on one side of the petals, then turning them all over and repeating on the other side. **4.** Making sure they're not touching each other and they're well protected from little hands or paws, leave them to dry in a warm, safe place for a couple of hours. They're then ready to use on cakes or desserts, and you can also store them in an airtight container for a few weeks.

Admire a beautiful orchid

Orchids may sound exotic and rare, but there are some species that are easy to find in the UK – you just need to know where and what to look for. They grow in some places you'd expect, like meadows and nature reserves, while others you might not, like parks or road verges. They're masters of disguise and have both enigmatic and literal names, like the bee orchid (which looks like a bee); the rather cheeky monkey orchid; or the elegant lady orchid. The easiest to find is the common spotted orchid, which you can enjoy in June and through the summer. It appears in a variety of habitats, and has a rosette of green leaves with dark purple spots. The flowers themselves are packed together in a cone shape, and range from white to pale pink to deep magenta. They have distinctive darker stripes and spots on their lower petals. Before you set out in search of them, do a little research as to where you might find them locally. Don't pick them as they're protected, but for this Random Act of Wildness do take a photo. These are the celebrities of the wildflower world and worth a little paparazzi attention.

Sample some seaweed

It may not look appetising when piled up on the beach, but many seaweeds are edible. None in the UK are poisonous. Some have distinctive flavours and are quite easy to identify, too. You must be wary when foraging seaweeds though. There's no common law that gives you the right to collect it – a little for personal consumption will be fine, but you need a licence to commercially harvest. It's polite to check with whoever owns the beach (a local council is a good place to start). Use scissors to snip away a few fronds.

None of the species sound particularly enticing – kelp, dulse, gutweed, carrageen – but can be made delicious with proper cooking. Don't eat seaweed straight off the beach. Pollutants collect along our shores that will need washing off, as well as any sand or salt.

For this Random Act of Wildness, next time you're at the beach, try and identify a few different kinds of seaweed: look for bright green, smooth strands of gutweed; smooth, leathery and brownish kelp, with long fronds; or sea lettuce, which is bright green in thin sheets, with wavy edges, and translucent. Take a little home with you and look up recipes that take your fancy – deep frying can produce a lovely texture for some seaweeds, while others are best used to flavour stocks.

Admire blooming buddleia

Beautiful buddleia in full bloom is a gorgeous sight in the summer. It can grow in huge clumps, up to 4m tall, and has tightly packed clusters of little flowers growing in spikes, which sometimes droop under their own weight. They can be purple, pinkish or sometimes white, and they give off a fresh honey scent. It's this smell that makes them so attractive to butterflies, bees and other pollinators.

Buddleia is an introduced plant, first brought to the UK from China in the 19th century. It escaped from gardens and collections and colonised railways and scrubland, and since then it's become naturalised. One reason it was (and still is) so popular is because of its ability to attract a whole range of insects, including butterflies. On a warm sunny day in the summer, when the flowers are in full bloom, see if you can find a fragrant buddleia bush near to you – maybe a neighbour's garden or growing near to work. You'll notice the buzzing straight away as hundreds of bees, moths and insects make the most of the sweet nectar. Butterflies will stand out though. See how many species you can count feeding off a single bush at any one time. My record is about six or seven species, including red admiral, peacock, small tortoiseshell, painted lady and large white, but there may be many more.

Get stuck to stickyweed

Stickyweed is the bane of parents across the land. Gardeners know it as cleavers or goosegrass, but this abundant 'weed' has many local nicknames, including sticky willy! It can grow in huge patches up to 3m tall and uses its 'sticky' texture to clamber up other plants and to spread around the countryside. Stickyweed isn't tacky in the same way that glue or tape is. It's covered in fine, tiny hairs that curve slightly, allowing it to attach like Velcro on to other plants and animals, including humans! In the summer, the round fruit appear as tiny balls on the plant, and these stick to anything passing by, allowing the plant to spread. Although it's considered a nuisance by many gardeners, it can be great fun to play with, growing commonly along rivers, in woodlands or meadows and in hedges. You can play a great game of tag with it. Collect some up and, as you're walking past one of your friends or children, press it against the clothes on their backs. Tag! They're it! They have to get it off themselves and chase others in your group, sticking it on to their backs in turn. A great game for getting children running around and enjoying wild places.

Enjoy an evening picnic

It's traditional to have a picnic at lunchtime, but why stop there? Whether you're on your own or with your family, an evening picnic as the stars are coming out, on a warm, balmy evening, is the perfect treat. Go somewhere within walking distance, like a local park, and allow the little ones to run free before bedtime – the evening air and exercise will wear them out. Take blankets to protect against the chill and play games in the dusk, like who can spot the first star, or listening out for night sounds (tawny owls hooting). This grown-up twist on a family favourite is lots of fun and will help you connect with the wild world around you, relaxing you before bed. If you're feeling really intrepid, switch it around and try a wild breakfast picnic one morning – sure to blow away any cobwebs from the night before.

Indulge in a natural facemask

So many of the products we put on our skin are full of chemicals, and you just don't need to do that to yourself – especially around your face. You can buy natural masks from some shops, full of vegetarian ingredients and absolutely no chemicals or preservatives: that's got to be better, right? And if you need a quick fix for tired skin, try hunting out some natural ingredients from the wild that will help you to detox and relax. You can buy some ingredients from shops, but you might be able to forage others. Herbs like mint make great additions to masks. Just remember to do a little patch test on your arm first, to check for allergies, and use your mask right away. Scrub it off the skin with a wet flannel after ten minutes. If you find one doesn't suit you, try using a different combination of ingredients.

Yoghurt Buy local if you can. A nearby dairy farm or farmers' market is ideal. Yoghurt is a bit of an all-round beauty whizz, being great for our insides and outsides, too! Yoghurt will gently exfoliate, soften and cleanse your skin, so makes a great base for a quick, refreshing mask.

Sugar Granulated sugar, mixed with honey, yoghurt or olive oil is a great exfoliating scrub. It'll help buff away dead skin cells and leave fresh, younger skin showing beneath. This is also great to use on legs and your bum, too, to scrub away any bumpy skin.

Mint Freshly picked mint from your garden – or wild mint – smells divine and will relax your mind and body. Muddle it into a paste and mix with any of the ingredients above, to feel refreshed and revitalised. The smell will be so enticing and leave you smelling fresh all day.

Oils Use oils with caution! My skin doesn't take too kindly to oils, making it greasy and spotty for days after. If you've got dry skin, though, a little coconut or olive oil might make it more supple, smooth and feeling less tight. Don't use too much, and make sure to wash it off thoroughly afterwards.

Lemon Lemons are antibacterial, so make an amazing deep cleanser. Don't apply lemon juice to broken skin as it'll sting, but over time can help minimise acne, reduce shine by taking away oils and hydrate your skin.

Bananas Bananas are a rich moisturiser. If you've got an old-ish banana lying around, try mashing it up and using it as a mask. You can add honey, sugar or even oats, to give it a bit of scrub – just try to avoid licking your lips!

Strawberries Wild, if you can get them! Strawberries are used across the beauty industry for a lot of reasons, mostly because they smell amazing and they're good for you. Try mashing some freshly picked, ripe strawberries with honey or lemon and rub across your face.

Down with pesticides

If you want a simple Random Act of Wildness today, make a pledge
to ditch the pesticides in your garden. That includes slug pellets.
Everything in your garden is connected to something else, and it's
not just about having the creatures that look pretty. When we rid our
gardens of slugs and snails, we're getting rid of a vital food source for
thrushes, like blackbirds. Worse still, if a hungry blackbird or hedgehog
eats a poisoned slug, they too can get very ill. The best way to manage
unwanted beasties in your garden, is to encourage in the things
that eat them – their natural predators. Forget the sprays and the
chemicals that are meant to help gardens blossom and flower – the
best kinds of gardens are diverse, bright, bold, beautiful and teeming
with all life. By having log piles, long grasses and compost bins, you
will encourage natural predators like beetles, birds and hedgehogs.
Give it time – your garden will take a while to re-balance if you've been
relying on pesticides. You may have an initial 'argh' moment as the
unwanteds flourish, but trust me and be patient. Encourage animals
up the food chain in, and they'll feast on your pests for breakfast,
lunch and dinner.

Gin three ways – part two

The second of our three gorgeous gin flavours, this time with refreshing, summery elderflower. (See pages 92 and 206 for more.)

Elderflower Elderflower gin has a subtle flowery flavour, soft, sweet and refreshing, that goes well with a good-quality tonic water and lots of ice. Look for creamy white flowers with a strong elderflower smell, rather than blooms that are going a bit brown around the edges. You can learn how to identify this flower on pages 89 and 107. You'll only need a few blossoms for this – about 5–8 per bottle.

To make up a batch, you'll need a bottle of gin and an empty, spare glass bottle (sterilised). Pour your gin into a glass bowl for safe-keeping. Shake off your elderflower sprigs under running water to remove any bugs or dirt, then add them to both bottles. Add a couple of tablespoons of sugar and a couple of strips of lemon rind, then refill the bottles with gin. Shake to mix everything together. After about a week, the gin should take on a pale yellow colour. Taste, and if you're happy with the flavour, strain through a muslin.

Build a moth trap

Moth traps are an easy way to discover lots of moths at once. You can buy very expensive traps, make your own, or why not have a go at building a makeshift trap in your garden? I have two ways to do this.

The first is simple. You pour a bottle of cheap red wine into a saucepan and heat it gently, stirring in 1kg granulated sugar as you go. You want it all to dissolve. Next, take long strips of old material (metre-long lengths about 2cm wide) and soak them in the wine solution. Hang them from a tree or washing line at sunset and wait for a couple of hours. Check back later with a torch. Moths will be attracted to the sweet smell of the wine and sugar, so should congregate around the material. Take photos (flash on!) to identify them later. If you position your strips next to bushes or trees, you might encounter some truly stonking moths, like the hawk-moth family. They come in the most beautiful colours and patterns – look for elephant hawk-moths, lime hawk-moths or eyed hawk-moths.

For the second moth trap, take a large white sheet and hang it from a washing line (at night, obviously). Turn off all lights, shine a bright torch on to your sheet and wait patiently for the moths to congregate!

Whirl with a whorl

Scouring the beach for shells can be hugely interesting and rewarding. If you're on holiday, or lucky enough to live near a beach, seeing what is washing up in the tideline is great fun. If you're by the sea today, see if you can find a whorled shell. These are the shells with spirals, a bit like snails; sea molluscs, like snails, build up this shell and live inside it, appearing through the hole to move about and feed, and disappearing inside at the first sign of danger. The shells are also inhabited by hermit crabs, which use these ready-made houses as shelter.

Walking through the tideline can give you the best chance of finding a whorl shell, lying among the seaweed and other debris. They can be very tiny, like wentletrap shells (which look like spiral staircases) or quite large edible whelks, which can grow to over 10cm. You're looking for that classic spiral shape. The best time to spot them can be after a storm surge, when lots of shells, animals and plants wash up along the shore. Pick your way very carefully, and if you find one, gently pick it up and look inside – be careful, though! There might be something living in there – maybe a crab looking to give you a nasty nip. You can feel the difference in texture between the rough outer shell and the smooth inside.

You'll need a photo of course – these are some of nature's most beautiful creations after all – but leave any whorl shells where you find them. No matter how big or small, these shells might go on to be home for another sea creature, and they won't be much use to nature sat in your bathroom. There might be something lurking inside, too, just out of sight, so pop it back among the seaweed when you've finished admiring it.

Dip your toes in the water

On a warm day, what could be better than a refreshing dip to cool you down? Wild swimming is a great way to immerse yourself in nature. Lots of people are swapping the pool for the sea, a river or a reservoir, getting fit and close to wildlife all at the same time. The waters of the UK aren't very warm, so only do what you feel comfortable with – whether that's wading ankle deep or diving in head first. Wldlife will tolerate swimmers much more so than walkers, so you might find yourself in the company of fish, kingfishers or birds.

If you've never tried it before, think back to your childhood. Did you ever go swimming or paddling in the sea? This is a great place to start. Pick beaches with lots of other swimmers and a lifeguard on hand, and only push yourself as hard as you think you can manage. Stay close to shore and take it easy. Make sure you've got towels and dry clothes to help you warm up afterwards as well.

You can also try wild swimming in rivers or reservoirs. There are maps online that show wild swimming spots that are tried and tested, and there are groups you can join for maximum safety and to swap some top tips. Staying in a group and learning from the pros is the safest way to get the most of this wild sport. You do need to be wary while wild swimming and follow some health and safety warnings, as it can be very dangerous. For guidance, see page 21. If this all seems a bit much, find somewhere you can dangle your feet in the water and see what wildlife comes to you.

Count the spots on a ladybird

Who doesn't love ladybirds? These tiny beetles are one of our most beautiful bugs, and one that we all recognise. But did you know that there are over 40 different species of ladybirds found living right here in the UK? There are loads of ways to tell the different species apart, but for starters check out the size, colour and the number of spots on its shiny shell.

The 7-spot ladybird is the most recognisable – bright red, with seven obvious black spots across its back (three on each wing case, and one that spreads across both). It's less than 8mm long. The 2-spot has only one spot on each wing case, is smaller and can change in colour – it can be red with black spots, black with red spots, or also orange. It is probably the most common ladybird, and the one you'll find hibernating indoors in the winter. A couple of species of ladybirds are yellow – including the 22-spot and the 14-spot, and there are even orange ones with cream spots! The eyed ladybird is our largest species, maroon red with very slight yellowish markings around each of its fifteen black spots.

There are non-native species, too. For example, harlequin ladybirds come from Asia and are hugely variable in their appearance – they out-compete our little bugs and can cause declines. They tend to be bigger, around 8mm. They can be anywhere between orangey-yellow to red to black, but most commonly will be orange with between fifteen and 21 spots, or black with two to four red spots. They never have white or cream spots.

It sounds very confusing but stick with it! If you find a ladybird, get up close and start counting those spots. If you can't ID it, take a photo and look it up online later. You're likely to find the most common species first, so start with these – look in parks, your garden, window boxes or in hedgerows. Ladybirds are beneficial in a garden as they predate other insects like aphids, which can be a nuisance when trying to grow plants. They should be encouraged, and a bug box is a great way to do this (ladybirds hibernate in winter and need somewhere safe to sleep!).

Nap in nature

A nap surrounded by nature can do you a world of good. Some people call it sunbathing, but let's call it well-earned meditation and reflection time just for you. Mindfulness and wildfulness to help you feel better, less stressed and less anxious. Pick somewhere safe, sunny and quiet. Lunchtime is my favourite time to indulge this Random Act of Wildness, especially on a warm summer's day when work is all getting a bit much or you're very busy. To help you switch off, allocate yourself a certain amount of time and set an alarm. If you're worrying about how much time you've got left, you'll never relax – let the alarm do the work for you. Cover your eyes, take a few deep breaths and concentrate on the natural smells, sounds and textures around you. Forget everything else for half an hour and take a nap in the grass; let the birds and the bees serenade you to sleep. You can use a blanket to lie on, but I prefer just to bundle up a jumper and my bag to rest my head on (keeping them safe, too) and lie back in the grass.

Find a chalky cuttlefish

If you've ever kept pet birds, or even visited a pet shop, you might have bought or seen cuttlefish bones. They're a favourite to give to budgies. These 'bones' wash up on beaches and are usually easy to spot – they're white, flat and shaped like a mini surfboard, with a hard wing around one pointed end. They bear little resemblance to a live cuttlefish, which is a multi-coloured rainbow of tentacles, with big eyes, strong bodies and related to the octopus. They can grow up to 45cm and live for about two years. Their skin can change colour, either to mimic their surroundings or to show off and attract a mate.

The white 'bone' that we see isn't part of a skeleton at all – it's a shell that's located inside the cuttlefish's body (called a cuttlebone) and helps control the buoyancy of the cuttlefish. When the cuttlefish dies, either of old age or from being eaten, the cuttlebone can wash up on shore: it's probably the closest that many of us will get to seeing a cuttlefish in the wild. It feels chalky when it's dry and extremely hard, but it can be snapped with pressure. See if you can find cuttlebones lying in the tideline.

Form a grass brass band

I've never been able to do this Random Act of Wildness. I've seen other people do it though, so I think it's just me – I was never very musical. It's a nifty trick if you can. You'll need a thick blade of grass, about the same width as your thumb. Hold it between your thumbs so that they're sitting side by side, and cup your hands together. Squeeze your thumbs together tightly. Then take a deep breath and blow with all your might on that blade of grass. If you're lucky and you hit it just right, you'll make a loud, proud, squeaking noise, not unlike that of a trumpet. If it doesn't work first time, keep practising. Try testing how hard you blow and how tightly you hold your grass. This can change the pitch of the noise and how easy it is to create. And if you can't do it, don't worry – you're not the only one!

Make a plant pot saucer drinker

Many butterflies (usually the males) like to partake in a little bathing now and then, also known as 'mud-puddling'. Although the nectar from flowers provides lots of sugars, there are some nutrients that butterflies need to get from other sources, and this is where mud-puddling comes in. On hot days in the summer, groups of butterflies will collect around a muddy puddle on the ground and sip the water. They're taking in nutrients and salts from the mud, which will help them to reproduce. They all sit around and quiver their wings, taking in the sunshine and the nutrients all at once.

   You can help butterflies in your garden by creating a puddling area for them. I recommend a large terracotta saucer (the kind you might have lying around in your shed) as the base – fill this with a layer of sand and soil, and drop in some smaller pebbles and larger stones as perches. Add a little water. You don't want it to be too deep, but you do want to make sure everything is nice and wet. Leave it in a quiet spot in your garden and see which butterflies come down to your puddling station on hot days. Remember to top up the water as it dries out.

Enjoy a tipple in the garden

This one is easy. If you're enjoying your favourite tipple in the evening, take it out into your garden or on to a balcony rather than sitting in front of the television. Take your shoes off and enjoy the feel of grass beneath your feet, the evening air and the buzz of nature. In the summer, enjoy the hum of insects and birds calling to each other; in the autumn and winter, take a blanket to cuddle up in. Leave your phone inside, too. You'll feel far more relaxed without the screens.

Think before you buy

When we see the adverts with those dreamy fragrances, it's easy to get sucked in and want to buy all those products that will feel so soft and smell so yummy. Just be wary, if it smells too good to be true, it probably is. Look for environmentally friendly laundry powders instead. They won't smell as strong for as long, but they'll get your clothes clean all the same and I find that they feel softer, too, without the need for additional fabric conditioner. Again, if you're not sure of where to start, read the reviews online or ask friends for their thoughts.

Learn a wild word

It's the end of the day, on a warm summer's afternoon. The dimpsey is upon us. A special time just before dusk, full of birdsong, dancing light and the buzzing of insects. This word comes from the southwest: Cornwall, Devon and Somerset. It's a great time of day to get your camera out. The light is rich and golden, and even if you're using a camera phone, get up close to something wild – like a wildflower – and enjoy the day as it gets a bit dimpsey.

Find the biggest leaf you can

In the summer, when it's hot and sweaty, don't you just wish you could carry around a great big fan with you all day? The little electric ones eat batteries and paper ones don't quite do the trick. Take some inspiration from the indulgent ancient civilisations, and look for a big leaf to keep you cool instead. You could even challenge any little ones in your life to help you find one. Ferns make great fans, with all of those different prongs, or you could go for big maple leaves. Gather up a few and see which ones are the most effective at getting a breeze going!

173

174

LAUNDRY POWDER

175

DIMPSEY

(n): The time in the evening just before dusk.

176

177 Hover with an emperor

You don't have to go far to hang out with emperors and you don't need to bow, curtsey or dress up. All you need is a bit of patience and any sort of wetland. You're looking for an enormous, stately dragonfly, patrolling around the edges of a river, lake or canal. These guys are one of the biggest species in Europe (nearly 8cm long!), so you're not going to miss them. They're vicious – if you're a smaller insect that is. They'll feast on smaller dragonflies and butterflies, which they catch in the air, making them an active predator. They are mostly blue in colour when you first glance at them – the males are boldly patterned, with a bright green thorax, light blue body and electric blue stripe down the body. The females are similar but duller. They're more common in central and southern parts of the UK, but even if you can't find one of these giants, there are other enormous species to look out for – golden-ringed, common hawker and brown hawker to name a few. Relax by some water nearby and wait to see what cruises along – you won't miss these beasts, and you can relax and take some 'me time' while you wait.

Hide and seek in the wild

Hide and seek is still the top wild game. It's easy to play, fun and a great way to encourage kids (and adults!) to switch off and immerse themselves in nature. You can split into teams, pick someone who's on or have a combination of both – when someone is found, they also become on! Give people plenty of time to spread out and hide – scramble up a tree, dive behind a bush or crouch in the long grass. Set a neat boundary area, too, and a time limit (so that if people aren't found, they know to come out). When someone is found, tag them quick! Woodlands and parks are a great place to play hide and seek – this isn't about identifying things or learning about wildlife, it's about immersing yourself in a natural area, having fun and switching off from everything else, even if just for a few minutes.

Press petals for decorations

This is one of my favourite memories from childhood and a simple Random Act of Wildness. My mum taught me how to do it, and it was the best use of the enormous dictionaries and encyclopaedias lying around! Gather up the petals and flowers you'd like to press – I always use fallen petals, from dog roses, or garden flowers that have gone over. To preserve their colour, you want to press them as soon as they're picked and dry them out as quickly as possible. You'll need some flat, smooth paper, like printer paper or coffee filters. You can use kitchen towel, but this may leave little bumps on your petals. Arrange your flowers between two sheets of paper, and place them in the middle of the heaviest book you can find. Beware – the book may absorb some of the moisture, so don't use books with sentimental value. Close the book gently and weight it down – with more books or even a brick. Stow it in a cool place and forget about it for a few weeks – about four should do the trick. When you open it up, be very gentle – lift up the paper and check that the flowers are completely dried out. You'll need a pair of tweezers to remove them gently. You can now use these to decorate cards and gifts or make displays for your house.

That time I nearly weed on a natterjack toad

Let's head to North Norfolk, a warm summer's evening, with the sunset casting long shadows in the sand. Holme Dunes National Nature Reserve. A beautiful spot, but sadly lacking in facilities. A leaflet helpfully indicates that the nearest WC is at the local golf course, which is a fair walk back down and simply not an option. So, I did what any naturalist would do: followed the path into the dark dunes, found a secluded spot and (ahem) dropped 'em. Incidentally, I don't know what the law is regarding peeing on nature reserves.

The first part of my strategy went according to plan; the latter caused something of a predicament. As I lowered myself (it's a lot more difficult for girls), a slight movement caught my eye in the sand. It was squat, dark, and crawling very rapidly towards the sound of running water. I swung the light of my phone up, and there before me was one of Britain's rarest amphibians: the natterjack toad.

Paul Sterry in *Collins Complete Guide to British Animals* describes the natterjack as 'a charming little amphibian' – I beg to differ when it catches you with your pants down! I will concur however that 'it can reach commendable speeds', and that 'they can disappear from view' as they wiggle down into the sand. Well, I squealed, the toad froze, and we ended up in an awkward bufonid stalemate.

In appearance it is much like a common toad, with the addition of a yellowish vertebral stripe, and is very scarce in Britain. Little pockets of distribution exist on habitats which offer free-draining sandy soils for burrowing, and shallow, seasonal ponds for breeding. Certainly, it was a rare natterjack toad, certainly it was quite confused by this turn of events, and certainly I had come very close to weeing on one of Britain's rarest species.

Do it yourself:

I really wouldn't recommend weeing on amphibians. It's just not ethical and natterjack toads are protected by law. You can have a great experience listening to them, though. They're only found in a few isolated locations now, in coastal sand dunes. Norfolk, the Solway Firth in Scotland and the northwest of England are top spots, and some heathlands in Surrey and Hampshire. Find your nearest location and, on warm, damp and cloudy evenings (spring is best), head to the nature reserves to listen to the chorus of the natterjack toad. They inflate their vocal pouches and sing away. Stick to the paths – they're so loud you won't need to get close!

Identify five buzzing bees

Bees are brilliant and come in all shapes and sizes. They're one of the top pollinators in the UK and we're completely reliant on them. They provide every third mouthful of food you eat (if you eat a healthy amount of fruit and veg). There are 24 species of bumblebees in the UK, and over 200 types of solitary bees. As you can guess from the name, solitary bees hang out on their own, whereas bumblebees live and thrive in colonies. There are also honey bees, which I've included here even though many of those you see will be from domestic hives. There's a common misconception that all female bees are queens and all male bees are workers; in fact, the workers can be male or female.

Buff-tailed bumblebee The buff-tail is one of the most quintessential of bumblebees, with the queen having a distinctive yellow and black abdomen (two stripes of yellow, black in the middle, and black underneath) with a buffy-white tail. In the males, this buffy line is much less defined, and they can have a white tail. Males also have black faces, which helps tell them apart from other big, common bumblebees. In urban areas, this bumblebee can be seen all year round. Look for them buzzing between flowers in your garden, particularly in the warmer months if you live in the countryside.

Red-tailed bumblebee Red-tailed bumblebees are very striking. They can be seen from early spring right the way through to late autumn. They are a large bumblebee: the females look huge, with a completely black body and bright red tail; the males are smaller and have yellow on the body, but still have the red tail. They are found in gardens, hedgerows, parks, along woodlands and near farmland. The only ones that hibernate will be the new queens; the old queen and males will die in the autumn.

Honey bee These are the bees that live in hives. They're almost unmistakable, having a black and gold abdomen and large eyes. They're not big and furry like bumblebees, but smaller and more streamlined. We've worked with honey bees for years, partly domesticating them by providing them with manmade hives, and harvesting the honey they produce within. They're not all domestic though, and may form colonies in woodlands. You'll see them busily visiting flowers in your garden or nearby park. It's always good to buy local honey if you can, as your flowers may have helped to make it!

Common carder bee The common carder is also a bumblebee, and one of the most commonly seen ones. It's orange and brown, with some darker bands going around the middle. The main abdomen is a rich goldy-brown colour. You'll see this bumblebee commonly in gardens, and anywhere else with plentiful flowers. The nests, which may contain up to 200 insects, are often built in burrows or cavities, like abandoned mouse holes, birds' nests or under lawns. They come out in early spring and will survive late into the autumn, so keep an eye out for them.

Leafcutter bee I've thrown this one in there to confuse you, but it's worth it. This little bee is a solitary bee, and it looks a bit like a honey bee. It's only distinguishable by its orange underside, but it has a very cool behaviour that makes it recognisable. They cut circles out of leaves in your garden and carry them back to their nests on their backs – you won't see a honey bee doing that! When they get back to their nests, they glue them together with saliva to form cells – this is where their larvae live. There are lots of species in the UK but they're very hard to separate. They are only active from April to August, so keep an eye out on warm, dry days and try to spot the holes in the leaves in your garden.

186   Count the arms on a starfish

Starfish are instantly recognisable and there are over 30 different species found around the UK. Whenever I went rockpooling as a kid, I was never lucky (or diligent!) enough to find anything as awesome as a starfish, but with a bit of patience, you might be.

Starfish may look pretty, but they're fearsome hunters – they munch on shellfish, prising open the shells with their strong arms. Then – and this is where it gets a bit gross! – they insert their own stomachs into the shell and dissolve the soft, chewy middle. They re-absorb their stomachs, along with that delicious shellfish soup, when they're finished. Nature is wonderful, isn't it?

Starfish come in all shapes and sizes, from the tiny cushion star which can measure just a couple of centimetres across, to up to 60cm in the case of the brittle star. Many have five arms and that classic star shape, but this can vary. Common sunstars, for example, can have twelve arms. If frightened, they can shed their arms and grow them back again. For today's Random Act of Wildness, have a mooch around in rockpools and see if you can spot a starfish. Don't disturb it – just snap a photo and see if you can identify it.

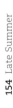

Make a wild splash

Two-thirds of our planet is covered in water, so it's no wonder we're drawn to it. We love to paddle, swim, splash, surf, bathe, relax and play sports in water – whether in lakes and reservoirs, warm pools or the sea. A good activity, especially in the summer or while you're on holiday, is a spot of kayaking. You can hire kayaks at beaches, rivers and lakes around the coast and enjoy a gentle paddle. If you're inland, rowing boats are a good alternative. When you get out on the water you'll find that the sounds of the land are muted – you can just hear the splashing of oars and the running of water. It's incredibly peaceful. Wildlife will let you get a bit closer if you're in a boat – birds don't seem to mind your presence as much if you're just floating along.

If there's no wildlife around, simply enjoy the sights and sounds around you. Remember, water can be dangerous if you don't know what you're doing, so check the conditions before you start to make sure it's safe and preferably go with a friend. Avoid areas like gravel pits or rivers with a strong current – they're especially dangerous because of the cold temperatures and fast-moving water respectively.

Build a sandy sea monster

Who doesn't love building sandcastles? Mixing the sand and the seawater together to get the perfect consistency, filling up your bucket and shaping your sandy fortress! It's great fun. Turn this lovely pastime into a Random Act of Wildness, by ditching the castles in favour of sandy sea monsters and creatures of the deep instead!

I have great memories of building sand sculptures with my dad. He took such things very seriously indeed. We made crocodiles, dolphins, lions and all sorts, decorated with intricate patterns of shells and seaweed (the lion's mane was made of kelp). We'd gather up great piles of sand mixed with seawater and get to work on a masterpiece.

Have a go at building your own sandy sea monster. It's much easier to start with things that are flat, rather than things that defy gravity. Starfish, for example, might be easy. Make them huge, though – don't settle for life-size! Once you've outlined your shape and built up your base, you have to get all those lovely, bumpy details in by gathering up shells (limpet shells work well) and decorating the arms and body. Try fish, dolphins and sharks, too. And remember to take a photo when you've finished – you'll want to savour your wild work of art!

Catch a crab

Crabbing is a very British pastime. It's a great way to get children interacting with nature while also teaching them about treating wildlife responsibly – and if you're doing it as an adult, well the challenge is just as much fun! It is simply the art of catching crabs, from rockpools, from the sides of jetties, and so on. Pick a spot with a varied seabed – with sand, rocks, pools, etc. You'll need some fishing line (tied securely around a stick or attached to a handle), a bit of bait (bacon and fish work well), a net and a bucket. Cover the base of your bucket with pebbles and seaweed, and add a few inches of seawater. Once the crabs are in there, you'll need to top up that water regularly (don't use fresh water). Tie the end of your line around your bait, and holding on tightly lower the line until it touches the seabed. Wave it around to get that attractive smell moving in the water.

When you feel a tug on the line, pull it up. If there's something on the end, you should feel the weight of it. Put your net underneath as soon as you can to stop the crab from falling and transfer it to your bucket. Don't put more than two in at once – they might start fighting! You can identify your crabs by gently picking them up – place your finger and thumb on the top and underneath of the shell at the back, so the claws are pointing away from you. You'll probably find shore crabs, but there are over 60 species in the UK. After a few minutes, pop your crabs back in the sea. Leave everything as you found it, and don't drop the line into the sea as it can cause serious harm.

Lounge with limpets

190

Limpets cling to cliffs, rocks, pools, piers and generally anywhere the sea can get to. The daily routine of the limpet seems monotonous to our land-loving eyes; if you head back to the same spot a few days in a row at low tide, you might notice that the same bits of rock are covered in the same limpets. Try measuring their shells to double-check – you'll find the same individuals repeatedly in the same place. It may seem that these little shellfish just cling to the same spot day-in, day-out, but once the tide comes in it's a whole different ballgame.

As the water rises, limpets go to graze in fields of algae. They roam around under water, searching for food, using their tongue to scrape algae off rocks, and leaving a trail which they can follow back to their favourite spot. When they reach home, they clamp down hard on the rock, sealing themselves in, which stops them from drying out when the tide goes out. If you look closely, you might find little rings etched into the surface of the rock – this is where a limpet used to live. They clamp on so tightly that it creates a scar in the rock – a home scar. Next time you're at the beach, marvel at the world beneath the waves.

Marvel at a mermaid's purse

191

You're not actually finding the handbag of a mythological being, but something much cooler – the egg case of a shark or ray! For most of us, this is the closest we'll get to sharks in UK waters. At least sixteen species of ray have been recorded around the British Isles, and over 30 species of shark. Of these, you're likely to find just a handful of different kinds of egg cases on beaches. These leathery cases contain the young of sharks and rays, which protect them as they grow. If you find one, chances are that whatever was living inside hasn't survived.

Most mermaid's purses are rectangular and come in a variety of sizes – most will fit in your hand. If they dry out, they will shrink. They're dark and rough, a bit like leather. If they have curly tendrils sticking out of the top or bottom and look elongated, it's a species of shark – probably the nursehound or the lesser spotted dogfish (to confuse things, the latter is also known as the small spotted catfish!). If the mermaid's purse has horns sticking up from the corners, it is probably a ray. The Shark Trust charity is looking for sightings all around the UK. If you're lucky enough to find one, head to their website, identify it, record it, and become a citizen scientist!
Check out **www.sharktrust.org**.

Hunt woodland beauties

A woodland in summer is an enchanting place, and worth exploring to enjoy some of Britain's most dramatic butterflies. Butterflies need bright, warm days with little wind, so this is a great excuse for a stroll in the sun. They'll congregate around brambles, especially where the sunshine reaches the woodland floor, or along pathways. Some woodland butterflies, like the rare purple emperor, even live in the treetops. Look out for fritillaries (small butterflies with intricate patterns); hairstreaks (the purple hairstreak loves oak woodlands); or white admirals (big and black and white). You'll also see more common species, like commas and peacocks.

Learn a wild word

Summer is the perfect time to see an osprey. This majestic bird of prey was once declared extinct in the UK, but is now making a comeback. They live exclusively on fresh fish, catching them in lakes, rivers and reservoirs. When they plunge into the water and emerge triumphant, they hang on to their prey tightly in their claws. They also turn the fish around in mid-air as they fly to a perch, making them more streamlined. To make this possible, they have a toe that can turn a full 180 degrees from the front to the back, so that they have two toes pointing forward, and two back (unlike the usual three forward, one back). This is called zygodactylism. Try slipping this word into conversation!

Think before you buy

This is a recent discovery for me, but I'm in love already. A friend recommended that I try an eco-friendly washing up sponge. We don't have a dishwasher, so we go through sponges at a rapid rate. Rather than a yellowy, plastic sponge, though, this was made entirely from coconut fibres. It was tough and durable, so you could really get in there and scrub, and when little bits did flake off, it wasn't the end of the world as they were all-natural fibres which would decompose. I haven't seen them in stores yet, but you can get them online. It lasted so much longer than a synthetic sponge, too – an absolute win.

Lunch in the wild

If you've been stuck inside all day – whether you're cleaning the house, chained to a desk or back-to-back in meetings – reward yourself with a nature fix at lunchtime. A wild picnic with friends will give you a much-needed boost. Find a wild spot close to home or work. A park is perfect. Take a blanket along and plonk yourselves under a tree; enjoy your normal lunch in a different setting. You'll feel better for socialising, and this simple wild place is way comfier than a desk or stuffy canteen. The fresh air will help you avoid the afternoon slump. You can combine this with other Random Acts of Wildness – try forging a daisy chain; listening to the birds; or foraging for some healthy food.

192

THINK! THINK! THINK!
THINK! THINK! THINK!
THINK! THINK! THINK!
THINK! THINK! THINK!

193

KITCHEN SPONGES

194

ZYGODACTYLIC

(a): (of a bird's feet) Having two toes pointing forward and two backward.

195

196 Sweep like an entomologist

Entomologists are scientists who specialise in insects. They study everything, from the most minute creepy crawlies to lumbering stag beetles. You can become an entomologist for the day by using a nifty trick to catch bugs without hurting them. Take an old fishing or rockpooling net and make sure it doesn't have any holes in it – you may have to sew up any tears so that insects can't escape. Find somewhere with lots of long grass or bushes and, moving as quietly and gently as you can, sweep your net back and forward, just skimming the tops of the grass or the bushes. Under trees can be a great place, too. You'll look a bit crazy to people passing by, but after a few minutes you should find that your net has some lovely insects crawling around inside. Gently take them out one by one and use a book to identify them (making a note of them as you go). You could also take photos to check later on. Release them back where you found them when you've finished.

197 Sleep under the stars

This Random Act of Wildness requires a warm night in the summer and somewhere safe near to your house – a garden is perfect. If you're going somewhere wilder, make sure it's safe and that you have checked with the landowner before pitching up. Camping is great fun when you go on holiday, but it's also a neat idea for a change when you're at home. Use it as an excuse to get close to nature. Pop up your tent (either one from the shops or something more rustic and homemade) and set up camp for the night. Settle in from sunset and make sure you've got a warm drink, some drinking water, a torch and some warm, comfy blankets. Enjoy the sounds of the night before you fall asleep – listen out for owls, foxes or just the wind in the trees. It should feel very peaceful. In the morning, make the most of this gorgeous opportunity to wake up with the world. Listen out for the first birds singing – you shouldn't even need an alarm clock!

Go organic

Organic food has been readily available for years now. It used to be expensive, but is now getting more affordable. Organic food has been grown without the aid of any chemicals – so no pesticides, fertilisers or other artificial nasties. The most you'll have to wash off your vegetables is soil. A cost-effective way of maximising your organic intake is to scout around online for locally produced and delivered vegetable boxes. You can order exactly what you need for the week or fortnight ahead, it'll turn up on your doorstep (usually covered in soil and a bit funny looking – carrots aren't poker straight and bright fluorescent orange, but they taste so much better) and you can have great fun planning meals. It's always local, seasonal, and you get to try things you wouldn't normally buy (the first time I ordered a veg box, I had to look up what something was: delicious golden beetroot). Organically grown food tends to lead to better soils, as no chemicals are added, which can also mean cleaner, healthier rivers. You can also get organic milk, meat, eggs, cheese and more. Have a scout around for farm shops rather than supermarkets to start with.

Share a tipple with insects

Butterflies and other insects have a sweet tooth. And in the middle of summer, they're as keen for a drink as we are for a glass of Pimm's. You can make a simple butterfly feeding station in lots of ways. Try suspending an old plate from a tree using string (make sure it's secure and can't fall). Add chunks of old, sweet fruit like oranges and strawberries, a small mixture of water and sugar (four parts water to one part sugar, boil until the sugar dissolves and allow to cool), and some brightly coloured glass beads to catch the light and the butterflies' attention. You can also soak sponges in sugar syrup and attach to branches. Pop your feeder somewhere to catch the morning sunlight, when butterflies will first be stretching their wings and foraging for food. Watch closely as the butterfly extends its long tongue, or 'proboscis', to drink. Count how many different species visit your feeder, and try identifying them. If the wasps move in, give them plenty of space (they can sting) and consider moving your feeder when it's cooled down and they've headed back to their nests.

Wasp, honey bee or hoverfly?

Wasps are one of the peskier insects, bugging us senseless on hot sunny days as they try to share our ice creams and picnics. They can sting you, too, which makes them a target of our displeasure. Wasps, like bees and many other insects, are pollinators though, and we need them for many types of food. It's so frustrating when parents stir their kids up into a panicked hysteria because there's a wasp or two nearby – all this does is teach the child that anything that buzzes is bad and dangerous, making them equally nervous of bumblebees, honey bees or hoverflies. Actually, our lives depend on them.

But how to tell the difference between all of those little yellow and black insects. It's a useful skill to have, as the stings can hurt and, of course, some people are allergic. There's three types of insect that are easy to confuse – the wasp, the honey bee and the hoverfly. All are pollinators and all of them are just trying to do their job. Wasps and honey bees can sting you, but hoverflies are completely harmless. A honey bee really doesn't want to sting you either – most that do will sadly die (the sting gets left behind).

Honey bees are hairy (like bumblebees). They're not naturally aggressive and will avoid confrontation. They are semi-domesticated and are responsible for making honey. They are black and golden. Wasps, in contrast, have smooth, shiny bodies. They are bright yellow and black and will buzz aggressively – it's this persistent behaviour that makes them so unpopular. They have much bigger eyes and their bodies are very narrow at the waist, with an obviously pointed rear end. Hoverflies hover and buzz quite quietly. They're mimicking the wasps as a survival strategy, but they can't sting you. They are also black and yellow, with a shiny body, but they have huge gleaming eyes and their bodies don't narrow as much at the waist.

If you can't bear to share your lunch with a wasp or two, just gently brush them off and try to keep hands from getting too sticky – they're attracted to the sugar. If they're really persistent, change spot. Don't get hysterical or worked up, especially with kids around – children aren't naturally afraid of buzzing insects, they learn it from adults. And what's to be afraid of? So for today's Random Act of Wildness, practise telling these little insects apart and make a new resolution to not be scared of them.

Identify five flowing grasses

Grass is grass, right? Wrong. Grass is so much more than the green stuff that grows in people's gardens and needs cutting once a week in the summer. Grass can grow tall in single stems or in little clumps. It can be different colours, different textures. The seeds look and behave in different ways, giving the plant different characteristics. Many people look at long grasses and think they're messy or untidy, but they're fabulous for wildlife and can be pretty, too. Often, you're best looking in unexpected places – pavement cracks, the forgotten edges of gardens, playgrounds, car parks. When you start looking closely, you'll see that there are different grasses everywhere. Make it your Random Act of Wildness to identify at least one, then see how many more you spot over the coming days and weeks. Lots of them look very similar, so use the internet or a book to help you, and don't worry if you get it wrong!

Yorkshire fog I love running my fingers through Yorkshire fog on a long walk. It's soft and silky to touch, with fine hairs all over, and can grow up to a metre tall (making it a great height to run your hands through). The flower heads are tightly packed together in long, slender nodes with downy stems. They have a purple tinge to the heads, giving a beautiful look and feel to the plant. It's often considered a weed as it's robust and can push out other species.

Smooth meadow grass This grass can be found everywhere, from roadsides to fields. This species formed, and still does form, the basis of hay meadows around the UK and abroad. The clusters of flowers spread out to give it a very spacious look and feel, with the flowers appearing pink or purple. It's smooth and almost hairless, and grows between 15 and 80cm tall.

Tall fescue Living up to its name, tall fescue can grow up to 2m tall if left unchecked. It likes damp places, so check along rivers or canals, in wet meadows or slightly boggy areas. The leaves are wide and stiff, and it has sheaths along the base of the stem. It is almost hairless, so won't have that downy feel.

Cock's-foot Cock's-foot is robust, tussocky and stiff, being almost hairless and having rough leaves. If you pull one the wrong way or rub yourself against it too hard, the sharp, rough edges can cut you. It has long, slim stalks with rounded flower heads, forming loose clusters. These can, rather optimistically, give the impression of a bird's foot.

Quaking grass This is a very beautiful grass and great fun, too. Balanced on very long, thin stems, the flower heads (which are shaped like little purple hearts) hang down like droplets off the grass, and literally quake in the breeze. They love chalky soils, and can be found in meadows across England and Wales.

Explore a summer orchard

Late summer can feel like an odd time for wildlife. Although it seems an age away, wild creatures are preparing for the winter ahead. Many habitats feel sleepy. Wildflowers will be dying back. Orchards, however, are about to come into their own. Apple, pear, plum and even nut trees begin to droop with their delicious fruits, and wildlife will be attracted to the sweet smells and shelter that an orchard provides. Lush hedgerows, long grasses and fallen treasures provide a wealth of opportunity for wildlife. Mammals, like squirrels, hedgehogs or badgers, might make the most of foraging; bees, butterflies and other pollinators will feast on the sticky fruits. Woodpeckers and beautiful finches, like bullfinch, love the gnarly trees. Make it your Random Act of Wildness to explore an orchard, maybe sample a ripe apple, or if you're feeling cheeky, take in a sip of locally made cider! Did you know that there are over 2,000 varieties of apple and 500 pears? Traditional orchards are quite rare now; the best ones are found in Worcestershire, Herefordshire, Gloucestershire, Somerset and Kent. If you can't get to one of these, look for fruit and nut trees near you, along hedgerows or in neighbours' gardens. Always check with the landowner before helping yourself to nature's treasures and leave plenty for the birds – no 'scrumping' please!

Stalk a wild tiger

Don't worry – these tigers can't eat you. Instead, I'm talking about the green tiger beetle, one of our most beautiful ground beetles found in sandy habitats, like dunes, heathlands, moors and dry grasslands. It is fabulous to look at – about 1.5cm long, bright metallic green with purple legs, and creamy spots on the wing cases. It has ferocious jaws and long, fast legs, making it an agile predator (if you're a smaller insect, that is). The best time to spot one is in the spring or the summer, when they're out hunting in their favourite habitats. If you know you're heading to one of the habitats above, maybe for a walk or a day out, keep your eyes peeled for one of these fearsome tigers, especially on warm, sunny days.

Forage the first wild blackberry

Blackberries are the ultimate foraged food for beginners. Plump, deep purple and juicy, there's always that moment before you bite in when you don't know what you're going to get – a sweet-and-juicy or an eye-wateringly sour explosion. Look for fruit which is completely dark, soft and round for a sweeter bite. Folklore has it that you shouldn't pick wild blackberries after Michaelmas, as the devil has ruined them (supposedly by spitting on them – or worse!). With blackberries appearing as early as July now, make a note of when you first see them and dare to try your first one of the year.

209 Sketch a fallen feather

Feathers are one of the loveliest treasures you can find in nature. Different birds will have different plumage, and you can often identify the bird from the feather lying on the ground. Whether they're little drab ones in greys and browns or something with a bit more flare, like a jay for instance, with its turquoise blue stripes, once you get up close you can see how varied and intricate they are. Sketching one can be therapeutic, as the detail and concentration required will encourage you to forget about everything else. Start by finding a selection of feathers – woodlands, parks, gardens, fields are all good places to look. You will probably find some of the more common ones, like pigeons, blackbirds, finches, sparrows and starlings, but keep a look out for some more intricate patterns, like pheasants. Gather them up gently and don't play with them too much or they may look a bit worn. When you've got a nice selection, take a very sharp pencil and good-quality paper, and see how much detail you can get into your sketch. You'll need to keep your pencil sharpened to capture the finest points.

210 Skim pebbles across the water's surface

This Random Act of Wildness takes a little bit of natural skill and a little bit more practice. I'm rubbish at skimming stones and always have been. My dad, on the other hand, is an absolute whizz at it. There's a knack to finding the right stones (round, light, flat pebbles); the right water (calm, flat, no waves); and the right hand and arm action. First up, find your location and rummage around for your stones. You may find some work better than others. Now, you want to stand right on the edge of the water and crouch down nice and low, so you're as close to the surface as possible. Take one of your stones in your strongest hand and pull your wrist back sideways – you don't want to throw upwards or downwards. Straight out. Rest the pebble between your thumb and forefinger, so that they form a 'C' shape around the edge. When you're ready, flick your hand and wrist very firmly, releasing the stone, so that it flies in a flat, straight line along the water. If you get it right, it'll skip straight off the top and bounce, sometimes multiple times! Don't worry if you don't get it the first time: just keep practising. The world record is over 50 skims and 75m! Just once or twice will do for your first time.

Blackberry vodka

Autumn is here! Well, sort of. The first blackberries of the year appear in August now, but the later you leave it, the juicier and sweeter they'll be. The bramble bush grows in abundance across much of our countryside, and for a few weeks of the year we all fall in love with it – especially the birds! Blackberries are distinctive, with thorny branches (watch out if you're harvesting) and little red-purple-black fruits made up of individual 'drupes' – little drops that hold the seeds and juice. Go for ones that are black and shiny, and give them a good wash to remove any dirt or nasties that could be lurking.

You will need:
- A mixing bowl
- A sterilised kilner jar or glass bottles
- A muslin sheet
- 400g blackberries
- 150g caster sugar
- Vodka – as much as will fit in your jar(s)

1. Freeze your washed blackberries in a bag or Tupperware box overnight. This will mimic the first natural frost, which will make them sweet and juicy. The next morning, mix the frozen berries with the caster sugar in a bowl. **2.** Pour the berries and sugar into the jar (or distribute evenly betwe your bottles). I've also seen recipes that add a sprinkle of cloves – 4 or 5 – at this stage, or a star anise, but this is dependent on your own taste. Top up with vodka, seal securely and give it a gentle shake. **3.** Pop your vodka in a cool, dry cupboard somewhere and shake it a few times in the first couple of weeks. Then forget about it for around three months. If you're harvesting in the autumn, this will make your vodka perfect for Christmas. **4.** Strain the contents of the jar or bottles through the muslin and into a bowl, leaving the rich, dark purple liquid free from bits of fruit. Decant into clean jars or bottles and serve as a Christmas drink with a mixer like soda water or lemonade.

212   Make some funky leaf prints

Leaf prints are a great way to admire the textures and veins in a
simple leaf, and they're easy and beautiful to make. You'll need
to collect a selection of your favourite leaves, so indulge in a walk
nearby. Try and get a mixture so that you have lots of different natural
designs: oak, maple, horse chestnut – whatever your favourite is. You'll
need to let them dry a little, but not become so brittle as to break.
Wipe off any dirt or debris. Next, you'll need some paper and paints,
a clean paintbrush and a little water. Simply coat your leaves with a
thin layer of paint using your brush – you don't want to use too much
or you'll lose the textures. Press them firmly on to your paper, hold for
a few seconds (don't move it around), then carefully peel off. It may
take a bit of practice to get the right amount of paint or desired effect,
so try a few times. The back and front will create different patterns, so
try them both to see which you prefer. You're looking to capture all the
detail of the veins spreading out across the leaf. Allow your picture to
dry – if your leaves are unbroken, you can wash and re-use them.

213   Bug-in-a-mug hotel

Got an old mug and some bamboo canes lying around in the garden?
Excellent – you've got everything you need to make a bug-in-a-mug
hotel. You simply need to cut up an old bamboo cane into several
short lengths (about 10cm), or some hollow stems or dried twigs will
do, and pack them into a mug you don't use any more. They need to
be held in firmly, so you can secure with twine if needed. If it's a dull
mug, you could decorate it with paint first, or just go with whatever
design you've got. Tie some twine securely around the handle and
hang somewhere sheltered from the wind, near to a hedge, bush or
log pile if you have one. Solitary bees will want the sunshine, but other
bugs might prefer some damp shade. Make sure it's slightly angled
down so that the rain can't get in and securely tied in place – you
don't want it waving around in the wind.

Show off on a nature table

Nature tables have gone out of fashion now, but they're a lovely way to engage people with natural treasures. You just need a table, strategically placed where lots of people will walk past and have a look (next to an office kitchen is good), and some labels on which to write what things are. Whenever you find anything weird, wonderful or interesting in nature, add it to the display, leaving a label nearby to identify it. Feathers, bones, fossils, leaves and seed heads are a great place to start. Sometimes you might find birds' nests or egg shells on the ground – these are perfect. Encourage other people to bring in their natural wonders too, and soon you'll have a lovely collection. Remember some basic rules: don't pick anything or disturb anything for your nature table; wash your hands after handling things; and don't use anything that has been recently deceased (basically dead animals) – clean bones are fine, but you don't want anything that might cause a health risk!

Search for sea glass

If you're looking for a memento to take home from the beach, then sea glass is perfect. It looks like little frosted pebbles scattered on the beach. Sea glass isn't exactly made in the sea, but its beautiful appearance is shaped by the tides, waves, seabed and currents. It is simply glass that has entered the ocean – whether from a bottle or a shipwreck – and been worn down over many years to create rounded pebbles of solid glass, with smooth corners and a gorgeous frosted effect all over. Sea glass will be completely matte and rough to touch, without any sharp bits sticking out. It can be found on beaches all around the UK – if you're lucky enough to pick up a piece, you're picking up a piece of history. It can come in all sorts of colours, but I've only ever found greens, blues and whites.

When you're strolling along a beach (especially one renowned for its tides or crashing waves), look out for the glint of sea glass lying along the tideline. It will mostly be in chunks a few centimetres across, and if you get a few pieces, they make lovely decorations or jewellery.

216   Put a wiggly worm in the grass

After a heavy downpour or continual rain, it seems like hundreds of worms fling themselves on to the pavement. It's easy pickings for birds and mammals to find them and munch them up, not to mention the fact that they can dry out if the sun comes out, drown if they end up in a puddle, or get trodden on and squashed. All in all, the concrete jungle is no place for a wiggly worm.

So why do they appear in abundance after rainfall? There's a few theories, but the most likely seems to be that worms breathe through their skin. In moderately damp soil, the home of the earthworm, there's a healthy mix of air and water. When the soil becomes saturated, to avoid drowning the worms must make their way to the surface to breathe. They become disorientated above ground, ending up on roads, patios and pavements. If you spot an earthworm wiggling its way along stone or concrete, give it a helping hand (they don't have any, after all). Lift it very gently and put it somewhere a bit more like home. A lawn or patch of grass is perfect, or generally anywhere with a bit of soil beneath. These little guys are nature's engineers and we're completely reliant on them to churn up our soils and grow our food. It's worth it, therefore, to rescue this little animal in distress!

Bust the myth of the daddy longlegs

If there's one insect I just can't bring myself to love, it's a daddy longlegs. In the summer and early autumn, they appear in great clouds. The gangly long legs, spindly wings and ungainly flight make them seem unpredictable and out of control.

The daddy longlegs is a species of cranefly, of which there are nearly 100 in the UK. As young larvae, they are known as leatherjackets, which live underground and munch on plant roots. This can make them very unpopular with farmers and gardeners, but they are a good thing for a healthy garden, and an important source of food, especially for birds. The most common rumour about daddy longlegs is that they are venomous, but that their teeth are too blunt to pierce human skin. Let's bust that myth right now. Daddy longlegs are not venomous (and they are unable to bite you!). It's likely that this urban myth has confused similar spindly species of spiders. For today's Random Act of Wildness, set the story straight with one person – even if you aren't a fan of them, take a moment to appreciate that they're an important part of the food chain. Doesn't make them any less annoying though!

Get tipsy with boozy berries

Boozy berries are a classy accompaniment to cocktail parties or desserts that you want to be a bit special. They're so easy to make and you can be as imaginative as you like. Foraged berries are great to use in the summer and autumn – like wild strawberries, pick-your-own raspberries and blueberries, or blackberries, damsons or bilberries. Any edible berries will work, and, even better, you can use any liqueur or spirit. Simply take a few handfuls of your washed berries and pile them into sterilised jars. Add a sprinkling of caster sugar, then top up with a tipple of your choice (don't fill the bottles all the way). Gin, vodka, rum (both white and dark) or any liqueur will work. Try out blackberry and dark rum; raspberry and gin; or blueberry and vodka. Shake gently to mix together, seal and leave for a few days to infuse.

Add a boozy berry to a glass of fizzy wine or prosecco and watch how the colours and flavours mingle together. Serve the fruit as part of a pavlova or atop a panna cotta. Or use the liqueur as a fruity base for cocktails. This is a versatile recipe, but watch out – those berries can pack quite a punch!

Sketch a wild landscape

What's your favourite view or landscape nearby? Is it a park, a mountain, rolling fields or a nature reserve? Whatever it is, try and connect with it in a different way and examine every detail, by taking a sketch pad outside and drawing that view. Start off with the big things you can see – landmarks, hills, roads, trees – and mark these in very faintly. Take your time getting your perspectives right. When you're happy with your faint outlines, start to add detail, again, working from the big stuff to the small intricate bits. When things are in the right place, you can go over your lines again, pressing hard for places where there might be shadows, or using lighter, thinner lines for places where the shadows aren't as harsh. You can use colour if you like, too, but get your sketch right first in pencil. Watercolours create beautiful landscapes, or try simple crayons. Ink also creates a lovely effect. Take your time with this Random Act of Wildness – genius won't come quickly if you're not used to it! This is meant to relax you, so don't get stressed if it doesn't look perfect.

Build a bank for beetles

Beetle banks are mostly found on farms, where there's enough space to build something huge, but there's no reason why you can't create a little one in your garden. It will encourage natural predators, which will protect your flowers and plants. They are simply grassy mounds positioned close to a flowerbed or vegetable garden, where the beetles will hibernate throughout the winter. You need to pick a location and dig out an area – as big as you can make it (but at least a half a metre long). You're looking to create an elongated hillock in the ground, or lots of individual mounds. Once you've marked out your area, remove the top layer of soil and grass and build up the mound with more soil, so that it's a few centimetres high (at least 25cm for a little garden bank). Seed it with native wildflowers and grasses and water regularly to ensure it's growing. You'll need to knock this back every now and then – a pair of secateurs is perfect. September is a great time to create a beetle bank, as they'll be starting to think about hibernating!

Enjoy a thunderstorm

Thunder and lightning can be very very frightening, but it can also be spectacular. You won't be able to plan this Random Act of Wildness in advance – it's spontaneous and reliant on very specific weather conditions. But if you see a thunderstorm approaching, either from the weather forecast or in the distance, enjoy every second of it.

You might see, hear or even feel a thunderstorm first. They are associated with warm, moist air, so it might feel humid and very still before the storm hits. Thunder clouds are 'cumulonimbus' – high, menacing clouds that tower into the sky. They can contain thunder, lightning, heavy rain and hail, so run for cover as they release all of that water and energy! Don't shelter beneath trees or other objects that stick up into the sky, like churches – they can attract lightning. The safest place to be in a thunderstorm is indoors or in a car. Watch as the sky darkens and flashes of lightning become more regular and obvious as they get closer. They'll be accompanied by deep rumbles of thunder, which is the sound of the air reverberating as it rapidly heats up around the electrical charge. Even if thunderstorms make you nervous, try and stick it out – guess where the next flash will be!

Share what makes you wild

Got social media? Fabulous. Not got social media? Well you'll just have to pick up the phone and call a friend, or chat to a neighbour. If you're feeling really brave, start up a conversation with someone in public – at a bus stop, on the train or in the supermarket. Today's Random Act of Wildness is to share your love of wildlife and wild places, by sharing your favourite nature story, photograph, idea, or simply why nature matters to you. You could tweet or post to your followers or indulge in some good old-fashioned gossip over a cup of tea. Tell people how important nature is to you and why. You might inspire them to do something wild, too!

Think before you buy

Plastic straws are one of the most common items picked up on beach cleans. Convenient? Yes of course. Good for the environment? Definitely not. They are used in their millions daily all over the world. Although you can recycle them, this is hard as they're so light and they mix so easily with other non-recyclable items. This also makes them easy to blow into drains, rivers and the sea, where they wreak havoc on fish and other sealife. Despite their size, they're durable, lasting for centuries into the future. Switch to alternatives, like paper straws, or re-usable alternatives, like metal or bamboo.

Learn a wild word

Autumn is the time to get to know your mushrooms and fungi. They appear poking up through the mulch and damp of woodlands and along hedgerows, a multitude of colours, shapes and sizes. An inkcap might refer to a range of mushrooms, some edible, some poisonous. The shaggy and glistening inkcaps can both be eaten by humans, while the magpie and hare's foot inkcaps are toxic. The shaggy inkcap is the most common one to forage for, also known as lawyer's or judge's inkcap. Never eat a mushroom that you can't confidently identify as edible, ideally by going on a guided walk with an expert.

Invite a friend into nature

Meeting up with an old friend or family member? This is a great opportunity to bond and re-connect somewhere wild. Pick somewhere close by with well-trodden paths, so that you don't have to concentrate too much on where you're putting your feet. After all, this is about spending special time together. Remember to dress appropriately – warn them it might be muddy, windy or sunny. For an added touch, take a flask of coffee, tea or hot chocolate to share. A wild wander makes a lovely alternative to a café or shopping trip: it's cheaper, more personal and more relaxing, and you can both soak up the lovely, wild atmosphere.

222

223

THINK! THINK! THINK!
THINK! THINK! THINK!
THINK! THINK! THINK!

STRAWS

224

INKCAP

(n): A widely distributed mushroom with a tall, narrow cap and slender white stem, turning into a black liquid after the spores are shed.

225

Sweeten it up with rosehip syrup

Dog roses are one of the most underrated flowers that appear in the spring. As the summer wears on, the petals will drop off to be replaced by the seedpod, the rosehip. Round, red and quite hard, these sweet little pods make the most amazing syrup.

You will need:
- Food processor or sharp knife
- Large saucepan
- Muslin or cloth to strain
- Mixing bowl
- Measuring jug
- Sterilised glass bottles
- About 1kg rosehips (leave some for the birds)
- 500g (or so) granulated sugar

1. Wash and shake your freshly picked rosehips, to remove any unwanted critters or dirt. Then pop them in the freezer overnight: this mimics a frost and will soften the fruit, leaving it sweet and juicy. Defrost before use. **2.** Chop your rosehips into a nice pulp, using a blender preferably, or sharp knife. You may need to do this in batches. Pop them in a saucepan and cover with water, about 1.5 litres should be plenty. Bring to the boil, then allow to simmer for 15 to 20 minutes. **3.** Strain the pulp through your muslin into a bowl, allowing plenty of time for all of the liquid to drip through. You can gently squeeze the cloth to help it along, but don't rush this step. Some recipes recommend straining the liquid again – if you're patient enough to do so, it's worth it. **4.** Once your liquid is nice and clear, it's time to add the sugar. Measure how much syrup you've got, then return to the pan. For every 100ml of liquid, add about 60g of sugar. Heat very slowly and skim off any scum that forms on top. Once the sugar has dissolved, you have your syrup! **5.** Decant into sterilised glass bottles and keep in the refrigerator to ensure it stays fresh. Serve over ice cream, as a sweetener in cocktails, or to give yoghurt an autumnal twist.

Be in it to win it

Need a good way to get friends, family or colleagues feeling enthusiastic about nature? Challenge them to a nature race and see how many species you can spot in an hour (or however long you've got). If you're all beginners, you can create spotting sheets or lend people field guides to help them, or just ask everyone to take photos so that you can identify things later. You could say whether you just want to do birds or insects or flowers or trees, or a mixture of all species. Split into as many teams as you like, and fan out over an area, giving everyone a meeting point and a piece of paper to make a note of what they've seen. Make sure there's a nice prize for the winners, too. This is a great lunchtime activity to do with workmates to get them outside, or even with children if you find yourself in need of an easy activity to fill an hour or two. Count the number of species each team saw at the end and announce the winners!

228   Let it rot

To you and me, a big old log pile might look a bit messy, but to a whole
host of creepy crawlies, this is their idea of the Ritz. Decaying wood
is the perfect hiding place for beasties. Place your log pile in a cool
corner of your garden, with sunlight to warm it up in the morning. If
you don't have easy access to logs, try speaking to a local tree surgeon
or gardener – they might be able to get you some logs for free. Build up
a nice higgledy-piggledy pile with different shapes and sizes, leaving
some tiny gaps between logs and some much bigger holes, too. To get it
all going, you can add a little magic by watering it gently. As the wood
rots down, lichens and fungi will begin to grow, making the most of
the damp, warm atmosphere. Leave bark on your logs, and try to place
on a patch of ground that's covered in grass or soil. Within no time at
all, lots of different animals will be making the most of this five-star
accommodation. Think of all those dark hiding places, safe spaces
and quiet homes. As the insects move in, so will other animals: frogs,
newts and small mammals, like wood mice, will love this new place to
live, and even hedgehogs will make the most of bigger spaces.

Mix up natural dyes

Dyeing things with natural colours can be great fun. See what colours you can create, then use them to make funky handkerchiefs, pillow cases or retro tie-dye scarves. You'll need to gather a few things together before you begin, and have a lot of patience with this Random Act of Wildness! Use the colour code below to decide what ingredients you need – and don't mix them together, or you'll just end up with a muddy brown. And wear gloves throughout to avoid dyeing your hands!

You will need:
- A large bucket or saucepan
- Washing up gloves
- A sieve
- A mixing bowl
- Tongs
- Salt or vinegar (salt if you're using berries; vinegar for everything else)
- Selection of berries, plants, roots or petals (see colour code below)

1. Start by filling your bucket or saucepan with water and the salt or vinegar. You'll need a cup of salt for every four cups of water for berry dyes (reds and pinks), or a cup of vinegar for every four cups of water for plant dyes (browns and greens). Completely submerge your fabric in the salt/vinegar water for a few hours. **2.** Remove the fabric from the water and squeeze out any excess. Rinse it thoroughly in cold water and squeeze again. If you want to create a tie-dye effect, now is the time to tie some knots in the fabric. **3.** Take your berries or plants and squash them in your rinsed-out saucepan, really mushing them up. Cover to the top with cold water and bring to a simmer. Allow the mixture to bubble away for an hour, adding more water if it looks like it's sticking, and stirring every few minutes. Once nicely stewed, strain the liquid into a bowl through a sieve to remove the seeds, twigs, skins and so on. **4.** When the liquid has cooled, plunge your fabric into it, making sure it is completely submerged. Use the tongs to stir it around. Cover and leave overnight to soak. **5.** When you're happy with the depth of colour, remove the fabric from the bowl and hang it out to dry, undoing any knots. You should have a great splodgy effect.

Colour code:
For reds, purples and pinks, use blackberries, sloes, rosehips and elderberries. For greens, use spinach, grass, nettles or red onion skins. For browns/oranges, use old teabags, turmeric or brown onion skins.

Paint some wild pebbles

This creative Random Act of Wildness won't just test your skill – it has the power to inspire other people and make them smile, too. You need some smooth rocks and pebbles of different sizes and some acrylic paint in different colours. Think about your favourite wild animals and plants, and have a go at painting them (one each) on a rock. You could practise on a piece of paper first, if you're really unsteady – just remember, they don't have to be masterpieces. I'd start off with things that are easy to paint with only a few colours – ladybirds, bumblebees, butterflies, and so on. If you make a mistake, you can quickly wipe off the paint with a wet cloth. Allow them to dry and then hide them in places where people might find them – in city centres, parks, woodlands, on your street – wherever. You could even leave a little note underneath asking people to share a photo on social media if they find it, with a hashtag that you can follow – you'll be able to see exactly who has found your stones!

Fly in the wind

Step outside on a breezy day and you realise that the air around us is a force to be reckoned with. Air likes to be in balance with everything else. When you get a high-pressure and a low-pressure system, the air will rush around to balance everything out. Because the earth spins and the sun warms some places more than others, air is constantly rushing around the planet (and always will be). This is wind!

  Wind can be a real nuisance – especially if you're trying to keep your hair neat and tidy, or don't want your eyes pouring with tears. It can be icy cold, making your ears and nose ache. It can buffet you around, whip things out of your hands, and generally cause a bother. But only if you let it. Rather than getting uptight on this windy day, try to have fun with the wind instead. Turn to face it full on and see how far forward you can lean, letting the wind take some of the weight of your body. Or get hold of a kite and launch it into the sky, watching as it whips around above you.

Whirl with a whirligig

Is this the best name for any animal? Possibly. Whirligig beetles are found in ponds and still water, like ditches. They glide around at the surface in large groups, looking for unwitting prey. They have two sets of eyes – one keeps a lookout for prey falling on to the water, while the other looks below the water for things swimming past. You don't need to get too close to identify them – their behaviour is unmistakable. Using their two back legs, which are flattened like paddles, they whirl frantically around the surface, literally spending their lives going round in circles. It really is fabulous to watch and a bit hypnotic. They're only about half a centimetre long, but when you get hundreds doing this at the same time it's great fun. Look for still water at any time of year, though personally I love to check it out on a warm evening in the early autumn. You'll find them easier to see if there isn't a breeze disturbing the surface, and of course you can look for other pondlife while you're there.

Nibbled by a squirrel

Red squirrels are not an easy species to see. They're now only found in a few places in the UK – the northern parts of England, Wales and Ireland, and in the forests of Scotland. They've hung on on a couple of islands off the south coast, too, including the Isle of Wight.

We were only there for a day trip, touring the island by car, discovering sunny little coves, fish restaurants and some of the quieter beaches. We'd called in at a nature reserve that was nestled in a woodland, with birds like tits, finches and sparrows all around. The hide we were in didn't have any glass in the windows, making you feel really immersed in the trees. We were enjoying the last of the luscious green, when there was a scrabbling sound overhead. Something was on top of the hide.

We went very quiet, looking all around to see if the culprit appeared, when a little red face appeared in the corner of the window. Tiny paws hung on to the window frame and it sniffed the air gingerly. Red squirrels bounce along confidently on the ground and will circle up trees like water flowing down a plughole in reverse, but when they're investigating something they'll make quick, darting movements coupled with long, frozen pauses. This little fellow wasn't afraid: he just wanted to know if we had food. I did – some nuts and seeds left over from the car journey.

I pulled out a handful and placed my hand flat in full view. He sniffed, looked, sniffed again, and then darted forward until he was inches away. Closer and closer he edged, before resting his tiny claws on my fingertips, gripping tightly. His beautiful tail swished behind him. He took a seed and nibbled it, and then another, relaxing a little. I didn't move, but just let him munch away.

And then, for no obvious reason, he sniffed my hand and nipped at one of my fingers, nibbling it thoughtfully before darting off and out the window. Ouch! He didn't break the skin but boy it made me jump. Maybe that was just his way of saying thank you? Who knows.

Do it yourself:
Red squirrels are only found in a few locations in the UK now. Scotland is still the stronghold, but there are populations in Wales, Northern Ireland, the north of England and a few islands off the south coast: Brownsea Island and the Isle of Wight. They have also been introduced on the island of Tresco, one of the Isles of Scilly. Do a bit of research beforehand on the most reliable spots. Lots of cafés have feeding stations outside where you can enjoy them running up and down.

Track wild creatures

There are probably more wild animals nearby than you realise. There could be little mice living in your garden shed, hedgehogs using your lawn as a highway, or owls in the local trees. Animals can be secretive, so one way to find out what's nearby is to have a go at spotting tracks and signs around your area. Patches of mud near puddles might show up paw or hoof prints, bird tracks or even the curving lines of a grass snake that's recently passed through. They might be from dogs or sheep of course, so if you spot some tracks, take a photo and look it up on the internet when you get home.

You might find owl pellets scattered on the ground underneath a tree – these look a bit like poo, but they're actually hard, regurgitated balls of fur, bones and seeds. If you find some of these, pick them up using gloves, soak them in water for a few minutes (they will fall apart) and see what's inside – you might find the skull of a vole or shrew. You could even make an ink trap for your garden. Take a baking tray and fill it with sand, smoothing it out and pressing it flat. Add a shallow dish of meaty dog food or mealworms in the middle. Leave it overnight in a quiet corner of your garden. In the morning, see what's come a-nibbling – you can use the internet to look up any paw prints.

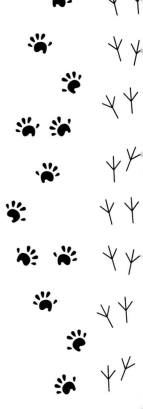

Try wild jam

A spot of autumn foraging can produce a real treat, especially if you'd like to have a go at making your own jams and jellies. Blackberries, bilberries, rosehips, crab apples, damsons and more can be used to make scrumptious preserves. This recipe is for crab apple jelly. Crab apples are notoriously sour, but the flavour can be brought out in a traditional and tasty jelly. It's great on toast or in cakes. You can't easily buy crab apples, so you'll have to forage them – the apples are smaller than shop-bought varieties, hard, and either green or flushed red.

You will need:
- A large saucepan with a thick base
- A jelly bag or muslin
- A large mixing bowl
- A measuring jug
- Sterilised jars
- About 4kg crab apples (try not to use bruised ones)
- About 1kg caster sugar
- 1 lemon

1. Wash the apples and cut out any bruises. Pop them into your saucepan and add cold water, enough to cover the fruit. Bring to the boil, turn down the heat, and simmer until the fruit is soft and pulpy – between 30 and 40 minutes. **2.** Strain the fruit in your jelly bag or in several layers of muslin over your bowl. This takes hours, so set it aside for the night and don't be tempted to squeeze the bag – your jelly will go cloudy if you do. **3.** Once the juice is strained, measure it out using your jug. For every 100ml of juice you'll need 70g of caster sugar. Stir in as much sugar as you need, and the juice from one lemon (this helps it set), and bring to the boil. You'll need to keep a rolling boil going for around 40 minutes, so be very careful at this stage – hot jam can cause serious burns. Don't try to taste it if it's hot! Skim off any scum that forms on top. **4.** To test if your jam is ready, take a chilled dessertspoon and coat it in the jam. Pop it in the fridge – if it forms a skin, you're ready. **5.** Warm your sterilised jars very gently in an oven, then add the jam (still warm, but not boiling hot). Close tightly and label. The seal on the jars should dip as the jam cools. If a jar doesn't seal, store it in the fridge and use the jam within two weeks. Sealed jars can be kept in the cupboard for up to six months.

Discover poo-dunnit?

A lot of mammals are hard to see in the wild, but luckily you can tell
if they've been nearby. You have to spot their poo! The golden rule of
this Random Act of Wildness – don't get too close or be tempted to
touch. Just look from a distance. There are some kinds of poo that are
easy to spot, while others are a bit harder. Rabbit droppings are the
most obvious. They are little, dark green, dry, grassy pellets, just a few
millimetres across and completely round. When you find some, you'll
notice that they're everywhere. Deer, which are much bigger but live
on a similar diet, have bigger versions of these pellets. Hedgehogs eat
a lot of beetles, so their droppings tend to be shiny and sparkly, and
3–4cm long. Foxes, which can eat a lot of meat, produce dark poo with
a twist at one end – and you won't miss the smell . . . it stinks!

Harvestman or spider?

You know those long-legged spindly things that totter along the
walls, curl up in corners and make us jump at inopportune moments.
You may think these are just super-skinny, long spiders, but don't
be fooled. While they may be related, you're actually looking at a
harvestman. Like spiders, they have eight legs, but unlike spiders,
they don't spin webs. They catch their prey with hooks at the ends of
their legs. Their bodies are tiny, just a few millimetres long, but those
gangly legs can make them up to 5cm long. They don't produce venom
and, if threatened, can leave a leg behind (which they won't grow
back!). They seem to totter as they move, and with such long legs can
cover ground quite quickly, moving silently and stealthily. If you see an
eight-legged friend today, take a second to see if it's a
spider or a harvestman. They won't harm you, so
if you're a bit nervous of spiders, you could even
try letting this fellow run across your hand.
They're so light, you won't feel a thing!

Run like the wind

I can't tell you the number of times I've decided to take up jogging, and within four weeks I'm back on the sofa. So this time I approached it differently. Rather than spending hours setting up an energetic playlist, I left the headphones at home and tuned into natural sounds instead. I used to hate running in the rain and wind; now I try to splash in every puddle. I use trees and bushes as markers to measure my speed and distance: 'just get to that tree and you can walk!' By distracting myself with wildlife – watching birds, noting the changing seasons, counting butterflies – I can run further and faster. I think it's because I've stopped thinking about how exhausted I am. I've found it's safer, too; without the distraction of music, I'm more aware of my surroundings – traffic, cyclists, pedestrians. I'm so focused on the wild world around me that time ticks by much faster; I've got my head up and I'm mindful of what's going on around me. When you're starting out, use these handy tips and see if they make a difference to your stamina, too.

MAKE IT YOURSELF

Make a magic wand

Magic wands can make great toys for children. Their imaginations can run wild with spells and potions and make-believe worlds. Don't spend your pennies on something plastic that will break easily, but never biodegrade. Instead, turn a magic wand into something personal and enchanting, by making it yourself. It's easy to do, will look better and will get you feeling crafty.

You will need:
- A stick, about 15–30cm long
- A potato peeler
- Wool, thread or string
- Pens/paints and a paintbrush
- Beautiful items in nature that you've collected, like leaves or feathers

1. Take your stick, and holding it away from you, peel off the bark using the potato peeler. You can sharpen one end a bit by peeling it more than the other, if you like. It can be a bit knobbly and it doesn't have to be perfectly straight. **2.** Take the thicker end in your hand. This will be the end that you hold while the other end casts the spells. Take your wool, thread or string and wrap it tightly around this end, so that it coils around tightly for a few centimetres. Tie it securely. You can use different colours to make it look pretty. Decorate the other end with pens or paint if you want to, or leave the wood on show to make it look rustic. **3.** Finally, add a mystical feel by incorporating your natural objects. You can tie these on or tuck them into the thread on your handle. Prepare to cast magical spells with your wand – where will your imagination lead you to?

Save a snail

Snails come in all shapes and sizes. Their swirling shells are examples of some of nature's most intricate and beautiful patterns and provide safety and shelter to the little mollusc within. There are lots of species of land snails, not to mention freshwater snails and sea snails, and most can be identified by their shell. The one that you always see in your garden or on a pavement is the common garden snail. Largely regarded by gardeners as pests, they're just going about their business like everyone else. They're low in the food chain, eaten for dinner by some of our favourite species: song thrushes, blackbirds and hedgehogs, for instance.

Snails love damp conditions, which is why you see so many of them when it's rained. Dodging them can be a nightmare, especially in the dark, walking on a slippery wet pavement. The kindest thing you can do if you see a snail is to move it. Gently pick it up by its shell (it'll probably retract inside, sensing danger), and gently place it out of harm's way – on a wall or on some vegetation, for example. It may stick a bit, suctioning on to the pavement, so be very gentle when you slide it off. You don't want to hurt it.

241 | Wobble with a red kite

Not so many years ago, the red kite was highly endangered in the UK. Thanks to protection and re-introductions, it's now one of our most noticeable birds of prey, spreading rapidly across the countryside (and even into towns and cities). Once upon a time, the red kite would have been an urban bird – they are said to have stolen ladies' knickers from clothes lines in central London! They love to decorate their nests, and a pair of pants would make a good addition, along with linen, sheep's wool and anything else lying around. They were taken to be predators, but they like fast food as much as we do, preferring to scavenge.

They're big and easy to identify, with angled red wings that tilt away from the body and a distinctive forked tail. You'll be able to see white and black in the wing, and up close they have a grey head. They also seem distinctly wobbly as they fly through the air. There are hotspots for them in Wales, the Highlands of Scotland, the south-east of England and the East Midlands, but they are becoming more common everywhere. They're drawn to big roads where they might find roadkill. Keep an eye out as you travel up and down the motorway, and look for the distinctive shape and rocking motion as they cruise up and down.

Search for woodlice

I remember going through a phase of collecting woodlice and storing them in jars in my dad's garage. They escaped, of course, and ran from this scruffy little urchin who seemed determined to squash them as much as help them. My dad didn't call them woodlice – he used the term 'slaters', which I think was passed down from my Scottish grandfather. Other terms I've heard are 'pillbug', 'woodpig' and 'roly-polies'. These tend to refer to specific species of woodlice, but folklore and biology seem to have become rather muddled in this instance.

Woodlice are fascinating. They're not actually insects at all – they're crustaceans, and the ones in your garden will spend their entire lives on land. Despite being related to crabs and lobsters, they do not taste nice. Their skeleton is on the outside of their body and acts like armour; some species can roll into a perfect sphere when threatened. Over 45 species of woodlice have been recorded in the UK, but only five or so are common. Find a few in your garden – look in pavement cracks, log piles and under rocks – and watch how they move. Do they curl up when they sense a threat?

Birdwatch on your bike

Does your bike sit in the shed, a bit dusty and forgotten? Or maybe you're out there all the time, pounding the roads? Either way, incorporating a bit of nature into your bike ride can help motivate you to get out more and to enjoy your surroundings, whether on your own or with friends and family.

Plan a few local routes that are both safe and great for wildlife. These could include cycle paths along rivers or canals, through country parks or along country roads. Chatting to neighbours or checking local webpages should also throw up some wild inspiration. If you're already out on your bike a lot, can you alter your regular routes to take in wild places?

When you're out and about, rather than speeding along, take a slightly more relaxed approach and see what birds you can spot or hear as you go. Make a list when you get home and add to it each time, noting the changing seasons and how this affects what you see or hear on your journey.

244 | Bathe in the woods

Immersing yourself in a woodland or forest is a magical experience. Shinrin-yoku, or 'forest bathing', has been practised in Japan since the 1980s, and is used to help prevent certain health problems. It's a simple idea – you visit a natural area and spend time relaxing in the surroundings. It's calming, rejuvenating and can restore your well-being. The idea has been used for centuries in different cultures, but it works, and we don't do nearly enough of it.

When you're in a forest, you get the same feeling as when you're in a cathedral: you are filled with awe as you gaze up at the canopy far, far away. Not only that, but forest atmospheres are good for us, too. A walk in a forest is supposed to boost your immune system, reduce blood pressure, accelerate recovery from illness, calm you and improve your sleep. When you're there, really take time to use all your senses to connect with nature, tuning out any annoying thoughts that might be worrying you or buzzing around your head. Walk and move slowly, breathe in deeply and make the most of being at one with nature.

245 | Take a shower beneath a tree

If forest bathing isn't your thing, or maybe you don't have that long to lose yourself in a woodland, try taking a quick shower beneath a tree. Please keep your clothes on – nudity is not required for this kind of shower! Find a tree nearby and get close to it. Inhale the smell, feel the bark beneath your fingers, examine the intricate textures and listen to the creaking bows. I think autumn is the best time of year to take a shower under a tree, when the leaves are turning fiery red and the wind can blow them off the branches. Let them fall all around you and wash over you, much like you would a real shower. If you get a big blustery blow, a whole load of leaves will cascade down at once. Make the most of this beautiful spectacle by being right there in it. Not windy? You can cheat and throw handfuls of leaves into the air. Just watch out for falling seeds – conkers and acorns might hurt if they catch you on the head.

Identify five funky fungi

Late August through to September is when fungi start to appear, springing up everywhere, from rotting leaf cover to a decaying branch to the middle of your lawn. Fungi aren't plants (not having chlorophyll) and they aren't animals either. They sit in a category of their own. Many species are famously edible, but many are poisonous, even deadly. The trick with fungi is to find a good spot to rummage around in, and go gently. Be careful not to kick any over. Unless you have experience foraging wild mushrooms or are with an expert, it's not worth the risk of eating fungi that you've foraged yourself. Sometimes the delicious and the deadly species are very hard to tell apart. If you want to have a go, though, start by booking yourself on to a guided walk or going out with an expert who can give some top hints and tips and recommend foraging books. The fungi I have listed here are my favourites to look at and always beautiful to find in the wild. Take a camera with you so that you can snap a picture.

Fly agaric This is the obvious fairy-tale mushroom, which everyone will recognise: the toadstool with a little pixie sitting on it. It comes in different sizes – from the very small to those up to 20cm across – and has a bright red cap with white spots on it. The gills (the bits underneath the cap) are white and so is the stalk. Although not reportedly deadly, it has been known to have hallucinogenic qualities: Alice in Wonderland was given some to nibble on, which might explain a lot. It grows in woodlands and on heaths.

Amethyst deceiver This is such a stunning fungus that it's hard to believe it's real. It is bright purple, going through many shades of lilac to deep indigo. It's quite small, growing close to the ground in woodlands, making it surprisingly easy to overlook. When it's been wet, the mushroom gets darker in colour, whereas dry weather leads to a paler colour. While you can eat this mushroom, it looks similar to other poisonous species, so it's best not to risk it unless you're with an expert.

Collared earthstar In the early part of its lifecycle, the collared earthstar is almost indistinguishable from many other mushrooms. It's found in woodlands across the UK, and starts off as a bulb about 3–5cm across, with a typical 'mushroom' colour. Then it bursts open like an orange breaking free of its skin, peeling back the outer layers in what look like petals, giving it the 'star' name. The spores come from a little hole in the top. Not one for eating.

Scarlet waxcap These pop up on lawns, grasslands, parks and in churchyards. They're not hugely common, but do grow in clusters, creating bright splashes of red. The cap is a bright burgundy red, which fades to yellow around the edges with age. The gills are orangey-yellow, with a similar-coloured stem. They're small – just 2–5cm across. They start off looking like a typical mushroom with a domed cap, but eventually they flatten out on top. It's thought that they're edible, but they're now quite rare, so leave them in peace.

Beefsteak fungus How could these fungi look like anything other than steak? They're soft, fleshy, large and red, and usually grow on oak or sweet chestnut trees. Rather than growing out of the ground, they grow out the side of the tree, resembling a raw steak. They even ooze red droplets that look like blood! They can grow as large as 25cm across and up to 6cm deep when fully mature. You can eat this one, but apparently it doesn't taste particularly nice.

251 Tell a deer by its rear

There are six species of deer in the UK – the native red and roe, and the non-native muntjac, fallow, sika and Chinese water. They look quite different, so identifying them is fairly easy, but you can also identify them from their bottoms! Parks and estates are some of the best places to see deer in numbers (Richmond Park is famous for them), but you can spot them anywhere in the countryside, in fields, woodlands, on nature reserves and near wetlands. They're quite shy, so you might need binoculars to get a good view.

When you spot your deer bum, you need to establish how far off the ground it is. Red deer are tall, like cows, whereas muntjac are tiny, like Labradors. How high up is that bum? If it's well over a metre off the ground, you're probably looking at a red. Its bottom should be a creamy red colour, paler around the legs and with a short tail. Muntjac, at the other end, are under half a metre off the ground, and can even be mistaken for foxes; they have a reddish bottom, though the tail might look like it's edged in furry white.

In the middle, you've got all the other species. Fallow deer are typically spotty, with gingery fur. They have white bottoms that are edged in black, and a longish black tail, so that the bum looks like the letter 'M' in black on a white background. Roe deer grow to about 75cm tall and have a very furry white bottom that looks like an upturned heart, with a tiny tufty tail. The white bum stands out from a distance. Sika deer are around the same size, but are seen only in certain places in the south and north of England; they also have very white fuzzy bottoms, but these are edged in black and their fur is a more muddy, dark brown. They can have little white speckles. The Chinese water deer is another small deer, just a bit bigger than the muntjac. They're only found in East Anglia and have a furry red-brown bum, without any white.

So next time you see a deer, get a view of its rear, and see if you can identify it for your Random Act of Wildness today!

Design a spore print

It's impossible to see a mushroom spore with the naked eye, but you can see them when they're all grouped together. There's a simple way to collect them and experience the beautiful patterns they create. Start by foraging some fungi from your local area. You're not going to eat these, but still make sure you wash your hands after handling them, in case they are poisonous. Try to get fresh but mature ones of different sizes and species, but don't make any of them too big – you need the cap to fit beneath a pint glass. They'll also need to have visible gills; something like a button mushroom won't drop its spores.

Gently trim off the stalk so that the mushroom lies flat on a piece of paper and sprinkle a few drops of water on the underside of the cap. Black paper will show up white spores, and white paper will show up dark spores. Place the cap flat on the paper, gills down, and cover with a big glass (like a pint glass) to keep off any wind or disturbance. Leave overnight. When you lift off the glass and the cap, you should have a beautiful print of the spores, which have fallen on to the paper.

Organise a wild outing

Got a team away day coming up? Or maybe a hen or stag party? Or a family gathering? These are all great opportunities to take your friends, family or colleagues outside and get them to experience nature, too. Not only is it cheaper than a restaurant or activity, but everyone will enjoy the different surroundings. All you need to do is find somewhere wild and beautiful to go that's close by, so that you don't spend a fortune on travel. Get everyone to dress appropriately, too – you don't want your time dampened by people moaning that they're too hot or cold. If you're looking for something active, set challenges for people to complete, like den building, tree climbing or a bird race. If you're looking for something more mellow, create some spotting sheets using photos of birds, bugs and flowers and get people to see what they can find when they're out and about. A nearby café or pub might hush any complaints (everyone loves tea and cake!) if people get cold or need a rest. This is a great chance to connect with colleagues or friends; be super enthusiastic before you go and get everyone really excited!

Spy an incy wincy spider

Incy wincy spiders may not always be so incy wincy, which is why they can make us jump when we're least expecting them to pop up in the shower! They're not everyone's cup of tea, and a common phobia, so I'm not going to ask you to start handling larger house spiders, wolf spiders or garden spiders. Instead, let's start small – can you find a cute little spider in your house, garden or neighbourhood that might make you a bit more confident with our eight-legged friends?

They're meant to be lucky, so focus on how rich you're going to be when you see a money spider! Money spiders are all less than 5mm long, and comprise lots of different species. They're so small that you won't be able to tell them apart unless you've got a PhD in arachnology. They are sweet, though, and very hardworking. If you see one, let it run across you. According to folklore, a money spider running across you has come to spin you new clothes, which will bring you good fortune.

255

PSITHURISM

(n): The sound of wind rustling through trees or branches.

256

257

258

THINK! THINK! THINK!

THINK! THINK! THINK!

THINK! THINK! THINK!

BOTTLED WATER

THINK! THINK! THINK!

Learn a wild word

Psithurism is a wonderfully onomatopoeic word. It simply means the sound of wind whistling through trees, branches and leaves. I think this is especially apt in autumn, as the slightest breeze can send clouds of leaves tumbling into the air, crackling and whipping around in a mini maelstrom. It's a complete tongue-twister and one that seems best whispered. But don't worry – no one will know if you pronounce it wrong, as you'll be the only person using it!

Take your colours outside

Colouring in is all the rage, and indeed it is very therapeutic. You can buy adult colouring books or print designs off the internet and use crayons or felt tips to delve into the detail. You don't have to worry about how accurate the colours are – the brighter and bolder the better. Find some nature designs to inspire you: they could be animals, leaves, patterns or landscapes. Take an hour to lose yourself in the detail of an adult colouring sheet and tune into the wild world at the same time. Let mindfulness become wildfulness and be as creative as you can. Don't worry about going outside the lines – I won't tell!

Track the autumn colours

This is a fun Random Act of Wildness to carry out with friends and family who might be spread out across the country. It takes a bit of planning, but only a few minutes of everyone's time. You're going to track the changing of the autumn colours as they spread across the UK, north to south, starting in September. Ask people to record when the leaves start to change colour and then drop from the trees. Get them to send you an email with a photograph when they first notice the changes. If you can get people doing this across the UK, you should be able to 'track' autumn as it moves south. You could create a montage of photos or share sightings on social media.

Think before you buy

Bottled water may seem like a necessary evil, but we live in a country with some of the cleanest drinking (tap) water in the world. Bottled water is expensive and can even be unhealthy – the plastic bottles release chemicals into the water if heated up. They're also awful for the environment. Instead, invest in a one-off purchase of a stainless-steel bottle which can be used again and again. Fill it up before you leave the house, and carry it with you instead of throwing away plastic bottles repeatedly. It's cheaper, better for you, and much better for planet Earth. Most cafés and restaurants will refill your bottle if you ask politely.

259 Eat the rainbow

When I was eight years old, I made the very noble decision to go vegetarian. My parents were far from impressed, and my grandma regarded the whole thing as frankly unnatural. For five years I kept my vow to stay meat-free. I finally cracked in my teens one Christmas. And not long after, my loving mother 'fessed up that she'd been slipping meat into my diet all along: so much for my lifestyle choice. Although I eat a small amount of meat now, I try to limit it. Meat and dairy products have a much higher impact on the natural environment than plant-based foods, due to the amount of land needed for livestock, the energy needed to farm them, and their carbon emissions (all those toots add up to a lot of methane!). By cutting down the amount of meat in your diet for this Random Act of Wildness, you'll be helping the planet. If you want to eat meat, shop locally, support nature-friendly farmers and try to avoid cheap, processed meats found in many supermarkets.

260 Win at a snail race

It's not exactly the most energetic of sports, but snail racing can be fun – especially if there's a few of you and you can make it competitive. You'll need different-coloured water-soluble paints and a paintbrush, a race course (just a bit of pavement will do) and some snails. Send everyone off to look for a snail to bring back with them – lift them very gently on to your hand by the shell and let them have a mooch around on your skin if they want to. Beware – they do poo!

When you've each got a snail, put a tiny dab of paint on the shell – ideally a different colour for each one. Line them up at your chosen start point, wave the imaginary flag and GO! Okay, so snails may not understand the word 'go', or be particularly inclined to race, but hopefully at least one will get the game and set off at, well, a snail's pace towards the finish line. You may have to coax them to stay in straight lines, but try to avoid picking them up – just see how they get on. Make sure you don't set your finish line too far away – this could take a while! The winner is the person whose snail crosses the finish line first – or the one that gets the furthest before you get bored. Wipe the shells gently with a bit of damp kitchen towel to take off that paint, and return the snails safely to where you found them.

Construct bug-ingham palace

Mastered the bug-in-a-mug hotel on page 170? Well done! Your next challenge is something more ambitious. Insects of all shapes and sizes are going to love this place.

The key to the perfect bug palace is to incorporate a range of textures, habitats and hidey holes. You can make this structure in any shape or size, so be as daring as you like. Enlist some help: a team effort will get the job done quicker and will produce something that everyone can be proud of.

Wooden pallets make an excellent structure, providing foundations, walls and rooms. Stack four or five on top of each other, making sure they're secure and stable. Pop your bug hotel somewhere with a good mix of sunlight and shade, then start filling in the gaps with old bricks, straw, twigs and branches, dead and decaying wood, pinecones, bark, loose pebbles, bamboo canes, ceramic drainpipes, upturned plant pots and old roof tiles. Recycle as much as possible. To finish, encourage climbing plants over the top, or even add a topper of wildflowers or turf to keep it insulated and warm.

Gin three ways – part three

The third of our three gin flavours – which has been your favourite?
(See pages 92 and 139 for parts one and two.)

Sloe Sloes are distinctive little fruits that grow on the blackthorn tree.
They look like miniature plums with a stone inside, purplish in colour
with a matte finish. Double-check your identification with a foraging
book or expert, though – some autumn berries can be poisonous. They
don't taste particularly nice raw, but sloe gin is utterly delicious, either
on its own as an aperitif or with tonic water. They appear in the early
autumn, often in abundance. Tradition has it that you're meant to wait
until after the first frost to pick the berries, as they'll be plumper and
sweeter, but this may not be possible in a warm year. Instead, harvest
your sloes and pop them in the freezer. This will mimic the frost and
break open the skins, making your gin even more delicious.

You'll need one bottle of your preferred gin and a spare, empty
sterilised glass bottle. Pour the gin into a mixing bowl. Place your
frozen berries into both bottles, until they're about half full. Add
enough sugar to coat the fruit and shake around to mix. Top up with
the gin and shake again. You'll need to leave it for about two months
to develop, by which time the gin will have taken on a strong, dark
purple colour. Taste, and if you want to leave it for longer, do. Strain
your gin through a muslin cloth and taste again – if it's not sweet
enough, you can add a splash of sugar syrup. The flavours will develop
year on year, so don't feel you have to drink this all at once!

Build a hedgehog home

Hedgehogs hibernate every winter, so they need a safe place in which to curl up and go to sleep, protected from the elements, warm and dry. By providing homes for them, we improve their chances of survival.

A hedgehog box is a great way to help our hibernating 'hogs. You can buy them from wildlife charities and gardening companies, or make your own. It needs to be waterproof, warm and accessible, so an upturned wooden or plastic box will do the trick. Cut some small ventilation holes in the sides, and make sure the entrance is big enough for a 'hog to get through (13cm square), and small enough to discourage predators. Ideally, provide a tunnel to create some shelter for your spiky pal as he's moving in and out. Cover the box with leaves, stones, earth and even turf to provide insulation and camouflage, but don't line the inside. Our 'hogs are fussy home decorators and they'll want to do this themselves. Position the box somewhere quiet, sheltered and south-facing, preferably with good foraging ground nearby and where water can't get in. It'll be really tempting to look inside to see if your home has attracted a tenant. Resist at all costs! You may cause disturbance, and this could be disastrous.

Follow a nature trail

Nature trails are easy to set up and a fun activity for little ones or big kids. You can make it as easy or as difficult as you like. The thing to remember here is that you're giving everyone a chance to delve into a wild place and look in detail at what's around, reflect on it and discover hidden wonders. You'll get them noticing and interacting with nature, even if they're a nature newbie. For an easy nature trail, give everyone a list of things that they must go and find in your local wild place or garden, and simply challenge them to tick each thing off when they have found it. For a harder trail, you could hide clues and riddles around a wild place and challenge everyone to find and solve them – the answers will be wild things that they have to spot or collect. Treasure hunts like these are an effort to organise, but great fun to participate in (and make great activities for children's birthday parties!). You could even include challenges like creating a wild work of art or building a den. Just remember, if you leave clues lying around on bits of paper, collect them up and recycle them when you're done.

Make a hedgehog from a pinecone

This is a great craft activity for the autumn, making some sweet little hedgehogs from pinecones. Have fun collecting the pinecones first of all – try and gather ones that have opened up a bit and are nicely dried out, with no damp, mouldy patches. The bigger ones will be easier to work with for little fingers. You'll also need some air-drying clay and some cloves (the kind you cook with). Dust off any dirt from your cones and balance them on their sides, so that the round end becomes the bum of the hedgehog, and the pointy end the snout. Next, you'll need to soften the clay in your hands and fashion a little cone shape to cover the nose of your hedgehog and create a face. You can also mould four little feet to help your cone to balance. Gently push the face and feet on to the cone, smoothing the clay as you go. You can add claws to the feet using a cocktail stick to add detail. Finally, push two plump cloves into the clay to create eyes, and another for the nose. You could use googly eyes, but they aren't recyclable, so I wouldn't advise it. Allow to dry and display your hedgehog with pride!

Go wild at work

The workplace can be dull and boring and distinctly unwild, and it's such a shame. Wild offices have been proven to be better for workers, making them feel more productive, happier and less anxious. So what can you do at work to help wildlife and bring a bit of wild into your office environment? Even if you're a few storeys up, is there a balcony where you could hang bird feeders or add some pot plants? Herbs are a great crowd-pleaser, as you can encourage colleagues to take a pinch here and there for their cooking in the evening. No room outside? Ask HR if you can put up some secure window boxes. If you're lucky enough to have an outside area, create a peaceful atmosphere by letting a patch of lawn grow wild or planting some wildflower seeds. If there's really no room at all, encourage people to grow plants on their desks or leave the office at lunchtime to go for a walk – you could put up maps or signpost people to local wild places so that they know where to go. Spotting sheets for the local area might be helpful, too. The publishers of this book even have a telescope focused on a peregrine nest in the centre of London – and they're on the sixteenth floor! There's no excuse – find a way to wild up your work.

267 Design a leaf picture

Gather up a selection of fallen leaves. Try and pick ones that are fresh, dry and a whole range of different colours, from bright lemony yellows to rich russet reds, chocolate browns to glowing golds. Find as many different shapes and sizes as possible to give you plenty of variety. Avoid leaves that have started to mulch or are a bit soggy – these won't keep as well and can make your picture look muddy. You can either create a picture to keep, or leave it somewhere wild for someone else to find. If you're keeping your picture, arrange the leaves into a design of your choice. The textures of the leaves can create beautiful images, like the fur of a red squirrel, the feathers of a phoenix or a brightly shining sun. Once you've arranged them how you'd like them, use tiny blobs of glue to layer them on to the paper. If you're leaving it somewhere wild, find a sheltered spot and arrange the leaves as you would like them. Take a photo to commemorate your creation and leave your masterpiece for someone else to enjoy.

Hunt for galls

Have you ever noticed those knobbly bits that seem to stick out of
the branches of trees or on leaves? You might be looking at galls.
These are little benign growths that are a bit like warts on a human.
They're harmless to the tree and are caused by insects, fungi, mites
and bacteria, which create the growth and control it as a sort of home
and larder. These structures are highly sophisticated and distinctive,
and different creatures will manufacture different galls to suit their
needs – for insects, they provide a safe place for the larvae to grow and
feed. For example, the oak marble gall wasp will produce little brown
marble structures (or 'oak nuts') for the larvae to grow in – these are
attached to the twigs of an oak tree and can be up to 2cm wide. In
autumn, after the adults have emerged from the safety of the gall,
you might see these dry, brown marbles with a small hole in them,
clustered on the twigs of oaks. Cherry galls, formed by the cherry gall
wasp, also grow on oaks, but these look like little red cherries on the
leaves. For this Random Act of Wildness, investigate the twigs and
leaves of trees (start with the oak) and see if you can spot any galls.

Think before you buy

Shampoo and conditioner don't have to cost the earth – they can be cost-effective and great for the planet. Simply ditch the plastic bottles and switch to solids instead. You can buy solid shampoo and conditioning bars online or on the high street. Like your normal hair products, you'll have to experiment with a few to find the right ones for your hair type, but that's part of the fun. They cost a bit more, but they last up to twice as long and I don't have to wash my hair so often. Read the reviews before you buy and invest in something to store them in, to keep them fresh even longer. They're handy for travelling, too, as they're so much lighter and smaller.

Learn a wild word

The world from the perspective of a little mouse or vole is very different to ours. Walls, fences and hedges are towering obstacles to be overcome and got around. A little smeuse here and there will go unnoticed by us as we lumber through the world, but could be a gateway to another field, another woodland, another garden for a little rodent. A smeuse is a little hole in a hedge or wall, perfect for a creature to venture through. Look for them in the autumn as leaves and grasses die off, making these short-cuts easier to spot, even from our great height.

Learn a wild word

The bouncing flight of the green woodpecker is very distinctive. It dives along, throwing itself through the air, occasionally landing on trees, but more often on lawns. It picks at ants in the grass, using its strong beak to dig into colonies. Green woodpeckers aren't just beautiful birds, with their bright green plumage and a red splash on the head. They are fabulous songsters, with a distinctive call – a 'yaffle' – like a cackling laughing sound as it flies along. Listen for it throughout the year – it's unmistakable.

Think before you buy

This Random Act of Wildness is a bit sneaky, but something I love to do. When you head to a counter in a supermarket to order cheese or deli products, they'll wrap your order in layers and layers of non-recyclable plastic. However, a lot of them will now allow you to take your own Tupperware. When you place your order, ask the server to put your order in the Tupperware after it's been weighed, rather than in the plastic, and take the label with you to the counter to pay. You might get some confused looks, but it's worth it.

269

SHAMPOO & CONDITIONER

270

SMEUSE

(n): A hole in a hedge or wall.

271

YAFFLE

(n): The European green woodpecker. It is noted for its loud, laughing call (also called a 'yaffle').

272

OVER-THE-COUNTER PACKAGING

Make a leaf tile

Salt dough is versatile, fun to make and great to get your creativity flowing. This easy Random Act of Wildness is perfect for autumn, when the leaves are falling from the trees. You'll need to gather up some of your favourites for this activity – make sure they're not too big though! Oak leaves are perfect.

You will need:
- A mixing bowl
- A wooden spoon
- A rolling pin
- A selection of your favourite leaves
- A sharp knife
- A baking tray
- A wire rack
- Your favourite paints and brushes
- 120g plain flour
- 300g table salt
- 250ml water
- 2 tbsp cooking oil

1. Mix your ingredients together in your bowl with the wooden spoon – flour, salt, water and oil. Shape it into a dough ball. **2.** Dust a little extra flour on your work surface and rolling pin, and roll out your dough until it's about 1cm thick. Move it around as you roll to stop it from sticking. **3.** Take your leaves and, one at a time, press them into the dough firmly, vein side down. Peel away carefully, leaving an imprint. Cut a square around the leaf to create a tile shape, with the imprint in the middle. Use the trimmings to create more tiles. **4.** Place all your tiles on a baking tray and bake in the oven at 100°C for two hours. Allow to cool on a wire rack. **5.** You can now decorate your tiles with paint, to make them look even more beautiful!

Spot mice on the underground

If you live in a city with an underground or metro, you'll notice how devoid of wildlife our subterranean stations can be. Once you're down there, you're lucky if you even see an insect on the walls. Nearer the surface, you might run into the odd pigeon. But next time you're at the platform, peer down on to the tracks and see if you can spot a little house mouse playing there. They forage for food down there, somehow surviving the endless vibrations and deafening noise from the trains. They look a bit darker, too, but they might just be mucky from all the dirt and soot! This must be one of our hardiest little mammals, and well done to them. They're showing us that nature can survive just about anywhere, and how adaptable animals can be. You might see house mice scurrying around on the platforms, too. If you do see one with the potential to get squashed by human feet, chivvy it somewhere a bit quieter. I scooped one up and moved him to the end of the platform, away from the hustle and bustle. And remember to stand well back from the tracks if a train is coming – don't worry about the mice. They've spent their whole lives avoiding those wheels!

Decorate with a mobile

A nature mobile is a great addition to your garden or to a child's bedroom (don't hang it over a bed though). They're easy to make and look better than manufactured plastic ones. Collect some natural items – pinecones, feathers, dry leaves, etc., and some twigs. You can make a mobile using one, two or three sticks.

For a simple one-stick design, you'll need one long, strong backbone. Tie lengths of string on to the stick so that they dangle down, then add your natural items by tying the string around them, spacing them out evenly. Add a loop of string to the stick to hang it from.

For three sticks, you'll need the backbone and two shorter ones. Tie two lengths of string on to the backbone, and about 10cm below, tie on the smaller sticks (around the middle), leaving plenty of string below. Add your natural items as above.

For a two-stick design, you'll need two long, strong sticks. Make a cross with them, weaving string around the middle of both to secure them together. Add more string or thread below the cross and attach your natural items, making sure to balance out your mobile as much as possible. Finally, you'll need one more loop of string above the cross to hang your mobile from. Hang it up and admire it with pride!

Identify five fiery leaves

Late in the autumn, as the leaves are tumbling off the trees in a riot of colour, see which ones you can identify and which you think are the most beautiful. This time of year is a great chance to test your identification skills for trees, and as they transform from lush and green to bare and naked, you can appreciate how different they all are. Have a go at identifying these five common fallen leaves that you might see every day.

English oak Oak trees are the most common native tree in the UK. Their leaves are around 10cm long, with four or five gentle curves along each edge, getting deeper as you reach the tip. They only have a tiny stalk. In the autumn they go a deep reddish brown.

Field maple If you're struggling with field maple leaves, think of Canada! They can grow up to 10cm wide and have five distinctive lobes, a central one and two on each side. Each lobe has gentle rounded teeth. They have a long stalk. In the autumn, they turn yellow-gold.

Ash Ash leaves grow in pairs, arranged along a stalk up to 40cm long, with a single leaf at the end of the stalk. The leaves themselves are typically 'leaf' shaped, with serrated edges. In the autumn, they glow yellow-orange, although they can fall when they're still green.

Horse chestnut Horse chestnut leaves are easy to recognise, with five or seven individual leaves growing from a single stem, ballooning out as they get to the tips, with serrated edges. The central leaves are bigger than those on the edge. In the autumn, they go every colour from brown to red to yellow.

Rowan Rowan leaves grow in pairs up a central stem, with between five and eight pairs on each side and a single leaf at the end. The leaves have lots of 'teeth' and are long, elegant and oval. In the autumn they can turn a rich, fiery red.

281   Salute a magpie for luck

Magpies really do get a bad press. They're associated with fortune
(good and bad), witchcraft and even death. No one can be sure
where all this superstition came from, although it might be
due to the fact that magpies are very clever and attracted
to shiny objects, which gives them (and other crows) a
reputation for stealing precious objects. They can also
be a bit brutal in their determination to survive, eating
pretty much anything. On the other hand, in some Asian
countries, magpies are seen to be lucky!

   You may have heard the rhyme 'One for sorrow, two for joy'.
There are many versions; some predict whether a baby will be a boy or
a girl, while others predict births and funerals. Either way, when you
see a single magpie, superstition has it that you must tip your cap at
the bird (I'm sure nodding will do!), say good morning and ask how his
wife is. This is seen as being respectful and the magpie won't pass his
bad luck on to you – it can't hurt and it might just bring you good luck!

282   Leave a pile in the corner

It's so frustrating when people put fallen leaves into garden waste
bins. They may look messy and make paths a bit slippery, but
when piled up together they create an amazing habitat for insects,
amphibians and reptiles. When you're sweeping them up, leave a pile
in the corner of your garden. As the season progresses, the leaves will
begin to mulch down and get all gooey and soggy at the bottom. This
is how compost is made. If you give it a good sniff, it should smell rich
and earthy. Add more leaves on top to keep the pile
nice and high, and let the different layers mix
together. This simple Random Act of Wildness
is perfect for helping wildlife survive the
winter – who knows who might move in?
And in the spring, you might have created
the perfect habitat for grass snakes to lay
their eggs.

Create a stained-leaf window

Have you noticed how stained-glass windows create the most beautiful patterns in churches? The light shines through the images, making the colours come to life. You can create your very own stained-glass windows in autumn using fallen leaves. They are ever so slightly transparent, so if you hold them up to the light you'll be able to see the skeleton of the leaf inside. If you've got a laminator, take a laminating pouch and arrange the leaves inside. For the best effect, overlap them a bit and don't leave any white space at all. Use different colours and shapes and sizes to create really multi-coloured designs. When you're happy with your window, seal the pouch and slide through the laminator. You can either hang the window up using string, or attach to a 'real' window using Blu Tack. Either way, make sure you choose somewhere really sunny so that the light shines through and creates some spectacular pictures. If you don't have a laminator, you can buy transparent contact paper, which has an adhesive on one side. Arrange the leaves directly on to the sticky side, then stick to a window.

Dolphin delight

The magic of being at sea on a boat is that you never know what you might see. The Isles of Scilly is my favourite place to go boating – the ocean can be flat, serene and calm, or crashing, rolling and stormy. Today was somewhere in the middle. The eight-foot swell meant I was beginning to grow nauseous. It was dull out there, too – no birds to delight or distract. We were three miles offshore – a long way when you're not feeling peachy. Then from nowhere: 'Dolphin!'

Self-pity abandoned, legs scrambling, I clambered over the fenders and leapt to the bow. Lying, stomach down, hanging over the front side of the boat, I waited a few seconds and then: 'Here they come!'

Beneath my outstretched fingertips they materialised, three, four, six, ten lithe, powerful shapes. They looked so close I could almost run my hand along their backs, but if I leant much further I would be in. They skimmed and crested the water, which played optical illusions on their size, shape and colour. As their blowholes opened, clouds of mist shot upwards. Mixed with the waves, I was soon soaked.

Common dolphins are the classic dolphins: quite small, with stormy grey and blue bodies and a creamy smear down the side. They rode the bow wave hard, sometimes shooting forward to leap playfully out, or hanging on to the side of the boat, swimming on their sides and looking up at this silly human who seemed to want to join them. I wasn't alone – the boat's resident dog, Bella, was barking, growling, screeching and howling next to me in an absolute frenzy. What were these strange creatures and why couldn't she join them? They hung on to the bow for over 20 minutes. Every time I glanced up, I could see more diving in towards the boat. They took it in turns to ride the wave, before peeling off to splash playfully alongside. It was mesmerising, enchanting. To share a few minutes immersed in the universe of the dolphin is a deeply emotional, life-affirming experience.

Do it yourself:

Here are some top tips for seeing dolphins wild around the UK. First, do your research. Off the Isles of Scilly is fabulous for common dolphins, while places like Cardigan Bay, the Moray Firth and Cornwall have resident pods of bottlenose dolphins. The Scottish coast has an abundance of sealife, including dolphins, and harbour porpoise can be seen around much of the coast. Either go on a boat trip specially to see them, or use a pair of binoculars or a telescope to scan the sea from land. Pick a calm day with a bit of cloud cover and look for fins breaking the surface.

Eavesdrop on a tawny owl

I remember once sitting in central London on a warm, balmy night, sipping wine with a friend. We were surrounded by the concrete jungle – blocks of flats, rows of houses, sirens in the distance. And I was stunned to hear the familiar 'ke-wick' call of a female tawny owl, very close by in some trees behind the flats. I could hear it more clearly and closer than I would in my own house in rural Leicestershire, despite the peace and quiet of the countryside. It sat calling for an age and we both listened in silence, just enjoying the sound.

You're more likely to hear a tawny owl than see one, although you may catch one in your headlights or spy one roosting in a tree. They're nocturnal, hunting and flying mostly in the dark. Most people think of the typical 'too-whit-too-woo' sound that we're taught about in childhood. If you're lucky enough to hear this, it's a male and female talking to each other – the female calls 'ke-wick' and the male answers 'hoo-hoo'. You're eavesdropping on a private conversation!

To maximise your chances of hearing a tawny owl, head to your nearest woodland or park, or find a nearby copse. They roost in the hollows of old trees and call from the branches. Leave it very late, and go in a group for safety. They're well camouflaged so you'll struggle to see one, but cup your hand around your ear to help you hear.

Blog about the wild

You may wonder what the difference is between keeping your wild diary and starting a wild blog. Well a diary is personal. You can add thoughts and feelings to it that you may not want to share with other people, and you can stick things in it physically, draw pictures or make notes. A blog is public and lots of people can read it. You could challenge yourself to start a blog to share your wild adventures. You can make this private, so only your friends and family can read it, or you can make it public and share it with a wider audience. Blogs don't have to be long – just a couple of hundred words – and you can add photographs, too, if you like. You can blog anonymously or add your name – it's up to you! Just write down what you've done and how it made you feel – happy, excited, sad. You can try different styles of writing – try to copy your favourite nature author. Hopefully you'll inspire someone you know to try a wild adventure or join you when you next go exploring!

Carve a wild pumpkin

There are loads of ways to get creative at Halloween, starting with making some special and wild designs in your pumpkins. Why not try a simple bat design, an owl or a spider? Carefully remove the top of your pumpkin and scrape out the insides. Don't waste this – pumpkin seeds are tasty when roasted with a touch of salt and pepper, and you can use the flesh to create soups, dips and even sweet things like cakes and pies (it tastes a bit like butternut squash). Try and get the skin of the pumpkin quite thin – it'll make it easier to carve! When you've prepared your pumpkin, you can either go freehand (brave!) or use a stencil to draw the outline directly on to the pumpkin. Use a knife or miniature saw to carve out your design. Personally, I love drawing a wise owl face, but get creative and see what you can do. Once it's ready, you're meant to pop a candle in it, but why stop there? If you want to take this Random Act of Wildness one step further, why not fill your pumpkin with a mixture of birdseed and fat (see page 236). Hang it from your feeder or leave it underneath, and let the birds enjoy this spooky time of year, too!

Bake a gingerbread birdbox

This is a cute way to make your traditional gingerbread house a little bit wild. It's yummy, looks amazing and makes a spectacular centrepiece at a Christmas party. For this Random Act of Wildness, make up a batch of gingerbread according to your favourite recipe and then take a wild spin on it…

You will need:

- A ruler
- A sharp knife
- Lined baking trays
- Cookie cutters, circular and, if you can find them, bird-shaped
- A piping bag with a medium nozzle

- A batch of gingerbread, made up into a dough but not cooked
- Flaked almonds
- 500g icing sugar
- 2 egg whites
- Sweeties of all shapes and sizes

1. Take your batch of gingerbread, roll out to the thickness of two £1 coins and measure out your house shape – use templates from books or the internet. Use your knife to cut around the templates. On the piece for the house front, ignore any doors and windows; instead use your circular cookie cutter to create a hole in the centre – just like you'd see on a birdbox. **2.** Slide each piece on to a baking tray and bake for around twelve minutes. You may have to do this in batches. **3.** Before cooking your two roof pieces, gently press flaked almonds into the gingerbread to create tiles. **4.** When each piece is cooked and gently browned, remove from the oven and, while still warm and soft, cut around the templates again. This creates straight, firm edges. Don't do this when cold or your walls will crack. **5.** Take any scraps of uncooked gingerbread and shape into a ball. Roll out again, then cut out some bird shapes. Bake for a few minutes. **6.** While your gingerbread cools completely, add the icing sugar to the egg whites a bit at a time, stirring until thick and glossy. Fill your piping bag and build your house one wall at a time, using generous lines of icing down each side. Line up the edges as neatly as you can, using a small bowl inside the house to add support. Wait until your walls are firmly set in place before adding your roof. **7.** Once everything is set (possibly overnight), decorate your box. I like to have a bird-shaped gingerbread biscuit peeking out of the hole in the front. Use sweets to make your birdbox really alluring (to people, not birds!).

Count the nests in a rookery

Rooks are sociable and intelligent birds. They are related to crows and magpies, from a family of birds called 'corvids'. They have been known to use tools and solve problems. Rooks aren't the most handsome, but you can tell them apart from their carrion crow cousins by their noticeably pale bill and face, and a domed forehead. Rooks gather together to form rookeries, which are like cities in the treetops. They nest high off the ground and forage together in groups; where possible, they will stick with their mate for life. In late autumn it's possible to see the nests high up in the trees (once the trees spring back into splendour this becomes much harder). There will be large groups of them together, often spread across lots of different trees, forming a colony of cawing, croaking birds. Look for them along roads, on the edges of woodlands, and around towns and villages – they make big nests from twigs, and you'll be able to hear the birds chattering to one another. When spooked, they will all take off at once, forming dark clouds above the trees and making a racket. If you can crane your head back for long enough, you might be able to count the nests in the treetops – how many can you spot?

Identify five fallen seeds

Autumn is the time to learn about some common seeds that you might find either clinging to the bare branches of trees or lying on the ground. If you're unlucky, a strong gust of wind might bring one bouncing down to land on your head. Ouch! Seeds are a valuable food source for animals like squirrels, birds and deer, with some species stashing the food away for the winter. Jays and squirrels do this, burying treats like acorns for when they're hungry in a few weeks' time. As well as seeds, you can also find nuts (like hazel or walnut), but if you go foraging, make sure to leave plenty for wildlife.

Conkers (horse chestnut) Conkers are beautiful seeds. When growing, they have a rounded shell covered in spikes. When they fall to the ground they split open, revealing the conker within. The husk of the conker, the spiky bit, feels wonderfully soft and silky inside. The conkers themselves are round (although they can be irregular), a deep chocolate colour with a white blob.

Catkins (silver birch) Silver birch catkins can be seen dangling from the trees in the colder months, with the golden, long males forming at this time. Both male and female catkins hang from the same tree, with the males hanging in little clusters at the ends of the twigs. The females (which are shorter and stubbier) form in the spring, releasing their seeds to the wind in the autumn.

Acorns (oak) Acorns are the fruit of oak trees. They are around 2cm long, with an oval-shaped, smooth seed held within a cup, which attaches the seed to the twig. They are bright green as they grow, but in the autumn they turn a brownish colour and loosen from the tree, falling to the ground below. Sometimes that rough cup will go with them.

Helicopters (field maple)
There are a few trees in the UK that produce helicopter seeds, including sycamore, ash and maple. They're called helicopters, because as they fall from the tree they spiral down, their wings making them fly like choppers! Field maple helicopters are tinged with pink. The wings are angled downwards in a shallow 'v', with two seeds close to the stem.

Cones (alder) The cones of an alder tree are female catkins. They start off green, but as the autumn presses on they become dark brown and wood-like, looking like little pinecones, opening to release their seeds. They grow in clusters of up to eight on a single stem. They'll stay on the tree all year around, but the autumn and winter winds can blow them off.

295 Wander through a woodland

Autumn is the perfect time to explore woodlands near you, on your own or with company. The ground will be all crunchy with the newly fallen leaves – you know you can't resist kicking your way through them. With fewer leaves on the trees, you've got a good chance of spotting birds and other wildlife that might be lurking in the branches, like finches, robins or woodpeckers. You might be able to see squirrels stashing nuts in the ground for the winter. Use all of your senses to tune into your wild woodland walk. Wood smoke always reminds me of autumn. Birds will be using their contact calls more than singing, but robins, blackbirds and thrushes might still belt out a tune. You'll be able to hear the slightest rustle in the bushes, too, as the dry leaves rub and shake together. Wellies and a warm coat are a must, though – if the sun goes in, the air will quickly turn cold.

Scale a wild obstacle course

This Random Act of Wildness is pretty hardcore and requires some creativity and a lot of guts: beware, you may fall off things, get bruises and/or get muddy! That's all part of the fun, though. If you're tired of running or walking and are looking for something more strenuous, find a local woodland and try setting up your very own obstacle course. You'll need to scout out what's possible first, and how to have fun on your course without causing damage to the nature around you. Look for sturdy trees that you can swing off, do pull-ups on or climb up. Eye up puddles or fallen trees to jump over. Find branches on the ground that you can walk along, testing your balance. This should liven up the same old running route; just make sure you don't stand on any flowers, disturb any nests or trample rotting branches: these are all great habitats for little beasties that we share our world with.

Wear it really wild

You can find nature almost everywhere now, including in clothing stores. Forget the eighties leopard print – a lot of clothes are now inspired by birds, feathers, butterflies, bees, fish and all sorts. Why not incorporate your amazingly wild dress sense with a fundraising event at work or school? Ask your colleagues and friends to come in their best 'wild' clothing and pay a pound for the privilege. You could then donate the proceeds to charity. Wild dress codes could take you anywhere, from simple animal print socks to full-blown fancy dress in a rabbit onesie. You can add wildlife-themed make-up or face paint, too. If people are shy about joining in, even a pair of socks will do! This is a great Random Act of Wildness to raise a few pennies and get people appreciating and noticing nature near you.

298 Create a poppy picture

This is a lovely, arty Random Act of Wildness to do with kids or on your own. You'll need some paper, acrylic red, green and black paint, paper straws, a little water and a paintbrush. First of all, wet your paper with a very thin layer of water (use your paintbrush to control the amount – you don't need it sodden, just damp). Mix a little red paint with water, so that it's not quite so thick, and then drop a few blobs on to your paper while it's wet. It should begin to spread out. Use the straw to blow the paint around a bit, to create a natural, red splodgy effect – these are the petals of your poppies. While they dry, add the stems in a similar way: water down some green paint and use a clean brush to paint on fine stems. Finally, when everything is nearly dry, repeat with a tiny dot of black in the middle of each poppy. Allow to dry completely and *voilà* – a beautiful, abstract poppy picture.

299 Enjoy nature's fiery beauty

As the clocks go back and the nights draw in, many trees will begin to glow a fiery red, orange and gold. This creates one of the most beautiful annual spectacles in the natural world, and for this Random Act of Wildness, find a way to admire it. You could climb somewhere high up and look down on a fiery forest or get up close with your camera phone and try and capture the rainbow. The trees that lose their leaves in the winter are called 'deciduous', which means 'to drop'. Other trees, like pines, are evergreen or coniferous, and they keep their needles all year round. But what makes the deciduous trees change colour and drop their leaves to the ground? Chlorophyll is what makes leaves green in the spring and summer. It's an essential ingredient that converts sugar into energy for the trees to survive. In the winter, with less sunlight available, the tree absorbs all the goodness from the leaves, leaving them brittle and dry; with no chlorophyll in them to keep them green, the yellow, red and brown pigments in the leaves shine through.

Check your bonfire for wildlife

It's nearly bonfire night! Remember the smell of burning wood, the sweet taste of toffee apples and the sharp crackle of sparklers in the air? If you're planning on having a bonfire this year, or even attending one with friends, make sure that you or the organiser checks the bonfire carefully for any wildlife that might have settled in for the night. To you it may look like a pile of old twigs – to a hedgehog, a newt or frog, this looks like the Hilton. An unlit bonfire is irresistible to many animals that might be looking to hibernate for the winter, so they must be checked very carefully before lighting, just an hour or so before the show begins. Wildlife will move in quickly, too, so a quick check the day before won't suffice. Hopefully you won't find anything lurking in there, but if you do, gently move it to somewhere safe and away from people and dogs. This Random Act of Wildness may not seem like much, but you could save a life, and you'll get a chance to educate others on the importance of wildlife, too!

301 Go bonkers for conkers

When I was a kid, we used to go crazy for conkers. There were enormous horse chestnuts on the walk to school, and every day we'd run down and collect as many as possible – the bigger and rounder the better. I think there was even a song about them at Harvest Festival. I remember two entrepreneurial kids in my class collecting bin bags full of them and selling them for 2p, 5p and 10p, depending on the quality! Children aren't encouraged to play with conkers any more, and I really don't understand why. There's nothing so satisfying as feeling that smooth texture beneath your fingers and admiring the chocolatey surface. We used to play conkers, too, using a pencil or screwdriver to drill through the seed (being careful not to split it) and threading it with a piece of string. You tie a knot in the end to hold it in place, then take it in turns to try and hit your opponent's conker with yours. Eventually one should crack. Apparently, this game can be too dangerous for children now (it's not!), so if this isn't your cup of tea, why not try simply planting them instead?

Grow your own chestnut tree:
Tip your potential conkers into a bowl of water. Discard any that float as these have dried out and won't grow. If they sink, they're fresh and ready to plant.

Plant your fresh conkers in individual pots in about 2cm of peat-free compost or soil, and leave outside in a sheltered spot away from potential conker-thieves, like squirrels. Keep them well watered, but don't be overly generous. Only move them in case of hard frosts; they'll need to survive the winter outside if they're going to grow to be trees, so a little cold weather shouldn't hurt them.

By the spring, they'll hopefully begin to germinate. As they grow bigger, re-pot them to allow their roots to flourish, and keep them watered. And finally, if you're going to plant them in the ground, make sure to ask the permission of the landowner first – these are big trees!

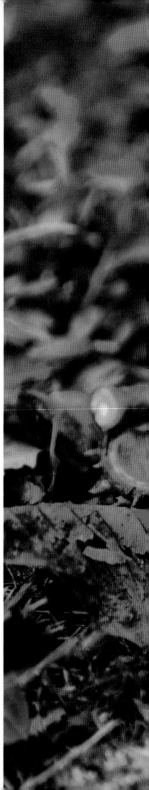

302 Spot a wild mammal

From urban squirrels and wily foxes to rutting deer and country hares, mammals can be hard to spot. They're often more shy and wary than birds, or secretive and good at hiding, like voles, moles and shrews. Many of them are nocturnal, like badgers and hedgehogs, so you'll be lucky if you see them out in the day. When you do find one though, you can have amazing encounters. The best place to start is close to home: parks are good for squirrels and deer, woodland for badgers or foxes, and riversides for otters and water voles. If you spot a mammal, you need to stay very still. They have excellent senses, so they'll be able to see, smell or hear you almost straight away. You need to show them you're not a threat, so stand very still and don't try to move any closer. You might spook them and they'll run off into the distance. Use slow movements and keep quiet – carefully sitting down might make things a bit comfier for you. A pair of binoculars will come in handy for watching from a distance, and if you're lucky enough to have a camera with you, try and quietly take a photograph. Otherwise, sit back and enjoy it – this is a special moment just for you.

303 Print your own Christmas cards

After the wild year you've had, you're sure to have some lovely photographs of wildlife and wild places that you've seen and explored. It would be great to share those with friends and family in the form of Christmas cards. You could take some specifically wintry ones if the weather is cold enough in November, or you could use others from throughout the year. There are loads of websites online that allow you to upload your photos and get them printed professionally on to cards, or just use some good-quality photo paper to print your own and stick them on to a card backing. Remember to plan ahead – if you want to send them out in plenty of time, you'll need to select your images and make your cards in November. Add a caption inside, letting people know about your wild year and what's on the front of the card – you might inspire them to go wild, too!

Make a Christmas wreath bird feeder

Christmas wreaths come in all shapes and sizes. This one is designed to help the birds in your garden, and it is great fun to make with family members or friends. Get a glass of mulled wine or a warming hot chocolate, some mince pies on a plate, and spend the afternoon getting crafty.

You will need:
- Several long, bendy, springy twigs (like willow)
- Garden wire
- A mixing bowl and wooden spoon
- A handful of pinecones
- Sprigs of holly, mistletoe and other festive leaves
- A block of lard (or vegetarian alternative), softened in the microwave for a few seconds
- A handful of birdseed or nuts, and dried fruit like raisins
- Some breadcrumbs and grated cheese

1. Start by making your wreath shape (as big as you like), by twisting your twigs together in bundles and fastening into a circular shape with garden wire. Make sure it's nice and secure, and make a loop of wire at the top to hang your wreath. **2.** Using your hands (if you don't mind getting messy) or a wooden spoon, mix together your softened lard (or alternative) with your seeds, nuts, dried fruit, breadcrumbs and cheese, until you have a nice sticky mess of birdy goodness.
3. Take the lard-paste and cover your pinecones in it, pushing it into all the gaps. If you've got any raisins left over, use them to decorate.
4. Decorate your wreath with the pinecones and your sprigs of holly, making it look as pretty as you can. Secure everything in place with more garden wire, and tuck in any pointy ends. **5.** You can now display your garden wreath to neighbours and the birds. Instead of hanging it on your door, choose a nice spot on a tree or near some bushes, away from disturbance, people and cats.

Write a wild haiku

Haikus are traditional short poems which originated in Japan. They're the kind of thing you learn about in school and then never think about again, but for today's Random Act of Wildness, try to rediscover your primary school English lessons and write a wild haiku about something in nature that you love. In most guides that you read, haikus consist of three lines and a set number of syllables – five in the first and last lines, and seven in the middle. This isn't a rigid structure, though, so don't worry if you go over or under a bit.

First up, you need to find your wild inspiration – pick something very small and detailed and see if you can really get into the detail of why it's beautiful, exciting, moving or mesmerising. A specific tree growing near your house; a feather you find on the ground; a bird singing in the park. A short walk outside should give you plenty of ideas. Next, make some notes. Try to imagine its story. Where did that tree grow from? How old is it? Where has that feather been and why is it here now? Why has that bird chosen to sing right here, and what does its song make you feel? This is all getting very deep, but try to be mindful and use your imagination to connect with the world around you.

Finally, when you've got your notes, have a go at penning your poem. I don't always write poems from beginning to end in order – sometimes a last line is easier to construct than a first, but see if you can capture all of that mindfulness in just a handful of words and syllables. It may take a few attempts, but play around with it until you're happy. It's all about choosing your words carefully to create a wild picture with your poem.

Check out this beautiful example by Joshua Johnson

Autumn leaves falling,
Drifting to the wet ground,
Crunching under foot.

Compile a wild playlist

This is a great Random Act of Wildness for a cold winter evening, when you're looking for something wild to do but can't bear to face the weather. Stay safely indoors and compile a playlist of songs that remind you of nature and the wild instead. You could look for songs that conjure memories of your favourite wild places (I love listening to Scottish music as it reminds me of holidays in the Highlands with eagles and otters!); songs that are directly about nature or animals; artists inspired by wildlife and wild places (Doves, Eagles, Guillemots); or even just songs with 'wild' in the title. This will keep you connected to nature, even when you're trapped indoors!

Learn a wild word

Gelid is a great word and perfect for this time of year. It means icy, frosty, bitter – the perfect word to describe a frigid, frozen morning. It can also refer to someone's personality if they're behaving in a cold manner or being stand-offish. It comes from the Latin *gelidus*, meaning intensely cold or frosty. Try using this one with your neighbour, friends or colleagues as you gossip about the cold weather that's set in.

Buy local produce

Our everyday staples – milk, eggs and vegetables – have come a long way to be with us: sometimes from different counties, sometimes from different countries! This means that our breakfast, lunch and dinner are stacking up a serious carbon footprint from farm to fork. If possible, buy food locally – from farmers' markets, farm shops or independent stores – and branch out from the big brands. Not only will your meal be a lot fresher, but you'll be doing your bit for the environment. And with fewer people in the middle – driving, packing, storing and stocking the food – more of your money will go directly to the person who grew it in the first place!

Leave footprints in the frost

Baby, it's cold outside. But you shouldn't let that stop you! This Random Act of Wildness is one for frosty mornings – maybe even the first frosty morning of the year. When you step out the door, admire the world around you as it's become dusted with silver, freezing cobwebs, leaves, pavements and blades of grass. If you've got a car to defrost, use your finger to draw a quick, wild picture on the windscreen before scraping it clear, or if you've got a lawn, savour being the first to stomp across it. So simple, yet so satisfying, and a fun way to enjoy this cold time of year.

306

307

308

GELID

(n): Icy,
extremely cold.

309

Mimic a pterodactyl

Did you know that pterodactyls fly among us? Okay, not strictly true, but you don't have to look far to see a creature that would have fit right in in the Cretaceous period. Cormorants can now be found all over the UK. They used to be confined to the coast and remain predominantly a seabird, but you can see them at lakes, reservoirs, rivers and wetlands as well. They nest on cliffs and in tall trees. They're big, shiny black birds with a 1.5m wingspan and prehistoric-looking features. They have piercing eyes and a long, hooked beak, which they use to catch fish as they dive underwater.

The cormorant, despite being a water bird, doesn't have waterproof feathers (unlike ducks and seabirds). Instead, it must dry its wings like we would dry a towel on a breezy day: by spreading them out and letting the wind help. The feathers on their wings and backs look like scales, so as they stand aloft with their wings spread in a distinctive 'M' shape, you can see the resemblance to a pterodactyl (or a typical cartoon bat). They're big and proud, so look formidable (even a bit scary). See if you can spot a cormorant drying out its wings – look on top of boats, dead trees, poles and big rocks near water. You could even mimic it on windy days and feel the rush of the wind around the sleeves of your jumper.

Kiss under real mistletoe

Mistletoe is an instantly recognisable plant, associated with everyone's favourite time of year (unless you're a Scrooge!). It's now more common to see the plastic stuff in supermarkets than the real thing growing wild. It grows high in the tops of other trees as a parasite, using the nutrients from these trees to flourish into its distinctive, globe-like shape. Apple trees, willows and poplars are favourites, but with fewer orchards around nowadays, the plant is harder to come by.

Mistletoe is made up of balls of leaves, which grow in pairs, and sticky white berries that are irresistible to birds. The mistle thrush even takes its name from its love of mistletoe. When the birds eat the berries, their beaks become sticky. They clean their beaks on the branches, leaving behind mistletoe seeds to colonise a new tree.

Rather than waiting for the Christmas party to pucker up, invite a loved one on a winter walk to try and find some real mistletoe. A clear, frosty day is truly romantic, whatever the outcome. Somerset, Herefordshire, Gloucestershire and Worcestershire are hotspots for mistletoe, but it can be found anywhere, even in central London.

Go natural when wrapping

Christmas is a time for giving. Watching someone open a present that you've chosen for them is such a warming feeling, and I love wrapping them all up, too. Once the gifts are open, though, you're left with a mountain of wrapping paper, ribbon, Sellotape and tags, many of which are coated in shiny plastic or glitter. While some of this can be recycled, far too much ends up in landfill.

Why not give Mother Nature a hand this Christmas by opting for natural, recyclable or up-cyclable wrappings? First, rather than the sparkly wrapping papers, try plain old parcel paper instead. It's cheaper, better quality to wrap with, looks classy and can be recycled. The glittery papers are covered in tiny plastics, which wreak havoc on natural environments. You can also get rid of Sellotape by using twines and strings to hold your parcels together – again, it looks amazing! Alternatively, invest in some lovely material and wrap your presents in this. Scarves are a great option, as the wrapping doubles up as a present. Finally, rather than using shiny bags to present gifts in, use ones made of hemp or burlap. These can be re-used all year round, so they're not limited to the festive period: more useful, and way better for nature!

Think before you buy

It's sad to know how many of the things we loved as children are so bad for wildlife and the planet. Balloons are one such thing. They look pretty and are fun to play with, but whether released into the sky or disposed of in the bin, balloons never biodegrade. Balloons that go up have to come down, and they can land in rivers and the sea, where they are eaten by fish, mammals and birds. The ribbon gets tangled around beaks, flippers and fins, causing starvation. It's not nice to think about, but it's true. Try to give up balloons for good. Use eco-friendly and natural decorations, and instead of balloon releases, think about planting trees or flowers instead.

Waste-not -want-not

In the UK alone, we waste about a third of the food that is grown. That's a lot of land that's not being used effectively; a lot of landfill; and a lot of environmental damage. This Random Act of Wildness is easy and can make a big difference to your purse, your lifestyle and the world around you. Try and cut down that waste. Pop a small bucket in your kitchen for a week. Instead of scraping plates into the bin after meals, put all the scraps in the bucket. You'll soon get to see who the main culprits are and have a clear visual guide as to how much you're wasting. Cut down on portion size so everything is eaten, re-heat leftovers for lunch, and only buy what you need.

Organise a work litter pick

A lunchtime litter pick is a great way to get colleagues involved in wildlife conservation, as well as being a good team-building activity. You'll need some sturdy gloves, a bag and some litter pickers. Mark out an area close by and sweep the area for rubbish, then pick it up with your gloved hands or pickers and pop it in your bag. When it's full, put the whole bag in the bin. You'll be amazed at how many people will stop and talk to you about what you're doing – be friendly and enthusiastic but explain how litter can harm wildlife and how a simple litter pick could save a life. Hopefully they'll be inspired and take up their own Random Act of Wildness.

Think before you buy

You either love or hate glitter. Sure, it's pretty, but it gets everywhere, and it hangs around, too. Because it's light and durable, it finds its way into rivers and oceans, where it causes chaos among sea creatures. It looks like tiny specks of food floating through the water, so builds up in the systems of animals. It can even turn up inside us if we eat fish! It can become toxic, which in small quantities is probably fine for us, but not so for fish. Try to cut glitter out of your life. Choose eco-friendly alternatives which break down much quicker. Ending the sparkly obsession is great for the planet and a fabulous Random Act of Wildness!

313

THINK! THINK! THINK!
THINK! THINK!
THINK! THINK! THINK!

BALLOONS

¡THINK! ¡THINK! ¡THINK!

314

315

316

THINK! THINK! THINK!
THINK! THINK! THINK!
THINK! THINK! THINK!

GLITTER

¡THINK! ¡THINK! ¡THINK!

Celebrate the humble stick

Sticks are one of the most wonderful toys you can give a child. They're free, versatile and encourage a huge amount of creativity and imagination. I will never, ever say no to a child playing with a stick – from magic wand to writing in the sand, a stick should keep a child entertained for hours. They're not bad for adults, too. I kept one on my desk for a while at work. When I was stressed or needed to concentrate, I'd twirl it in the fingers of one hand like a baton, which would calm me down. I've also seen people use them to jog their memories – if they need to remember something, they think about it while holding the stick, and then next time they see the stick or pick it up, it reminds them. There are hundreds of things you can do with a stick – challenge yourself, your friends or young family members to think of 100 things. Here's a few ideas to get you started…

317. Pooh sticks I used to love playing Pooh sticks with my dad on the canal. Inspired by A.A. Milne's *Winnie the Pooh*, the game simply involves finding some different-sized sticks and dropping them off a bridge over a river, canal or stream. Make sure you can tell the difference between the sticks and let everyone pick one. Let them drift under the bridge, then run to the other side and see whose stick appears first!

318. Lightsaber or sword When I was about eight or nine, pretending to be battling evil was the main weekend game. My best friend and I would venture into one of our gardens with two long sticks and clash swords for hours. There would be the inevitable and painful thwacks on the fingers of course, but it was great exercise and amazing fun.

319. Journey stick Journey sticks are a lovely way to keep children entertained on long walks, especially if they're the kind of kids that get easily distracted or bored with simply tromping along. Take some string with you, collect a stick each near the beginning of your walk, and get everyone to find natural items, like feathers, leaves and so on, to tie on to their sticks. When you compare them at the end, you'll have a record of everything you did. Get everyone to explain what each item is, where they found it and why they picked it up.

320. **Walking stick** A simple but surprisingly useful Random Act of Wildness. Take a big, chunky stick or branch and use it as a walking stick as you're exploring. You can lean on it, turn things over with it, test how deep water is by dipping it in, and use it to knock aside nettles and brambles that may sting or cut your legs.

321. **Toast marshmallows** This is a great use of a stick – yummy and lots of fun. It does require adult supervision and a huge amount of common sense though, so be very careful. You'll need to make a little fire somewhere easy to control. Your back garden is usually a good place. Simply get some skinny twigs, skewer on some marshmallows and roast them for a few seconds in the heat of the fire. They should go dark, bubbly and sticky. Leave to cool for a few seconds before taking a bite – they're boiling hot!

  Remember some basic fire safety tips: make sure you have water on hand to douse it; don't light up anywhere near dry or brittle plants (like grass) as fire can spread easily; and keep a close eye on it. Sand or stones around your fire can help to stop it spreading, and avoid anywhere near buildings.

Revel in a raptor roost

For many species, winter is simply about endurance. And when you're watching wildlife in the coldest months of the year, that's what you must do too – endure. Wrap up warm against that frozen wind, keep your extremities tucked in, and be thankful that for you, at least, this isn't life or death (unlike the wildlife you're watching).

In the winter, many of our birds of prey will gather in something called a raptor roost. They're bleak places, usually marshland, and to get a good view you need height – this means that you're even more exposed to the elements. A banking is a good place to watch from, where you can survey the whole area, waiting for movement. Late afternoon is perfect, just as the sun is slipping in the sky.

On this occasion, despite the many layers of clothing, I was still shivering. Every time I picked up my binoculars to scan the marsh, the heat from my face and breath would cause the lens to mist over. Conditions were perfect though (the end of a sunny day with only a gentle wind), so we would persevere.

At first we were joined by a peregrine, racing from one side of the marsh to the other at breakneck speed, undoubtedly in pursuit of a rabbit. A pale barn owl quartered up and down on silent wings next, hovering in the air to pounce on a mouse or vole. A short-eared owl, too, gliding away from us on large, outstretched wings, and a marsh harrier, with wings crooked upwards in a deep 'v' shape. You can see why these places are worth the cold.

Then the ghost appeared. This phantom was pale grey with dark black, pointed wing tips. Poised and very powerful, he materialised (no one saw where from) and began to haunt the marsh, back and forward, listening for his next meal. Up close, you would see piercing yellow eyes. The last of the sun caught a glowing white rump. This was the hen harrier, and this was his domain now. He heard something, quickly reeled in the air and landed on the ground, disappearing into the gloaming. He didn't resurface. The other owls, raptors and falcons continued to hunt for their supper, but the star of the show had already scored. And so had we.

Do it yourself:
Winter is a great time of year to look for birds of prey. They may come together, usually on lowland marshes or wetlands, to form winter roosts. This happens all around the UK, so look for your nearest nature reserve. Wrap up warm, take a pair of binoculars and be patient!

Set a wild ringtone

This is a great way to confound people when they're least expecting it: set yourself a wild ringtone. When you're out and about in public, or even at work, the air will suddenly fill with birdsong as your phone rings! Not only will you really confuse people (why can I hear a bird singing in the supermarket?!), it'll take you back to a wild place every time you take a call. You can download different bird songs from the internet to use as a ringtone, or you could record your own. The dawn chorus is when the birds are at their loudest, but you could also use the buzzing of bees or waves crashing on rocks – whatever your favourite wild sound is!

Learn a wild word

Winter is the perfect time to witness a murmuration. They are magical to behold, and come in many sizes. As the weather grows colder, starlings (like many birds) join forces and group together, sometimes in flocks of thousands. As dusk falls, they meet near a safe place and fly together, forming intricate patterns in the sky. The birds weave together, creating shapes and undulating designs that look like dark clouds. It's a spectacular sight, and even with just a few hundred starlings it's magical to watch.

Create a calendar

Creating calendars with family photos is a wonderful keepsake for loved ones. There are loads of websites that allow you to upload your images directly, position and edit them, and get a calendar printed. With so many snaps from your 365 Days Wild, why not treat yourself to a calendar to remind you of your adventures? Select your twelve favourite seasonal photos and get creative. You can add in special dates, like birthdays, and captions explaining your different Random Acts of Wildness. You could even add little Random Acts of Wildness on certain days to encourage others to go wild, too!

Gaze at the moon

On dark nights when the moon is bright, don your binoculars and gaze up at the orb in the sky. When we look at the moon with the naked eye, we're seeing the side that's lit by the sun. We might see shadows and distinctive craters, but not much detail. You'll be amazed at the difference a pair of binoculars can make. You'll need a clear night, and it's more interesting if the moon is full. Focus in on the shadowy craters, the pale higher areas, and the darker shallow areas known as 'seas'. Even with a basic pair of binoculars you'll be able to pick out craters just a few miles across. Scan the rest of the sky, too, and see how many more stars are visible now you've got those binoculars!

323

324

MURMURATION

(n): A flock
of starlings.

325

November

326

Make some reindeer food

Ho ho ho! Santa is coming! But how will he know to stop at your house (assuming you've been well behaved, of course)? A lot of shops now sell something called 'reindeer food', which is essentially glitter and sequins mixed with oats. It may look pretty, but these microplastics are harmful to wildlife – they don't break down, so they last for years, ending up in rivers and seas, or harming creatures in your garden, like birds and hedgehogs. There is an alternative, though: it's great to make with any little people in your life, or on your own if you want to give wildlife a helping hand this Christmas.

Collect together some leftovers from your cupboard to make the base of your reindeer food: an apple, a carrot, a lump of cheese, porridge oats, dried fruit (like raisins) and, if you've been making mince pies, some leftover uncooked pastry. Grate the apple, carrot and cheese into a bowl (or chop into tiny cubes) and mix together with your hands. Stir in the porridge oats and the raisins. Crumble the pastry into the bowl using your fingertips – as if you're making the topping to a crumble. Mix everything together.

If you're making this with children, divide it into little paper bags so that they can have one each, and, on Christmas Eve, scatter on to your garden. Remind them that the carrot is to help Rudolph see in the dark; the apple is to give him fresh breath; the cheese is a little treat; the oats are for energy; and the raisins and pastry are like a reindeer mince pie!

Of course, what you're actually doing is helping local wildlife (as well as attracting reindeer!). This delectable mix will make a great Christmas treat for the birds.

Give a wild gift

Do you ever get that feeling of mild panic: what on earth do I get for people this year for Christmas? Did I get them socks or a scarf last year? Has it been long enough to justify another pair of slippers? Did they really like those toiletries?

Take the stress out of Christmas shopping by thinking of some wild presents instead. They're cute, original and always have a personal touch. You could encourage green-fingered relatives to think about wildlife in their gardens by buying them a bird box, a bug hotel or a bird feeding station (better still, if you're feeling ambitious, make one from scratch for them). Would an outdoorsy friend enjoy receiving a field guide for birds or butterflies? Maybe the bookworm in your life would enjoy a copy of your favourite nature book. It's easy to spread the wild love at Christmas, so make the most of it.

Of course, if you want to go a step further, give the gift of wildlife by adopting a wild animal from a charity. This works a bit like sponsorship – you choose your animal, pay a small amount of money (usually around £30 for the year) and this allows the charity to carry out amazing conservation work for that animal, helping to create new habitats, look after them and protect them. In return, you get photos, updates on your wild animal, magazines and all sorts, including sometimes a little present like a cuddly toy. There's loads of animals to choose from, like squirrels, badgers, dormice, birds, whales and dolphins, so there really is something for everyone.

Membership to a local wildlife charity also makes a great gift. In return, most charities offer a magazine and regular updates, discounts to events or access to special nature reserves and a membership pack when you join. You can often pay monthly, which helps spread the cost, and this personal gift allows everyone to feel like they're making a difference.

Check out your local Wildlife Trust for gifts, adoptions and membership for starters.

329 Sketch a naked tree

Winter is the perfect season to appreciate the raw beauty of our trees. With the leaves stripped off and the branches exposed, you can appreciate the intricate patterns in the bark, the maze of branches and twigs, the deep and twisting roots. They may not be at their prettiest, but naked winter trees have a wild beauty about them. This is the perfect time to sketch them.

Pick a tree that you see quite a lot – a tree on your street, in a nearby park, near work or somewhere close to home. Wrap up warm: if you can brave the cold, sketching out of doors and in the elements will get you feeling really close to nature; just make sure you've got gloves, scarf and hat, as well as a good coat, because you're going to be sitting still. The fresh, frosty air will ignite your senses and shake away the cobwebs. Next, pack up your materials – at the most basic, you'll need some paper or cardboard and pencils. A hard book to lean on (or a clipboard) will also be handy, and a flask of your favourite warm drink is recommended.

Find a spot where you can sit and see the whole tree from top to bottom. Mark out the proportions on your paper, then start to fill in the detail – the trunk, big branches, the roots. Add your texture, your twigs and shadows next, building your sketch in layers. Remember to use a sharp pencil to capture the fine twigs, and a softer pencil for chunky lines and cast shadows. You can change your perspective and sketch from different angles, move in close to examine the rich texture of the bark, or take photos on a camera phone to work from. You can even change your medium, working in charcoal or inks to create a different atmosphere and capture the naked beauty of your tree. Your sketch could take five minutes or an hour – it's up to you, and it doesn't matter at all how accurate it is. This is your drawing – you don't have to show it to anyone else if you don't want to.

Get starry-eyed

On those clear winter nights when everything gets frosty, settle back to gaze up at the dark sky and enjoy the twinkle of stars far away. The key with stargazing is to try and minimise light pollution, so head to the darkest place you can find. In the countryside this can be much easier, as there's fewer towns and cities to obscure the view, but even in the city it is still possible. Large parks can do the trick, or try the tops of hills or even tall buildings – anything that gets you above the streetlights and gives you a view straight upwards.

You can stargaze with or without binoculars. Binoculars will show you thousands more stars that you never knew existed; a clear view just using your eyes might help you hone in on familiar constellations and practise a bit first. Just make sure you're wrapped up warm and you've got a clear night. If you want to take notes or sketches, have a pencil and paper handy.

You need to spot the difference between stars, satellites and planets. Stars twinkle gently to themselves, although some are much brighter than others. Satellites move purposefully across the sky – they don't twinkle and, unlike shooting stars, they don't fade away. Planets shine out brightly without twinkling, and, depending on what you're looking at, can appear different colours (so, for example, Mars has a slightly reddish glow).

Start with the easiest constellations, and then figure out how they fit together. The Plough, or Big Dipper, is quite obvious and looks a bit like a giant saucepan. It's made up of seven stars, four making the bowl of the pan, and three making the handle to the left. If you take the edge of the saucepan without a handle, and head up in a straight line from these two stars, you'll find the North Star (or 'Polaris'), which glows brightly. The entire starscape in the northern hemisphere wheels around Polaris. I also like to spot Cassiopeia from here – first find the Plough, then the North Star, then work your way the same distance again, and look for a big 'W' in the sky. The North Star will line up roughly with the middle.

When you're stargazing you're looking back into the past. It takes light such a long time to reach us from the stars, that you're seeing history in action. These same stars guided sailors and explorers all around the world, acting as a natural map.

Dabble with ducks

Who doesn't love ducks? They are charismatic and full of personality, and winter is the best time to see them. From tiny teal with yellow bottoms to wigeon which whistle to each other, lots of species arrive in the UK in the winter, gathering together in big numbers on lakes, reservoirs and wetlands to stay safe and well-fed throughout the season. There are far too many to talk about all of them in detail, but here are some of the ones you're most likely to see.

You will recognise a mallard straight away. The males have bright green heads with an iridescent shine, while the females are brown and streaky. There's no doubt about it – these guys go 'quack'. Tufted ducks, or 'tufties' for short, are black and white, smaller and hang out in the middle of lakes, so you'll need a pair of binoculars. The males have a tuft at the back of the head, giving them their name. Teal are smaller again. They 'dabble' at the edges of the water, sifting the mud for tasty treats. They are largely grey in colour, with reddish faces, a green band through the eye, and yellow bums that make them look like they've sat in custard.

Gadwall are very underrated ducks: they look largely grey, but when you inspect them closely through binoculars, they're made up of lots of tiny hatchings and markings. They have black bottoms and a white patch in the wing when they fly. The aptly named shoveler has a huge bill which is flattened, much like a shovel: they look a bit like someone has sat on their beaks. The males have green heads, a chestnut patch on the side and a white breast. When they fly, you can sometimes see powder blue, too.

Can you identify the next duck you see, paddling about in a pond?

Spot winter ghosts

Owls are one of my favourite families of birds, and many people will say the same. Their eyes point forward, meaning that they can look straight at you with their piercing stare. There are five species that occur regularly in the UK: long-eared, short-eared, little, barn and tawny, and the last two are iconic animals in the countryside.

Barn owls are probably our most famous owl. They are undeniably beautiful, with long, graceful wings, pearly white coats and dark eyes. Winter is the perfect time to share an encounter with them; when the days are shorter, they come out in the daytime to find food, so you might see this ghostly creature glide past. They are completely silent when they hunt, sneaking up on prey unnoticed, and excellent eyesight and hearing allows them to detect the slightest movement in the grass. They fly up and down fields, especially along hedgerows and margins, searching for small rodents. When they hone in on their dinner, they will hover above it and suddenly drop from the sky.

The best chance of seeing one is late afternoon as the sun is setting, around the edges of fields or wastelands where voles and mice might be common. Often, you'll just catch a glimpse in your car headlights as they glide ahead of you down a road. It's a haunting experience as it's so silent.

333   Paint your wild photo

The perfect rainy day Random Act of Wildness – recreate a recent wild memory by painting, drawing or colouring it in your favourite artistic medium. Whether it's a wide landscape at sunset, a close-up of a butterfly or a blooming flower, find your favourite wild photograph and try to copy it. It could be your own photo or one that you find in a book or online – it's entirely up to you. You can do it as quickly or as carefully as you like, with abstract patches of colour or intricate detail. Pens and inks create a lovely effect and are great for capturing detail; chalks, charcoal and acrylics are good for broad strokes of colour; and watercolours create beautiful landscapes. Even if you don't have specialist art equipment in the house, simple printer paper, pencils and biros can unleash your inner artist. As you work, think about how that wild experience made you feel.

334   Cuddle your favourite tree

Afraid of being a tree-hugger? Don't be! Trees are awesome and deserve a little respect. They are essential to life on earth, are home to thousands of wild animals, and make many of the things we take for granted (like paper, fire, houses) possible. Your favourite tree deserves a well-earned cuddle from you. If you've got an oak that is three adult hugs (or more), a beech measuring two hugs or a skinny rowan tree that's one hug round, then you've got yourself an ancient tree that could have been alive for hundreds of years. In the open, such as in a park, most trees grow an average of 2.5cm of girth (length around) for each year of their lives, so a tree with a girth of 250cm would be about 100 years old! In a woodland, they grow slower, about 1.25cm a year, so a tree of the same size would be 200 years old!

Ice some owl biscuits

This is a great Random Act of Wildness to try out with little ones, especially on a rainy day. If you've got a great recipe for your favourite biscuit, you can make your cookies from scratch, or you can cheat and use readymade shortbread, Digestives or Rich Tea biscuits. Owls are perfect to pipe because they're made up of geometric shapes, and they look cute because their eyes face forward (unlike most birds).

You will need:
- A mixing bowl
- A baking tray or wire rack
- An icing bag with a thin nozzle
- Icing sugar and water, according to the packet instructions
- Food colouring (three colours)
- Your favourite circular biscuits
- Flaked almonds (if you like)

1. Mix up some icing according to the packet instructions, so that it's thick and glossy but still runny. Add a couple of drops of food colouring – any colour will do. We don't need to be accurate with these, so if you want some bright purple owls, go for it! You can do different colours of course – I recommend at least three different colours. Leave some of it white, though. **2.** Next, fill a piping bag with the icing, and attach a thin nozzle. Take a biscuit and very carefully pipe two circles right next to each other, in the white icing, just above the centre. These are your owl's eyes. Fill them in with white icing.
3. Next, you need to pipe little wings on to each side, heading down to the bottom of the biscuit. They can be any colour you like – they just need to be simple half-moons, coloured in. You could also use a flake of almond, attached with a dab of icing. **4.** When your eyes are dry, you need to add ears and a beak. The ears should be little triangles pointing up, above each eye, and the beak should sit in the middle, just below the eyes. You can add feet in the same colour as the beak, too.
5. Finally, add a little spot of dark icing (black or something else dark) to the centre of each eye, to give expression. Allow them to set in a cool, dry place.

Think before you buy

If you're wrapping cakes or sandwiches, you simply don't need clingfilm anymore. You can now buy products, like beeswax wraps, that work in exactly the same way – but you don't have to throw them away when they get stuck together! It takes a few uses to make it nice and pliable, but a reusable sandwich wrap can hold its shape (and some come with poppers or Velcro), be wiped or washed clean, and fold down to the perfect size to transport your sarnies. There are lots of makes to choose from with different textures, features and funky designs.

Learn a wild word

A flash of turquoise darting down a stream, accompanied by a high-pitched whistle as it whizzes past, so fast that you hardly know what you saw. It's a kingfisher. One of our most beautiful birds, that electric shade of blue is an optical illusion, caused by pigment shading in the feathers, creating an iridescent shimmer. The common kingfisher found in the UK isn't of the genus halcyon, but it's related. Halcyon days are calm and tranquil, idyllic, like those we can look forward to in the coming spring.

Learn a wild word

In the New Year, when it's cold and brisk, watch the clouds part and feel the apricity on your skin as the sun shines through. It'll warm you, remind you of spring and give you something to look forward to at the darkest time of the year. Sunny winter days are great for exploring the wild world around you: admire how the light changes at this time of year.

Think before you buy

Plastic cutlery comes with a lot of takeaway meals. Often, it's thrown in without you asking for it. So, before someone has a chance to force it on you, make sure you're prepared. Carry around a re-usable and washable knife, fork and spoon in your bag (along with a handful of napkins) and when someone offers you plastic cutlery, you can politely decline. You can even get little envelopes now to keep them in if you don't want dirty cutlery rattling around at the bottom of your bag.

336

CLING FILM

337

HALCYON

Halcyon (a): Denoting a period of time in the past that was idyllically happy and peaceful.

Halcyon (n): A tropical Asian and African kingfisher with brightly coloured plumage.

338

APRICITY

(n): The warmth of the sun in winter.

339

PLASTIC CUTLERY

Find a flock of finches

Winter is a great time to enjoy finches. Not only do we have more species in the country – birds like hawfinches spend the winter here – but they become more obvious, too, coming into our towns, streets and gardens to find shelter and food.

Finches are often brightly coloured and have distinct calls. They usually hang around in flocks, enjoying seed on bird tables, on the ground and in feeders. They're quite small as a rule (around sparrow-sized, with some variation), and have triangular bills that are adapted for the different kinds of seeds that they eat. There are between ten and fifteen species of finches that are regularly seen in the UK. Here are some of the ones you're most likely to see in your garden or neighbourhood; if you can make it into the countryside, finches love hanging out in messy field margins, too, so look out for them on a winter walk.

Goldfinches look like little warriors, with bright red war-paint on their faces, a golden back and striking yellow and black on the wing. They love niger seed, which is commonly available for feeders. Male chaffinches can look very smart, with blue-grey heads, pinky-red breasts, and strongly marked black and white wings (which become obvious when they fly). The females have similar markings but in greys and browns.

You can't mistake a bullfinch for anything else. They are chunky birds with thick, bull necks, a black cap and (in the males) a bright pink breast and blue back. They often hang out in pairs, with the female looking demure. When they fly they let out a shrill whistle and show off a big, white bottom!

Greenfinches used to be common in gardens, but they've been hit hard by disease (which is why you should always clean your feeders thoroughly). They have a wheezy song and are greenish all over, with a bright yellow patch in the wing. And although usually found in the north of England and Scotland, in winter siskins get much easier to see all over. They move around in noisy flocks, bouncing through the air to land in the tops of trees. They are bright yellow streaked with black, with a black cap on the males.

Find a flock of finches for your Random Act of Wildness and see what species you can identify.

341 Catch a snowflake on your fingertip

The moment the snow starts to fall, there's a chance to catch and examine, if only briefly, a beautiful natural wonder – a snowflake. Snowflakes form in the atmosphere when tiny drops of cold water freeze on to specks of dust before drifting down to earth. There are several things that affect the way a snowflake forms, including the humidity of the atmosphere and the temperature. The most intricate ones are formed in slightly wetter and warmer conditions (but obviously not too warm!). When it starts to snow, grab your coat, head outside and try to catch a snowflake on your fingertip. They're so delicate that you'll need to be incredibly gentle. Once you get one, examine it closely – is it a little cluster of snowflakes, or a single, beautifully formed one?

342 Make a fairy garden

Fairy (or elf) gardens are a great way to get little ones interested in wildlife gardening. They add a spot of magic and sparkle, which can capture the imagination. You can make a fairy garden several ways, depending how much space you've got. A shady corner is a perfect spot – remember, there might really be fairies at the bottom of the garden! You can buy plastic accessories for fairy gardens, but try and use natural products that you can forage instead. It's about detail, so have loads of fun planning your garden before you start. You'll need a little area where your fairies will live – you could make a mini tipi out of twigs, for example. You need to add some features – a little pond (or wishing well) made from an old saucer; a table and chairs (you could use cross sections of branches); a washing line (made from twine tied to two twigs – you could even attach leaves using little wooden craft pegs); and so on. You could build a fence from twigs or create a wall from pebbles, or use the tops of acorns as cups and bowls. Let your imagination run wild! Encourage kids to keep adding more at every opportunity and use it as a great chance to develop their sense of discovery, imagination and awareness of wildlife.

Rise with hedgehog bread

This is a fun way to do some baking and feel inspired by nature at the same time! Hedgehog loaves, whether big or small, are a great way to get little ones baking and in the kitchen, and you can have great fun creating the most lifelike hedgehogs. For this recipe, I'm encouraging you to make your own favourite bread recipe (try a simple one off the internet if you've never done it before) and have fun shaping it.

You will need:
- Scissors
- A damp tea towel
- A baking tray, lightly greased
- A batch of your favourite bread dough made up, kneaded but not proofed
- Flour, for dusting
- A handful of raisins

1. Take your ball of kneaded dough and snip it into five or six smaller equal parts – one for each hedgehog. On a dusting of flour (to prevent sticking), roll each part into a ball and then pull one end to create a nose for your hedgehog. The gluten in bread makes the dough bounce back, so be firm with it. Repeat for all your pieces. **2.** Cover your hedgehogs with the damp tea towel and leave in a warm place to rise for about an hour – they should double in size! **3.** Once the 'hogs are risen, take a pair of scissors and snip spikes all over the back at an angle, leaving the face and nose spike-free. You can then add the raisin eyes and nose – make sure to push them in very firmly, or they pop out during cooking. **4.** Bake your bread-hogs in a preheated oven (about 200°C), checking them at 15–20 minutes. The exact time will depend on your recipe and the size of your hedgehogs, so keep checking. Your kitchen should smell divine! **5.** Remove from the oven and allow your bread-hogs to cool – they should be golden with no burned spikes! Don't worry about resisting them until they're cold; fresh warm bread is a treat worth having.

Spot colourful thrushes

You may have noticed that, in the coldest winter months, we are treated to a visit by some gorgeous birds. They'll hang out on hedges and in fields, venture into our gardens to eat berries, or perch on the tops of trees. These are our winter thrushes, and the two you're most likely to see are fieldfares and redwings.

These lovely birds are related to blackbirds and song thrushes. They're about the same size, with redwings being slightly more petite and fieldfares being a bit bulkier. Both bird species are after berries, fruit and worms, so they love trees like holly and apple. In fact, the best way you can encourage these visitors into your garden is to leave out apples (piled up on the ground or skewered on to trees) and to grow berry-bearing bushes. When the weather gets colder, they might need this larder.

Redwings and fieldfares are easy to identify. The redwing is brown on top and streaky underneath, with obvious pale stripes going across the face, just above and under the eye. They have a rusty patch beneath the wing. Fieldfares are chunkier, with a blue-grey head and bottom, chestnut head and pale tummy, that has etchings all along it. If you see huge flocks of birds erupting from the tops of trees in country lanes or suburbia, these could well be thrushes. The species will hang out together, so spot a flock and see if you can identify which is which.

Create ice decorations

This Random Act of Wildness is great for frozen days in mid-winter. The decorations you create will only last a few hours, depending on the weather, but that's what makes them so magical. You can always cheat and use a freezer if the weather isn't quite cold enough! You're going to create beautiful outdoor gems to hang from trees. Boiling your water first may seem strange, but it will ensure that your decorations are crystal clear, rather than clouded.

You will need:
- Some saucers
- Natural twine
- Natural items like feathers or fallen leaves
- A kettle full of freshly boiled water, allowed to cool
- Maybe a freezer

1. Start by laying out your saucers on a table, and add a piece of twine to each – it'll need to stretch from the middle of the saucer to about 10cm beyond it at least. Lay your feathers, leaves or other natural items over the top of the twine in the saucer. **2.** Pour in your cool boiled water so that the string and the items are covered and leave outside on a frosty night (or you can cheat and pop them in the freezer). **3.** In the morning, take your saucers and place them in a baking tray of cool water – this should be just enough to loosen the ice decorations from the saucers. **4.** When they've come loose, very gently carry them outside and hang them from a tree or bush in your street or garden.

Enjoy an edible pond

An edible pond makes a great addition to a kid's birthday party – or even an adult's party! They look spectacular and taste yummy, too. If you're vegetarian, you can now find vegetarian jellies in most supermarkets, or make your own using vegetarian gelatine, food colouring, water and flavours. The blue one can be the hardest to find, so you may need to use a mixture of packet gelatine, water, food colouring and a flavouring of your choice.

You will need:
- A big clear glass bowl
- A measuring jug
- Three different colour jellies (purple, green and blue/blackcurrant, lime and mixed berry), made up according to the instructions
- Jelly sweets, including snakes, worms and fish
- Apples, sliced into 'reed' shapes
- Dragon fruit or passion fruit
- Green grapes, halved

1. Start by making up your purple jelly and pouring it into the bottom of your bowl. When it's cooled, but still liquid, pour in some gummy snakes. Allow to set completely. **2.** Next, make up your green jelly and separate into two halves. If you have some blue food colouring, add a couple of drops to one half to make it turquoise. Pour this over your set purple layer and add some jelly worms and fish. When nearly set, stick some apple reeds out of the top so that they stand up straight. **3.** Pour over the next layer using the remaining lime green jelly, and add any remaining fish and jelly snakes. **4.** Finally, add your blue layer and spoon in some dragon or passion fruit (for frog spawn), some sliced grapes (for lily pads) and any remaining reeds around the edge. *Voilà!* Allow to set completely and serve with pride.

Make room for birds' nests

The two most common garden species to use nest boxes are great tits and blue tits. As we've cut down more trees and our woodlands have shrunk, nest boxes have become increasingly important. There are loads of different types and you can even build your own if you're feeling adventurous. The type of nest box you need will depend on your most likely species, so for example, tits like a closed box with a little hole at the front for access; bigger birds, like thrushes, prefer an open box. You can put up a nest box at any time of year, but winter is best, as they may start staking out potential sites before the spring. Attach your nest box to a tree or wall, out of direct sunlight (so not south-facing). Make sure there is cover nearby for the babies when they fledge. Fix it high up, at least 1.5m off the ground. If your box is used, make sure to clear out the old nest in the autumn, to make way for new residents the following year.

Volunteer your wild time

Volunteering is something that anyone can get involved with, no matter where you live or what you do. The great thing about volunteering for a wildlife charity is the array of work on offer. You can head outside and indulge in some industrial-strength gardening – great for meeting new people and getting exercise. This involves carrying out conservation work like coppicing trees, clearing scrub and building bonfires, all with the help of trained professionals (who will make sure you stay safe). If you're not so physically able, you can volunteer to help in a shop for a few hours, or fundraise, do a bit of office work, or even join education teams, inspiring children to go outside and get a bit mucky. If you're great at making cakes, why not ask a local nature reserve if they need an extra pair of hands in the café? No matter what you're good at or able to do, wildlife charities are always looking for volunteers, so even if you can only spare a few hours a week, it's worth it. It's great for your health – you'll get active; you'll meet other people; and you'll be giving something back, too. Your Wildlife Trust is a good place to start – contact them and see what's on offer.

Identify five winter wildflowers

Winter is not the time of year usually associated with wildflowers, but look close enough and you can find hardy flowers growing all year round. You have to know when and where to look. Depending on where you are in the UK, and what the weather's been like, you might see different flowers coming into bloom at different times of year. When it's mild in the south of England, flowers like daffodils and lesser celandine will burst open as early as December. Climate change is bringing flowers out earlier, but traditionally you want to be looking out for them in late February. Some plants really do like to blossom when it's cold though, so challenge yourself to find one in the depths of winter. A lot of them look a bit scruffy, but don't discard them as weeds. They're great for wildlife – and respect to them for growing when nothing else will!

Shepherd's purse Shepherd's purse is often labelled as a weed. It grows in gangly sprigs with tiny white flowers with minuscule white petals and seedpods that look like hearts. It'll grow in the cracks in pavements and up walls, or in bare wasteland areas around car parks or buildings.

Snowdrop Snowdrops are instantly recognisable, growing low to the ground in little clusters. If they grow in woodlands or beneath trees, they can sometimes form a carpet of white nodding flowers that droop down in that droplet shape. They can grow everywhere, including in your garden, but they are worth a special trip to a nature reserve if you want to see them covering the ground in their thousands.

Chickweed Chickweed grows all over the place, close to the ground in little clumps, from gardens to roadsides to field edges. It has star-shaped flowers with little white petals that splay out like fingers. Lots of animals like to eat it, including (unsurprisingly!) chickens.

Daisy Daisies pop up all over the place at any time of year. We associate them with spring and summer, but they will flower in colder months, too – in fact, they're one of the flowers you're most likely to see. You probably know what they look like, but just in case, they are little, growing in lawns, pavement cracks, wastelands – wherever! – in little clumps, with white flowers and a bright yellow centre. They go to sleep at night, too, closing their petals around them.

Teasels We are cheating slightly with this winter wildflower, as we're not actually looking for the plant in flower. Instead we're looking for the brown, spiky seed heads that you can see in autumn and winter, and which make an amazing food source for goldfinches. You can see them all over scrubland, wasteland and around field margins. In the summer, the flowers are tiny and purple, bunched together on the flower heads. The teasel is a tall plant, reaching over 1.5m. They are thorny, and the seed heads are spiky, so beware if you're handling them.

The humpback whale I never thought I'd see

If there's an animal I never expected to see in the UK, it was a humpback whale. I thought I would have to travel the world in search of this leviathan, maybe to Canada, Iceland or Hawaii. Who knew Devon would turn up the goods? The whale had been spotted a few days before, and we'd made the journey specially to see it. We arrived early afternoon and were amazed by the crowds that were already forming: news was out, and everyone wanted a piece of the action.

By late afternoon, the air of expectation had grown. We were scanning the sea for any signs. Then from further down the beach it became clear that someone had seen her – a long way out through a telescope, but she was back. Directions were shouted and we set our scopes on the spot – a minute or two passed where everyone around us fell silent, and then the shape broke the water. Dark, elegant, accompanied by the gentle arc of the bumpy back and huge tail. A humpback whale in UK waters.

A little girl was hopping up and down next to me. I handed her mum my binoculars and pointed her in the right direction. It took a few minutes, but I'll never forget the moment the little girl first saw that whale. She squealed, sighed and caught her breath. She held on to those binoculars for over an hour, not once taking her eyes off it.

The whale drifted closer inshore until it was no more than a couple of hundred feet away. Everyone could see it and share in this magical moment. The whale stayed close by until night had fallen, and we could no longer make out the dark shape in the sea. It was a long drive home, but that kind of adrenaline will get you an awful long way.

Do it yourself:
You can see whales around the UK, but it is tricky and does take some hard work. Prepare yourself, you're not going to see much more than the back and fin of the animal, especially from the shore. You can go on boat trips, and I've always found the West Coast the most productive: Wester Ross in Scotland, Northern Ireland, Cornwall and the Isles of Scilly. The East Coast can be good, too, seawatching from places like Flamborough Head. The whale you're most likely to see is the minke whale, which grows about 8m long. Orkney and Shetland are excellent for more unusual species, like orca. Summer is the best time to get good sightings. You'll need a lot of patience, some height to get a good view, and a pair of binoculars to scan for the shape of the whale breaking the surface.

Enjoy mini murmurations

Murmurations of starlings can reach many thousands, even millions of birds, all swirling and dancing at dusk. There are special spots where you can see them every winter, such as the Somerset Levels, Gretna Green or Brighton Pier. You might be lucky enough to find a mini one near you though. Even a few hundred birds moving in formation can look and sound impressive.

Starlings like to roost in numbers, so they'll go for reedbeds, trees or even the ivy growing up the sides of walls (if it's thick enough). When they've eaten enough in the day, they'll all join together to put on a show before bedtime, evading any predators in the process. Then suddenly, they'll pour into their roost, emptying from the sky and chattering loudly. It's thought that this incessant gossip is an exchange of information between the birds, like where the best places are for food. At night, packed so closely together, they're warm, too.

I've been lucky enough to enjoy mini murmurations locally, so keep your eyes open. All those starlings must roost somewhere, so see if you can find your local hotspot and feel the magic.

Plant a mini nature reserve

Nature reserves can be vast, beautiful places – or they can be tiny, quaint and totally manmade. This is a great chance to make your own nature reserve, using any leftovers that you might have lying around your garden or shed. All you need is a plant pot (a large ceramic one or a long, thin one will do) or a window box. Fill it with a layer of peat-free compost (or soil from your garden), then bury a little dish of water in it (a yoghurt pot will do) and add a lump of decaying wood. The soil is your ground, the water is your mini pond, and your decaying wood will add life. You can add a rock, too, which will provide shelter for any bugs that come along. Don't be tempted to add plants. See what nature brings instead. Leave it somewhere outside where you can add more water or inspect your nature reserve as needed. Plants should start to grow as the spring kicks in, and bugs will make a home there. Cut back any grasses that get out of control, but make a note of what turns up!

Pen an acrostic poem

Acrostic poems are great fun to do, either as an adult or with children. They're not the most subtle or elegant, but that's what makes them so much fun. They don't need to rhyme, they can be as long as you like, and there's no counting out syllables or searching for similes. Instead, you just need to pick a subject in nature and have fun crafting a poem all about it using its name to start each line. So, for example, if you chose 'robin', your poem would have five lines and each line would start respectively with 'r', 'o', 'b', 'i' and 'n'.

Pick something in nature that inspires you and that you can easily describe. Birds are good as they make lots of noise and look very beautiful. Flowers, butterflies and beetles all work well, too. It's up to you how long your word is, but if this is your first time, maybe pick something a bit shorter. Make some notes before you start to help you out as you write: what does your animal or plant look like, sound like, smell like, feel like? Where does it live and why? Doing this thinking now will help when you start writing.

Finally, write out the letters of your word going down the left-hand side of your page. You don't have to start at the top, but think about how each line can flow. The only rule: each line must start with one of your letters in the right order! This sounds simple but it can be quite tricky. There may be some crossing out and scribbling involved.

Check out this evocative acrostic poem by Rowan Cormack

```
Warmth echoes like a siren
Inside the lunar cold;
No leaves reaching to heaven,
Their stories lie untold.
Exposed and bleak horizons
Rewatching time unfold.
```

Watch a real swan lake

In the winter, we're treated to an influx of birds that visit us from the cold north, finding our shores balmy in comparison to the frozen Arctic. Ducks, geese and swans arrive in huge numbers. Most people will have seen a mute swan. These are our classic swans: big, white, a bit scary when they hiss, and with the red knob at the top of their bill. They are with us all year round, and easy to spot at parks and on canals and rivers. In the winter, two more species of swan join us though, and it's well worth trying to see them.

Whooper and Bewick's swans are the stars of our wild winter ballet. They arrive in flocks to wetlands and marshlands, and a local wetland nature reserve may see some of these elegant birds. They become the real swan lake, more beautiful and elegant than any dance. As dusk falls, the swans gather on a lake along with ducks and geese. They've come here for safety, using the water to protect them from predators, and to look after each other. They make a haunting, mellow honking sound. Some nature reserves provide food for them, and you can enjoy the spectacle from the comfort of a warm hide; they'll swim much closer at the prospect of a good meal of grain.

Whoopers and Bewick's both have yellow on their bills instead of red. The Bewick's swans are smaller than the swans we normally see; they have lots of black on the bill with a little blob of yellow, and shorter necks. Whoopers, in contrast, are bigger, with longer necks, a sloping forehead and a wedge-shaped yellow bill (like a chunk of cheese) with some black on it. They can be hard to separate, so attending a walk, talk or swan feed will give you a good chance to learn about the different species.

Stalk a dinosaur

Not a real dinosaur of course, but a bird that looks truly prehistoric – the grey heron. They are tall, with a long neck and legs, pointed dagger bill, grey plumage and black cap. They're widespread across the UK and one of our most obvious water birds. You can spot them easily on rivers, canals, reservoirs and even garden ponds – and now they've moved into our city centres, too, where they make the most of lakes (like St James's Park).

When they hunt – there's not much they won't eat – they stand stock still on the edge of the water. If they must move, they stalk through with stealth, their big feet barely making a ripple. They're looking for fish, frogs, toads, small birds, mammals – anything that happens to be passing.

You can see a grey heron at any time of year, but my favourite time is in the late winter. Herons are usually solitary, but will come together to form heronries high in the tops of trees. They build huge nests from twigs, lay eggs in February and perform elaborate dancing displays on the ground. When they fly, they unfurl their wings into a distinctive 'M' shape, like the famous McDonald's sign!

Take a few minutes from your day to find a grey heron nearby (just look for water) and watch how it moves. Can you see the dinosaurs walking among us?

Find the first frog spawn

One of my favourite memories from school involves frog spawn. When I was about seven years old, our teacher brought some frog spawn into the classroom and popped it, with some pond water, into an old fish tank. We were learning about lifecycles and this was the whole process in action. We had to observe the jellylike frog spawn, with its obvious black centre, slowly transform into tadpoles. A few days later, the tadpoles started to grow legs. About this time, we had a very sunny half term and our teacher, in her infinite wisdom, forgot to secure the lid to the tadpole tank. We came back to school to find baby frogs, or froglets, all over the classroom. We were rounding them up and releasing them for days! We never knew if we found them all.

I'm not endorsing releasing wild froglets in your classroom or your kitchen, but it's worth looking out at the end of winter for frog spawn in nearby ponds. With climate change affecting our weather, frog spawn can now appear in the middle of winter, but traditionally it's found in February, or a bit later in the north of the UK. Look for the jellylike substance just below the surface of the water, in ponds, ditches or slow-moving streams. Frogs like the shade, so areas with dappled sunlight are usually best. Want to know if it's frog spawn or toad spawn? Frog spawn clumps together in bundles or patches; toad spawn has long lines of eggs, laced together like the beads on a necklace. Make a note of the date you find your first frog spawn.

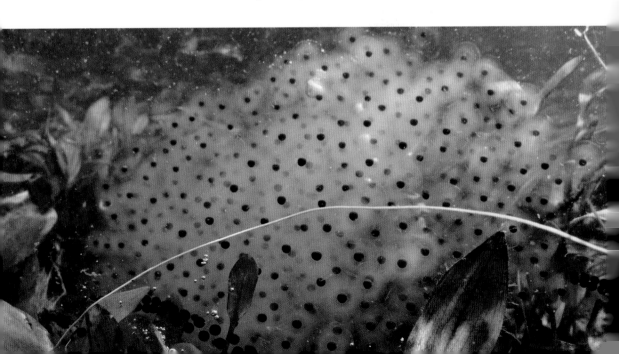

361 Catkins calling

Many catkins start to appear at the end of winter. They dangle from trees in little drooping bunches – they are little clusters of flowers hanging around a central stem, although the petals are either non-existent or impossible to see. They are male or female and are part of how trees reproduce. They feel velvety or downy to the touch, very soft and pliant. The word 'catkin' comes from the Dutch for 'kitten', as they look and feel like a kitten's tail. They also have the nickname 'lambs-tail'.

In January and February, when the trees are bare, it's easy to spot catkins hanging from some trees. They begin to lengthen and turn a rich colour as their pollen comes in. On hazel trees, they are golden in colour and hang from bare, skinny twigs and branches. On silver birch trees, the catkins will be at their most obvious when the leaves are also starting to burst open; the male catkins are long and hang down, the females are short and point upwards. Alder trees produce catkins a bit like hazel, but they are darker and longer, and they collect at the ends of twigs rather than all the way along.

See what you can spot near you, and make a note of the first catkins of the year. They're a sign that spring is on the way!

Become a wildlife champion

Sharing your love of wildlife can have a big impact, especially if you share it with politicians. Not many of us contact our politicians, when we really should – they work for us, after all! It can be hard to know what to say or how to say it, and it's easy to think it won't make a difference, but if we all stood up for wildlife we could make some real changes. For this Random Act of Wildness, think about something you'd really like to see done differently to help wildlife. Would you like to see more wildflowers in our countryside? Would you like there to be more trees? Would you like birds to be better protected, or a local wild place to be saved from development? There's so much you can say and so much you care about, so say it to your MP by writing them a polite and passionate letter. You don't have to get technical – that's their job. They just need to know that you care. You can find their address online, or even send an email if that's easier. If that's a bit daunting, start out by contacting a local newspaper.

Build a wild snow creature

Have you been lucky enough to get some actual real-life snow (not just the utterly depressing slush that we're so often treated to throughout the winter)? Well first, I'm jealous, and second, get outside right now! There's no age limit on building a snowman, and now you're a bit more grown up you have an exact creative vision for what it's going to look like. No more wonky twig arms and lopsided heads for you – your snowman will be a work-of-art!

   Rather than going for the traditional snow-human, though, let's think a bit wilder. This is your opportunity to show the world just how creative you are, and how much you love nature. You could create an entire snowy woodland scene out there, full to the brim with animals – a fox is a good start (don't try and make him stand up on four legs – opt for a sitting down position: we're artists, not scientists), or a hedgehog (which is basically just a rugby ball of snow with some twigs stuck in). A hare with pointy ears might be a bit more ambitious, and a bumbling badger would be lots of fun. Let your imagination run wild and see how creative you can be.

Admire the setting sun

This is a great Random Act of Wildness to do no matter what the season. In fact, try doing this once in winter, spring, summer and autumn, and watch the way the sunset changes at different times of the year. Pick somewhere with a good view west, and leave yourself plenty of time to enjoy the whole beautiful effect. Make sure you've got some height – at the top of a hill or in a tall building. For a wilder experience, get outside. A warm blanket might not go amiss!

Don't forget the folklore saying: 'Red sky at night, shepherd's delight'. This means that a red sunset might indicate that good weather is on the way. A red sky occurs when small particles, like dust, get stuck in the atmosphere. This scatters the blue light of the spectrum and leaves only red light, sending the sky crimson. Even better, there is an element of scientific truth in this: a red sky in the west can mean that good weather is heading towards you; high pressure is moving in from the west, bringing fair weather with it.

What do you notice about wildlife at this time of day? It'll change depending on the time of year. In the winter, the atmosphere will be frosty and cold, so wrap up warm. Birds like owls are crepuscular, so this is the perfect time to see them hunting along hedgerows. In the spring and summer, evenings will be long and stretched out. The air can be full of birdsong, and bats might flitter around like shadows. Moths might flutter by, too. If you sit still, you might hear a mammal shuffling around, or even see one.

Watching the sunset is relaxing after a long day. Make time to enjoy every second, and let any worries slip away with the sunlight as it disappears below the horizon.

Reflect on your wild year

This has got to be your final Random Act of Wildness. After a year of learning about nature, identifying bugs and birds, transforming your garden, ditching your plastics and inspiring everyone around you to love wildlife too, take an hour to yourself to re-read your wild diary – the one you started a full year ago. What a wild adventure you'll have had. You won't have managed to do all of the activities in this book and you certainly won't remember everything – I don't! But that's why you kept the diary: to remind you of this wild journey you've undertaken either on your own, or with the people around you. Turn the pages and lose yourself in all the wonderful things you did, and think back – how did each of those things make you feel? There will have been plenty of days when things didn't go to plan or Random Act of Wildness didn't work out, or you simply didn't feel up to it. And that's fine. You might have skipped whole days (or weeks!) by accident, but think again. Did you really miss them, or did you find yourself doing something wild totally subconsciously – like enjoying the play of rain on your face, appreciating the buzz of a bumblebee or admiring the trees in autumn.

I hope you've loved your 365 Days Wild as much as I have loved writing every word of this book. It's been a magical experience, incredibly hard at times, but totally inspired by the Random Acts of Wildness I see people performing every single day. And if enough of us do those Random Acts of Wildness, enjoying wildlife, learning about it and taking action for it, we could make a real difference and save the natural world around us. It all starts with you. Don't stop now – your wild life is only just beginning.

Acknowledgements

This book has been made possible by a great many people, who have shown their support by offering inspiring ideas, taking me on wild adventures and showing unending patience as I wrote through the scorching summer of 2018.

Martin Redfern, Diane Banks and the whole at Northbank Talent Management provided the confidence and guidance I needed to start out on this great venture, and Robyn Drury was the first to put her trust in me. I must extend my utmost thanks to Myles Archibald, Hazel Eriksson, and the team at William Collins, who have taken the jumble of ideas in my head and turned them into a book.

The Wildlife Trusts have given me tremendous support in this project. Principally, Adam Cormack, has offered endless encouragement, wisdom and inspiration. He also coined the term 'Random Act of Wildness'! Stephanie Hilborne, CEO, and Janel Fone and Patience Thody made it possible. My colleagues in the Communications Team and wider office have shown great friendship and tolerance, most notably Leanne Manchester, Liz Carney, Emma Robertshaw, Ben Cook, Eden Jackson and Tom Hibbert. Former colleagues Michelle Househam, Catherine Middleton, Anna Guthrie and Ellie Lewis must be thanked, too.

Many nature enthusiasts have opened up doors of opportunity for me and often shared in those wild experiences around the UK and further afield. They include the Allen family, Tim Appleton and the Birdfair team, Joe and Traci Badcock, John Badley, Nick Baker, Peter Cairns, the Carter family, Carl Chapman, Andy Clements, Mark Constantine, Dominic Couzens, the Craig family, Mike Crawley, Ken Davies, Nick Davies, Mike Dilger, the Eaves family, Ieuan Evans, Robert Flood, Dick Filby and the team at Rare Bird Alert, Pete Gamby, Neil Glenn, Jo Greenlaw, Isla Hodgson, the Holden family, Conor Jameson, Tony Juniper, Denise Landau, Jim Lawrence, Ceri Levy, Sir John Lister-Kaye and the team at Aigas, Ruth Macpherson and Bob Farley in Western Australia, Duncan Macdonald, Dallas and Howard Martenstyn in Sri Lanka, Michael Miles, the late Derek Moore, Nick Moran, Paul Morton, Stephen Moss and family, Rebecca Nason and Phil Harris, Mel and Charles Oldershaw, Joe Pender, Hugh Pulsford, Nigel Redman, the Ross family at Leault Farm, the team at Rutland Water Nature Reserve, Megan Shersby, Paul Stancliffe, Isabell and Graeme Steel, Mike Toms, James Walsh, Hugh Warwick, the Whittredge family in New England USA, the Wilde family, Matt Williams – and to anyone else I might have inadvertently forgotten!

To Beth Aucott, Ellie Henman, Kate Richards and Sarah West – our friendships have given many years of love and laughter.

And finally to my family: my mum, Alison, who was my rock, my guide and my best friend. I miss her every day. My dad, Eric, and close family, who gave me my wild childhood and provided me with the strength I needed to carry on after mum passed away. My stepmother, Steph, and mother-in-law, Joan, both trusted friends; and my stepson, Hamish, for a wild Australian education. And my husband, Rob, who has been endlessly patient and supportive. We share in almost all my wildlife adventures (from common dolphins to natterjack toads…), and he has supported me in my ambition to publish a book before I turned 30. He has challenged me, pushed me and been a critical friend. I have him to thank for my wild life. Our daughter, Georgiana, will share in our adventures.

Long Clawson, Leicestershire. Autumn 2018

Index

Picture credits

All reasonable efforts have been made to trace the copyright owners of the images in this book. In the event that there are any mistakes or omissions, updates will be incorporated for future editions. With thanks to Alexandra Hoadley for help with sourcing photographs.

Illustrations by Nathan Burton.

4 – Matthew Roberts; 24 – Nick Upton/2020 Vision; 25 – Guy Edwardes/2020Vision; 27 – Ben Hall/2020Vision; 28 top – Steve Waterhouse, bottom – Bertie Gregory/2020Vision; 31 – Lauren Heather; 32 – Joy Russell; 34 – Philip Precey; 35 – Andrew Parkinson/2020Vision; 37 – Terry Whittaker/2020Vision; 38 bottom – Lee Schofield; 40 – Andrew Parkinson/2020Vision; 41 – Steve Waterhouse; 43 – Elliot Smith; 44 top – Jon Hawkins, bottom – Bob Coyle; 45 top – Steve Waterhouse, middle – Bob Coyle, bottom – Neil Aldridge; 46 – Guy Edwardes/2020Vision; 47 – Chris Gomersall; 48 – Bob Coyle; 54 – Matthew Roberts; 55 – Tom Marshall; 57 – Matthew Roberts; 59 – Ross Hoddinott/2020Vision; 60 – Richard Burkmar; 63 – Chris Lawrence; 64 top – Philip Precey, bottom – Dawn Monrose; 67 – Zsuzsanna Bird; 71 top left Amy Lewis, top right and bottom – Matthew Roberts; 75 – Matthew Roberts; 76 – Chris Gomersall/2020Vision; 79 – Jon Hawkins; 80 – Amy Lewis; 83 – Katrina Martin/2020Vision; 84 top left – Katrina Martin/2020Vision, top right – Stefan Johansson, bottom – Matthew Roberts; 87 – Ben Hall/2020Vision; 90 top left – Adam Cormack, top right – Vicky Nall, bottom left – Chris Lawrence; 95 – Dawn Monrose; 96 – Tom Marshall; 98 – Tom Marshall; 101 top – Alamy; 103 – Rachel Scopes; 104 top – Jim Higham, bottom – Amy Lewis; 105 top – Chris Gomersall/2020Vision, bottom – Jim Higham; 106 – Richard Burkmar; 108 – Paul Hobson; 109 – Derek Moore; 113 – Dale Sutton/2020Vision; 114 bottom left – Richard Burkmarr, right – Katrina Martin/2020Vision; 116 bottom – Gemma de Gouveia; 117 top – Chris Gomersall/2020Vision, middle – Katrina Martin/2020Vision,

bottom – Niall Benvie/2020Vision; 119 – Ross Hoddinott/2020Vision; 121 – Mark Hamblin/2020Vision; 128 – Margaret Holland; 129 – Derek Moore; 132 – Katrina Martin/2020Vision; 134 – Jon Dunkelman; 138 – Chris Lawrence; 141 – Matthew Roberts; 143 – Matthew Roberts; 144 – Malcolm Storey; 148 – Ross Hoddinott/2020Vision; 151 – Philip Precey; 152 top – Jon Hawkins, bottom – Ed Marshall; 153 top and middle – Nick Upton/2020Vision, bottom – Gillian Day; 154 – Neil Aldridge; 156 – Matthew Robert; 159 top – Don Sutherland, bottom – Matthew Roberts; 162 top – Paul Hobson, middle – Nick Upton/2020Vision, bottom – Chris Gomersall/2020Vision; 166 – Ross Hoddinott/2020Vision; 167 top – Ross Hoddinott/2020Vision, bottom – Alan Price; 172 – Tom Marshall; 177 top – Kathryn Edwards, bottom – Matthew Roberts; 179 – Alan Price; 180 – Scott Petrek; 183 – Chris Lawrence; 185 – Gillian Day; 186 – Philip Precey; 189 – Ben Hall/2020Vision; 191 – Alan Price; 192 – Jon Hawkins; 195 – Mark Hamblin/2020Vision; 196 top – Guy Edwardes/2020Vision, bottom – Karen Lloyd; 197 bottom – Faye Durkin; 199 – Ross Hoddinott/2020Vision; 200 bottom – Matthew Roberts; 202 top – Ross Hoddinott/2020Vision; 205 – Matthew Roberts; 206 – Alan Price; 207 – Dawn Monrose; 210 – Paul Hobson; 211 – Amy Lewis; 216 bottom – Adam Cormack; 219 – Katrina Martin/2020Vision; 221 – Joseph Pender 222 – Damien Waters; 226 top – Alan Price; 227 top – Alan Price, bottom – Adam Cormack; 228 – Ross Hoddinott/2020Vision; 239 bottom – Katrina Martin/2020Vision; 240 – Derek Moore; 243 top – Peter Cairns/2020Vision; 245 – Tom Marshall; 246 – Mark Hamblin/2020Vision; 249 top – Andy Rouse/2020Vision, bottom – Peter Cairns; 254 – Nick Upton/2020Vision; 255 – Gary Cox; 261 top – Mark Hamblin/2020Vision, bottom left – Neil Aldridge, bottom right – Adam Jones; 264 – Jon Hawkins; 272 – Danny Green/2020Vision; 275 – Gillian Day; 276 – Terry Whittaker/2020Vision; 277 – Linda Pitkin/2020Vision; 278 – Bob Coyle; 281 – Mark Hamblin/2020Vision; 282 – Rob Lambert
All other photographs copyright © Shutterstock.